My heart is warm with the friends I made;
And better friends I'll not be knowing;
Yet there isn't a train I wouldn't take;
No matter where it's going.

Edna St. Vincent Millay (1892–1950)

Trains in My Heart

Trains in My Heart

Connie Luna

ABOOKS
Alive Book Publishing

Additional copies may be ordered from the publisher for educational,
business, promotional or premium use.
For information, contact ALIVE Book Publishing at:
alivebookpublishing.com, or call (925) 837-7303.

Book design by Alex Johnson
Cover art by Mike Swan, BC Creative

ISBN 13
978-1-63132-051-4

ISBN 10
1-63132-051-3

Library of Congress Control Number: 2018943486

Library of Congress Cataloging-in-Publication Data
is available upon request.

First Edition

Published in the United States of America by ALIVE Book Publishing
and ALIVE Publishing Group, imprints of Advanced Publishing LLC
3200 A Danville Blvd., Suite 204, Alamo, California 94507
alivebookpublishing.com

PRINTED IN THE UNITED STATES OF AMERICA

10 9 8 7 6 5 4 3 2 1

To my Mom who gave me unconditional love.

To Sharron
Life's short —
be happy

Connie Luna

Table of Contents

Foreword

Lamb-sicles? A Luna Fizz? Something about humping off the back of a private car? The Grandma Rapper? Birthed by two mothers? Just an American mutt?

Welcome to the entertaining world of Connie Luna, nee Collins. When I was asked—a gesture I am both humbled and proud to accept—to write the foreword to this, Connie's autobiography, I knew her only as a private railroad car chef, a relationship she generously explains somewhere here. Little did I know she was one of those "light up the room" dames. You know the type. A comedic hard-worker who can create both lifetime memories for rail travelers, and also a heart warming and hilarious account of that specialty.

We are, of course, provided with the basics. In an opening chapter we learn a date of birth—funny, I note we share a birth year—and of early memories, of growing up in a hard-working family, of a failed first marriage (mentioned in one sentence), and single parent-hood (with not a trace of bitterness), of work and her entry into the travel industry, of the experiences that exposed her to rail travel, and finally of her unusual Christmas Eve engagement and eventual marriage, this one to her life's partner, Henry Luna.

But this is merely the warm-up. The headline act—in chapters 2 through 6—accounts for Connie's emergence as a highly regarded chef on that highest end of rail travel and cuisine: The Private Varnish. And a hysterical account it is. She comes to this work almost as a calling. She learns the ropes working as a travel agent and a tour manager. Entering the world of private rail car travel— working primarily on the *Native Son* (now the Bella Vista), the *Plaza Santa Fe*, the *Royal Gorge*, and of course the

Tamalpais—she hits her stride. Fittingly, Chapter 2, titled *My Destiny*, is the book's longest. Throughout, we are entertained by story after story of what it is like to work managing a private car and its movements, all while cooking for and entertaining guests that ranged in number from two or three to, in several instances, hundreds. Every challenge appears to have been met with resilience and good humor.

Spoiler Alert: We eventually share an account of a late-in-life medical crisis that would buckle most of us. The manner in which she handled it, as well as its outcome, should come as no surprise. People like Connie Luna survive the longest because they are recognized as the hardest to replace.

What Connie may not know about me is that I am drawn to and collect first-hand accounts of people who work for the railroad past or present. So it is not the words or phrases cited above, or the numerous chapter sub-heads that kept me reading. It is the stories that make the pages move.

Here, from the very beginning, you are "on board." And what a fun trip it is. These episodes may seem to only roughly follow a strict chronology, but that does not matter. They are timeless for the setting. Anyone who has ridden a train, or better, one with a dining car, and best, on a Private Varnish, will relate in an instant. Besides, like for those who work in the enclosed space of a moving train, timing and location of a passing setting does not matter. It is just a moment to enjoy.

Connie ends with her "Grandma's Rap"—it will be available for eternity on YouTube at:

http:/www.youtube.com/watch?v=d3aD0Ei3_O0

—with a lament: That she is not still twenty-two. One of mine is that I never road a private car with her. But like me, you are about to read the next best thing.

Have fun.

James D. Porterfield Author and columnist

Elkins, West Virginia,

Introduction

"You should write a book!" I heard this so often that I guess the idea of actually doing so finally became a reality. By nature I am a story-teller, and after twenty-five years as a private railcar chef, I had so many stories to tell (all true!). As I was recalling my experiences with trains, it became quite apparent that the stories were reaching farther and farther back into my life, so to simplify things I took a hint from the Bible and started "In the beginning......." As I never kept a diary, the chronological order of things may not be perfectly recounted, but the stories themselves are definitely non-fiction. One of my greatest regrets is not keeping a journal of all the private railcar trips I did. Life itself is quite a journey, and how fortunate for me to have spent a good portion of it riding the rails.

Chapter 1 Preparing for my Destiny

The Early Years

"The war is over! The war is over!" we chanted while banging on pan lids with wooden spoons. We were children, and at three years old, I was the youngest reveler. Our little impromptu parade is my first real memory—as clear as if it had just happened.

I was born February 1, 1942 at St. Francis Hospital in San Francisco, where my mother had trained as a nurse. Our family, Mom, Dad, and two sisters, Pat and Letty, moved from The City down the Peninsula to Burlingame, shortly before my brother, Bill, was born, exactly one week after my third birthday. Our house was a couple of hundred feet from the street that was adjacent to the Southern Pacific rail line that went from San Francisco to Los Angeles, and you could see the trains from our front porch. Parallel to the train tracks were the streetcar tracks that ran between San Francisco and the city south of us, San Mateo. The little SP depot, three blocks south of our street, is still there.

At night, the steam whistles would blow their mournful and beautiful tune, music to accompany the chirping crickets. I think it was this, more than anything else, that made the romance of trains infuse into my heart.

All the trains southbound originated in San Francisco. (To a native, San Francisco is "The City." It's okay to say San Fran, but a grievous mistake to utter the unforgivable moniker of "Frisco!") The freight trains ran mostly at night, and the day was filled with commute trains going to San Jose and the *Del Monte* going to Monterey. Two long distance trains, the *Lark* and the *Daylight* went to Los Angeles, and in the summer on Sundays,

the *Suntan Special* made its way to the Boardwalk at Santa Cruz.
The *Lark* was an overnight train, and it would pass by our street
in the morning on its way back to The City. This was my favorite
train and sometimes we would walk to the tracks to watch it go
by. You could see people in the diner eating breakfast and
porters making up the rooms on the sleepers. I'd think, "When
I grow up, I want to be on the inside, looking out at the children
like me."

One of the engines on these trains, the 4449, is still running
and is quite famous. It pulled the *Freedom Train* all around the
country in 1976. When you are young and small so many things
seem awfully big, but when you grow up you realize they
weren't so big after all. That certainly wasn't the case with the
4449. When I went to see the *Freedom Train* as an adult, I found
that the wheels of the engine were as tall as I was. No wonder it
so impressed me as a child.

Number 4449 is a huge 4-8-4 (that means that front to back
there are four small wheels followed by eight large wheels then
four more small wheels), and is now based in Portland, Oregon,
running on occasional excursions.

A steam train engine is so much more than just a big hunk of
steel. There is something about them, both large and small, that
makes them almost like living entities—the steam breathing life
into the engine, the sounds and smells, the ground vibrating, the
clickety-clack of the wheels on the track, like a fast-beating heart,
the language of the whistles blowing and the bells ringing. Ask
any of the steam train engineers and they'll tell you that just like
people, each engine has its own personality—some sweet, some
cantankerous, but all distinctly individual.

My family lived in that house for forty years, so trains were
part of my entire childhood. The house is still there and trains
still run by. There is no more steam on that line, and the *Lark*
and *Daylight* and *Del Monte* and *Suntan Special* and streetcars are
all part of history now. Only memories keep them running.

When Mom took us kids to The City, we usually went on the slower, less expensive streetcar on the 40 line that ran between San Mateo and San Francisco. Back then, everyone dressed up to go to downtown San Francisco, even children. We would sit in the front of the car facing my mother. If we started to act up, she would raise one eyebrow, and we would settle right down. We could be, and usually were, wild at home, but, oh boy, did we ever have to behave in public! A schoolmate from grammar school, Paul, also remembers riding the streetcar with his Mother to San Francisco to visit his grandmother. He would sit behind the motorman so he could watch him maneuver the controller and step on the brass button on the floor to ring the bell. His mother sat watching him but no raised eyebrows were needed as Paul was a very well-behaved child. My dad worked at the *Chronicle* newspaper in The City and commuted by train. When he came home in the evening, streams of commuters would walk from the train in all directions to their respective homes. I would watch for the train to go past our street, slowing to stop at the station and run to the corner to walk with my Dad, taking long strides, trying to keep pace with his. Looking back on that, perhaps I was practicing to be a commuter myself.

A little boy in my kindergarten class, Henry, lived about a block away from us. His father also commuted by train, and he would walk up Broadway and down Paloma Avenue to get home. Henry couldn't see the trains from his house like I could, but he could hear them, and when he grew up he was one of six young guys who started the Pacific Locomotive Association (PLA). Now, over fifty years later, it is one of the largest and most active rail organizations around. He also wrote a book— *Niles Canyon Railways*. But I digress. More about that kid later.

The SP Derailment

The freight trains did a lot of switching during the night and early morning. Usually, you would just sleep right through the noise, but sometimes they would really get to banging those cars around and it would be pretty noisy. One early morning when I was about eleven years old they were especially loud, crashing and banging, waking everyone up. Well, the switching turned out to be a big derailment. Oh my, was that ever exciting. It was pretty close to our street, and practically the whole neighborhood went to see it. Hardly anyone owned a TV then, so, unless news was huge and got in the newsreels shown in movie theaters, you had to witness events in person, hear about them on the radio, or read about them in newspapers.

My most vivid memory of this event is of a freight car on its side with its contents strewn all over—thousands of cans of beer. Henry was there with his Brownie camera, recording the event for posterity, a precursor to his lifelong hobby of railroad photography. Many of his photographs can be seen in books about trains.

The Forbidden Railroad Tracks

In the forties and fifties, with no television, we played outside (unless it was raining). The way things are today, it's hard to imagine the freedom we had. We roamed all over and had to be home by whatever came first, dinnertime or darkness. The only place we were told not to go was across the tracks. Of course, that was a favorite destination! There was a kind of a swamp on the other side of the tracks and some kids had built a raft. It was so much fun to pole the raft through the trees. We'd also look for hobo camps. Once in awhile we'd find a camp, but we never did meet any hobos!

One time my friend Harriet (who was also forbidden to go across the tracks) and I were trying to launch the raft into the water when she fell in. We ran to my house, where I hid her in our basement. There was a big, old-fashioned furnace down there and it was on, so it was warm. I phoned her Mother, "Hello, Mrs. Bigelow, could Harriet please stay for dinner?" I sneaked a towel and some food to her, and while I was upstairs eating dinner with my family, she was in the basement, drying her clothes. Somehow, she got home and our mothers were none the wiser, but we lived in fear for weeks, just waiting for our deception to be discovered. Sometimes, I wonder if our mothers really did know and let our fear be our punishment. It seemed like your mother knew everything, with those mysterious eyes in the back of her head!

Did it stop us from going back to play across the tracks? Of course not!! We kids would walk on the rails, seeing who would lose their balance first, but nobody ever got hurt. There were a lot more trains then, but you rarely heard of anyone getting hit by a train. I think what's different now is the use of cell phones for talking or texting, listening to music on iPods and the high use of alcohol and drugs, both legal and illegal. Perhaps all our parents warning us to stay away from the tracks at least made us cognizant of the inherent dangers. We were all well aware that trains had the right-of-way and couldn't stop on a dime or, as we kids used to say, you'd end up in quarters.

Train signals are universal. The bell ringing indicates the train is about to do something. On steam trains, the bell was rung by the fireman and the whistle was blown by the engineer. On diesels, the engineer can do both. One short whistle means stop, two short whistles means go, and three short whistles is for backing up. The whistle configuration indicating the right-of-way is two long, one short and one long. I like to tell children the train is talking to them, warning them to stay off the tracks at the street crossings. (Perhaps this should be told to truck drivers!) If they listen carefully, they can hear the train saying "Heeeeere Commmmmes the Traaaaain." This is actually a very old right-of-way signal from the days when ships and boats in England had to yield to make way for royal vessels entering or leaving a harbor. Another old English tradition determined the width between rails on standard gauge used all over the world. It is exactly four feet eight and a half inches. Why? Because that was the width between the ruts left by Roman chariots in England.

It seems like the English are the most tradition-obsessed people in the world. One time, I stayed in a fairly modern hotel in England. There was a modern bathtub in the room, but it was quite high with a false bottom. Why? Because it was the same height as the old claw-footed tub it had replaced! The water faucet in the bathroom had one spigot, but the water coming out of it was hot on one side and cold on the other. I foolishly thought the purpose of one spigot was to mix the water for a uniform temperature. There used to be an English cooking program on TV featuring two "old fat ladies". It was very entertaining, but they used to take a metal spoon to empty a bowl—scrape, scrape, scrape, scrape, scrape, scrape! I'd find myself yelling at the TV, "They've invented rubber spatulas!" I actually thought about sending them some, but didn't, because I knew what would happen. They would take the rubber spatula and scrape, scrape, scrape, scrape, scrape, scrape the bowl!

The Earthquake

I was a freshman in high school and had a crush on a boy in my church group. He lived in the Burlingame hills, quite a distance from the railroad tracks. After I had gotten up enough courage to invite him over to my house to study, we were sitting at our dining room table when a train went by. Well, our house shook and the windows rattled. He jumped up yelling something about an earthquake. None of us knew what he was talking about. He must have thought we were crazy, but we were oblivious to the effect of the trains on the house. We honestly didn't hear or feel anything. Funny, he never came back.

El Camino Real is a main road that runs through Burlingame. In fact, this is the highway that connected the California Missions, all situated approximately a days journey apart. The name itself translates to The King's Highway (referring not to the King of Spain, but to God the King). In Burlingame, the high-end real estate is on the west side of El Camino where the hills are. The train tracks are four to five blocks east of El Camino toward the San Francisco Bay. Looking back on my school years, I feel kind of sorry for the kids who didn't get to experience the trains like I did. Of course, it took quite a few years to come to that conclusion.

The Suntan Special

My oldest sister, Pat, was rather shy and very smart. She was the best student in our family, and I can still hear my Latin teacher saying to me, "Are you sure you're Pat Collins' sister?" Letty was cute and popular and the most social one, then I heard "Are you sure you're Letty Collins' sister?" I was a skinny, scruffy little tomboy, who got attention by being funny and talking too much. One year, Letty wanted to go on the *Suntan Special*. Mom thought it was too wild of a train for a teen-age girl, and I still can't believe Letty talked her into it, but she was finally allowed to go. While Letty was on the train, Mom drove to Santa Cruz with my brother and me, so we could meet the train. I remember being amazed that the train ran right down the middle of the street in Santa Cruz. There was an All Day Lunch Car on that train that now is part of the collection of the Niles Canyon Railway. I never got to ride on it to Santa Cruz, but have spent many hours working on it in the Canyon.

The Lark

I was about seventeen and talked my mother into letting me

go by myself on the train to Southern California to visit someone, and was finally going to be on the inside looking out, onboard the *Lark*—my childhood fantasy coming true. Mom was
a bit reluctant to let me go as I was probably the most naïve,
gullible, innocent, street-dumb kid ever! But looking back on my
life, I'm sure I've had an angel, a very exhausted and exasper-
ated angel, riding shotgun on my shoulder, keeping me safe and
out of trouble. I could have gotten into soooo much trouble on
my own!

The *Lark* didn't stop at the Broadway station, so passengers
had to board at the Burlingame Depot, a mile south of Broadway. My boyfriend, Tod, and my mother were seeing me off,
and watched from outside the train while I walked through the
car to find my assigned coach seat. They could see this tall, handsome boy stand up, tip his cowboy hat and with a big grin, greet
me, his new traveling companion. As the train pulled out of the
station, I could see Tod and Mom running alongside the train
with this strange, stricken look on their faces. These days, I probably would have gotten a call on my cell phone instructing me
to get off at the next station, But then, in that simpler time, you
were allowed the freedom of non-communication that allowed
you to experience and enjoy life on your own terms. The boy on
the train was an eighteen-year-old, out visiting from Texas. The
Lark was an overnight train to Los Angeles and we talked half
the night. I've loved hearing a Texas drawl ever since that trip
on the train! Of course, when we arrived at the Union Station in
Los Angeles we went our separate ways, ships in the night.

The fabric of life is woven with memories creating, at least
for me, a very warm blanket indeed. Cell phones have dramatically changed our way of life and today, almost everything is
recorded. In some ways this is a good thing, but I imagine that
if this technology was around during the expansion of our country, not too many pioneers would have ventured west after witnessing in living color the massacre of a wagon train. Sometimes,

ignorance really is bliss!

Aunt Ellis and Ted

Looking back on your life, you can recognize the various people who had a tremendous influence on you, both good and bad. But at the time they don't necessarily stand out. My mother's oldest sister, my Aunt Ellis, was a fearless pioneer, bravely entering uncharted territory. She was the first airline stewardess in the world. I made a promise to myself to correct an accepted historical inaccuracy, and am using this narrative as its vehicle. Her name was Ellis Crawford, a registered nurse who was hired by Boeing Airlines to test the public's reaction to an onboard attendant. She traveled with a photographer, who documented her trips for six months. The airplane on which she flew was tiny—holding just eighteen passengers. It was a two engine, double-winged propeller plane (model 80A) She was so favorably received that United Airlines then created what was referred to as "The Original Eight." Aunt Ellis was one of those eight, and was used as the model for the uniform. One of the other women of the group has been listed in history (in error) as the first stewardess as she headed "The Original Eight", but my aunt had been flying for six months before her. Aunt Ellis tried in vain to correct the record, and one newspaper actually had a picture of her with the other woman's name underneath.

As Aunt Ellis had no children, I ended up with her pictures and papers. Before she died, I told her that one day I would set the record straight. My proof is a dated newspaper—the *San Francisco Call-Bulletin* (April 24, 1930) with her picture on the front page, "Local girl first "flying stewardess". My aunt was pretty, smart, and extremely funny. (Funny genes run in our family!) So, here's to you, Aunt Ellis, and I know somewhere you're smiling!

Ellis was married to Ted, who was from Germany and was a

top chef in San Francisco. He was the best cook I've ever known. If I had only known the path my life was to take, I could have apprenticed under him, but what makes life so interesting and adventuresome is not knowing what paths lie before us.

One more memory of Aunt Ellis—we kids would stay overnight with her in her house, which was in the Richmond District of San Francisco. She could only take two of us at a time, and I always went with my brother, Bill. My fondest memories are trips to the zoo, Playland at the Beach, her cuckoo clock, and the foghorn and sirens we could hear at night from her home.

The Train to San Jose

After graduating high school at seventeen, I commuted by train to college (San Jose State). I had a distant connection with San Jose, as my great, great grandfather had been born there in 1799. (His father, Jose Larios, was one of the early settlers of San Jose.) The train left Broadway, Burlingame at 5.33 a.m. (Funny, how I've never forgotten that time!) It was dark out, and I was always late. With a pile of books in my arms (only hikers used back packs back then), I would run to the end of my street and pace alongside the train as it pulled into the station. The rear brakeman on the last car would leave the platform up and cheer me on as he gave me a hand up the steps onto the train. It usually took two more stops before I could catch my breath. By 1959 the big steam engines had been replaced by the more efficient diesel engines. The first time I saw a diesel engine I thought it was the ugliest thing. Even its whistle was jarring and ugly. Of course, over time, you got used to them, but I still miss the steam trains, especially the whistles. Progress is so accelerated now, things are obsolete before memories can even be established in our minds.

The train to San Jose consisted of low-level coaches. The double-decker commute trains came later. You would always have the same conductor and car attendants on the train and see the same passengers, so there was a friendly, comfortable atmosphere onboard. I traveled the farthest, but other students would board along the way. The San Jose State campus was quite a ways from the station, and we'd all walk there together. Coming home, I was usually alone, arriving at Broadway around 6:30 p.m. There were some girls on the train who had gone to Mercy High School—an all-girl Catholic school. The girls from Mercy were really good students, but all they could talk about was boys. It appeared that attending school with boys was the most important aspect of college for them, but, to me, who had always attended public school, it seemed so odd for them to be that excited about it.

The thing for me was going to school with black kids for the first time. The only exposure I'd previously had to integration was church camp. At San Jose State, I sat right behind a black boy in my history class. He was the smartest kid in the class, and I remember thinking, "What's the big deal about integration, he's just another kid." You must remember, this was 1959.

The other thing I remember specifically about the train was the fare. I was given a weekly stipend of $5.00. My round-trip commuter ticket cost $3.50 for a week. I had a minor in art and the supplies were an added expense, so I worked at odd jobs on the week-ends (babysitting, ironing, etc.) to supplement my income. I don't remember anything about student loans in those days. Parents often used to save for their children's college education and I knew many kids who worked their way through school. There were quite a few scholarships available for deserving high-achievers and students excelling in sports. Also, a lot of the boys would go into the military right out of high school and then go to college on a GI Bill. It wasn't easy to work and go to school, but I think it was a lot easier than starting your adult life with a big debt.

The World's Fair

The Seattle World's Fair was in 1962. I was twenty years old, working, and had been out on my own since I was eighteen. I announced to my family that I was going by myself on the train to the Fair, but I don't think they believed me. Of course, this was after I'd revealed my plan to get a yellow (my favorite color) jeep and a German shepherd dog (for companionship and protection), and travel by myself around the country. I figured I could stop along the way and get jobs (washing dishes—whatever), see the land, meet its people, and absorb America like a sponge. At the time it seemed like such a grand plan. (Coincidentally, it was also about this time that my mother's hair started to turn white!) Common sense prevailed, and I scrapped the plan. I'm sure my angel, who probably threatened to go on strike, was greatly relieved.

But I did go to the Fair. After taking the train to San Francisco and a bus to Oakland, I boarded the *Cascade*. The Southern Pacific had an automat car onboard, dispensing pre-packaged food from a vending machine. The only good thing about it was that I can today claim to have personally experienced the automat car. After decades of great dining on the railroads, the automat car wasn't very popular. There was a dome car being dead-headed to Portland, and the attendant let me sit upstairs in the dome for a while. The car was dark and I was in my own magical world, watching the moon and stars through the glass dome. Twenty five years later a Union Pacific dome car (possibly the very same one) would re-enter my life and help fulfill my destiny. I've often thought my life is proof positive of the theory of predestination.

Eventually, I had to return to my reserved coach seat. Although the leg rest came way up and the seat reclined way back, it was hard getting to sleep because it was so cold. Across the aisle from me were two nuns. In those days they still wore their long habits, and I enviously eyed what came to look like blankets to me. It seemed as if they were the only warm people on that car. I was planning on waking up early and going to the ladies lounge to freshen up, but when I awoke my head was resting on the window sill and all that could be seen were trees, thousands of acres of dense trees, as far as you could see—my welcome to Oregon. The scenery was so beautiful it was mesmerizing. The heck with my rumpled looks!

All the hotel space in Seattle was sold out, and three ocean liners were brought in to be "boatels". I had a small cabin on the *Dominion Monarch*, a grand old steam-driven cargo liner built in 1939. What a beautiful ship. Sadly, after the Fair she went to Japan, where she was scrapped. In those days, I was doing a lot of oil painting, so my little cabin doubled as my studio. I had brought my art supplies with me, but there was no way wet oil paintings could be transported back on the train, so they became gifts for newly-made friends in Seattle. I was there for ten days. The weather was nice the first day and the last day. The rest of the time it rained. There was even a parade in the rain, with all of the girls on the floats wearing formal gowns covered in plastic. I really loved Seattle, but, oh my, the rain!—a little too much for this California girl. Wonder if any of those painting still exist….

Commuting to San Francisco

I later worked in San Francisco and commuted by train, not only as my father had done, but also my grandfather. My mother's parents had lived in Redwood City with their three little girls, and my grandfather worked in San Francisco and commuted by train. When my mother was just six years old my grandmother died, and my grandfather died before I was born, so I never knew them. But the house where my mother grew up (that my grandfather had built in Redwood City) was on Lincoln

Avenue and the house in Burlingame where I grew up was on a Lincoln Avenue too. The house in San Francisco where my mother had been born was on Buena Vista Terrace (I have a picture of that house I painted for my mother). The house in Walnut Creek where I still live is on Buena Vista Avenue. (Life is chock full of odd coincidences.)

By all accounts, my grandfather was a wonderful, caring man and a loving father, and I've always been sorry that I never had a chance to know him. While riding in those old commute cars, the knowledge that they were the same cars he had ridden, and chances were good that I sat in some of the very same seats as he, gave me such a warm feeling of connection.

A funny thing happened on my way home from work one time. The old SP station in San Francisco was at Third and Townsend. What I remember most about the station was the old blind man who ran the magazine stand. He was totally blind, but he could accurately tell you what to pay and always gave you the correct change, and no one ever tried to cheat him. There would be several trains in a row, and commuters could board early before each train left. They were mostly very conservative businessmen, who would get on the train and quietly read their evening newspapers. I boarded early and sat in a window seat, and must have dozed off with my head resting on the window sill, not waking when the train pulled out of the station. There was an engine parked on a siding facing our train, and as we passed it, I opened my eyes to see a train coming straight at me, causing me to jump up and scream. The impending disaster did not occur, however every newspaper was lowered and every eye was on me. I just sat down and wanted to crawl under my seat, wondering if anyone realized what had happened. It is an odd sensation on a train when sometimes you can't tell if you are moving or if the train next to you is, or If you both are.

Back to Henry

Remember that little boy in my kindergarten class? I used to like to play at Henry's house because he had the neatest model train layout. I was such a tomboy and preferred playing with boys rather than with dolls. A group of boys in my class had a "Boys' Club" that met at Bobby Williams' house and I was the only girl invited to join! There was a lot next to Paul's house where his dad had built the best treehouse. It was built in tall black acacia trees and you would climb up one tree and then walk across a bridge to the house in another tree—quite an adventure!

Almost all kids had a model train that would go around the Christmas tree, but Henry had a whole train table in his bedroom that was up all year, with tunnels and everything. He was a rather spoiled and protected only child. I, on the other hand, was a scruffy little tomboy. The only way Henry was allowed to play with me was at his house, where his mother could keep an eye on me, so I wouldn't beat him up. Really, I never, ever beat anybody up! We kids used to "Indian-rassle" and I would win, even though I was a shrimp of a kid. Admittedly, I did call him names though. His last name was Luna, so, depending on my mood, he was Loony Tunes, Loony Bird, or Lunatic. I think God, who I am convinced has a great sense of humor and of justice, was looking down on me, saying, "Oh, someday I'm going to get you, little girl."

Anyway, Henry was like "the boy next door" and we were always friends. In high school, Tod was my steady boyfriend. Henry was pretty shy with girls and spent most of his free time chasing and photographing trains with his other rail fan buddies. I never would have dated him; he didn't even like to dance, for heaven's sake! In the mid-sixties, Henry joined the Air Force. It was during the Vietnam War, but he was lucky enough to be stationed on Wake Island. Seeing his father around town, I would always ask how Henry was. To tell the truth, I really did-n't care that much and only half listened, but knew it just made his father's day to talk about the "light of his life". What I didn't know was that he was writing to Henry, relating how little Con-nie Collins was asking about him again.

One of Henry's favorite stories of Wake Island is when he was due to be discharged and was scheduled to leave. It was right before Christmas, and Bob Hope was going to stop at Wake Island on his way to Vietnam. Henry said he didn't want to leave because he wanted to see Bob Hope, so he was allowed to stay a little longer. There were only about twenty five Air Force per-sonnel, so they, along with the Commander, hosted Hope's troupe to dinner. Henry's dinner companion was a young starlet by the name of Raquel Welch. Before dinner, he was assigned to drive Hope's band leader, Les Brown, around the Island to search for a plastic lei of little vodka bottles like the one he had gotten the year before. Apparently, this item could only be found on Wake Island and it took five stops to find it. Henry got home before Christmas and was walking down Broadway, seeing peo-ple he hadn't seen for four years. In going into McClellan's hard-ware store, he exchanged greetings with a man coming out. When he got in the store, Mr. McClellan said "Do you know who that was?" "No", said Henry "But he did look familiar." "That was Bing Crosby!" (The Crosby family lived in Hillsborough—about a mile from Broadway.) Henry has always been sorry he didn't recognize him so he could have said "Hey, I just had din-ner with Bob Hope two weeks ago!"

In 1969, I was visiting my parents and had just walked out of the house when Henry drove by. After the Air Force he had moved back home with his parents. He stopped his car, rolled down the window, and asked me if I was going to our ten-year class reunion. I told him I didn't think so. I was recently divorced with two small children and really didn't feel like facing anyone. (As if I were the only one! Hah!) In high school, I was voted the girl athlete of my senior class. (I could have been voted as the girl least likely to ever be divorced!) What did Henry say? "Go with me, and everything will be just fine." He reached above the visor for a pen and paper to write down my phone number. They fell on the floor and Henry was so nervous he dropped them two more times before he took my number. I didn't laugh, but it was pretty funny watching him fumble around.

Before the reunion, we spent a day together in San Francisco to get reacquainted. What a day! We rode cable cars, and went to Fisherman's Wharf and Chinatown. We drank strawberry wine on the Marina and went to the Cliff House, where we walked around the ruins of Sutro Baths. In 1896 when Sutro Baths was built, it was the world's largest indoor pool establishment featuring six salt-water pools, fed from the adjacent Pacific Ocean, and one fresh water pool. We had gone swimming at Sutro Baths for our sixth grade graduation. It burned down in 1966.

We ate dinner at a restaurant on the site where Henry's grandparents had a restaurant that was destroyed in the 1906 earthquake. We had both been born in San Francisco and both moved to Burlingame as toddlers. We even liked the same music. So now, the nerdy, shy, little rail fan had gone into the Air Force and morphed into Mr. Personality—cute, charming, funny, and confident. I, on the other hand, had the stuffing knocked out of me in my personal life, so now we were on an even playing field. Somehow, I really didn't care that he didn't dance!

The Truckee Limited

The PLA had arranged a special excursion train to Truckee in April, 1970. It was twenty-two cars long and the end car was the *El Dorado*, an observation lounge car built in 1924 (SP #2902), the car featured a barber shop (in a separate room), with the original chair. It's hard to imagine being shaved with a straight razor

on a moving train! The train left Oakland in the morning and returned late in the evening, traveling around 400 miles round
trip. The excursion featured a newspaper, printed onboard with
a mimeograph machine. I did the artwork for the newspaper
heading and also for the drink menu (the menu featured cartoon
chipmunks wearing railroad uniforms), and I also served drinks
on the *El Dorado*. This was the very first time I worked on a train.
I wore a very short dress (the style in 1970) and high heels. (had
the legs in those days!) During the trip our car ran out of ice and
the car attendant and I had to go back through about ten cars to
get some. The ice was in a plastic bag, placed inside a cardboard
box. On the way back, it started to leak, so I ran ahead, clearing
the way for the attendant to come through with the ice. The
coaches were all old and their vestibules were around a corner
(not straight through as they are now). At one of the vestibules
the attendant said, "Stop, Connie. I can't hold it anymore." He
punched a hole in the bag and the water noisily cascaded out.
Just then, two elderly women came around the corner, looking
shocked and disgusted. They turned their faces away from us
as they passed by, so I'm not sure if they ever realized it was just
an innocent bag of ice water!

There was a photo run-by at shed 47 in the high Sierra. In a
photo run-by, the train stops and those who want to take pictures get off the train and form a line. The train backs up and
runs on by the group while they take their photographs, and
then returns to pick them up. The *Truckee Limited* was pulled by
diesel engines (when a photo run-by was done with steam engines it was really spectacular as the engineer would pour out
the smoke for the pictures). When the train stopped to let off the
passengers, I stood on the steps of the car, watching. Henry was
out in the deep snow, organizing the photo line. Suddenly, I got
pelted with a snowball from Henry's direction (revenge, perhaps, for my having beat him at Indian rassling or calling him
names). Without a thought of my bare legs and high heels, I

jumped into the snow and the battle was on. Everyone on the train was cheering me on, and the photographers on the ground got an added attraction. The *El Dorado* is part of the California State Railroad Museum now. Fully restored, it runs on the Museum's Sacramento Southern Railroad for excursions.

New Career: Travel Agent

Before he went into the Air Force, Henry had a job at Pacific Airlines fueling airplanes, and he had returned to his job when he got out. I had gone back to college to study drafting and had a job as a draftsman. I loved drafting, but hated doing it eight hours a day, and Henry wasn't all that happy fueling airplanes, so we decided to go to travel agent school together in San Francisco. It was a night course lasting four months, so we could go after work. The funniest thing happened after class one night. It was a rare warm evening in The City and lots of people were out walking. We decided to go get an ice cream cone. With our cones in hand, we walked past some stairs that led up to a place where a house had stood. All that was left were the foundation, a chimney, and a tree in the yard with a rope and a tire hanging from it. We climbed the stairs and sat on a wall eating our ice cream. A couple walked by below us, obvious tourists with cameras around their necks. They appeared to be a couple of country bumpkins, looking all around as if they had never seen a city before. Henry suddenly called down to them, "Hey, have you seen our house?" Startled, they looked up at us, "No, no we haven't." Then, with a straight face, Henry said, "The darnedest thing happened. We just went out for ice cream, and when we came back our house was gone!" Wide-eyed, with incredulous looks on their faces, they said, "We're sorry, we really didn't see what happened." We watched as they walked on down the street, muttering to each other, shaking their heads and glancing back at us. For every time I've told this story about Henry's crazy joke, there's a couple somewhere telling the sad tale of a San Francis-can couple who went out for ice cream and lost their house.

Connie's Fun Tours

After graduating from travel agent school, I worked at a cou-ple of different agencies in San Francisco. To supplement my in-come I started a little side business escorting bus trips to Reno. It was 1970 and we lived in a rented house, two blocks north of my parents. I was a single mom with a two-year-old son, Michael, and a seven-year-old daughter, Jade-Lynn. I was again commuting by train to San Francisco, going on the bus trips on the weekends. (Not every weekend, only when I had enough passengers to fill a bus.) While onboard the bus, I'd serve drinks and lead the singing, having learned the words to a hundred old "sing-a-long" songs. I practiced at home with my kids, so they learned all the songs too. Michael was possibly the only two-year-old in the country who could sing *Casey would waltz with a strawberry blonde*, *The Bowery*, and *The man on the flying trapeze*. I also had a game on the bus, where the passengers would try to guess the minute we'd arrive in Reno and the minute we'd get home, so there were sixty guesses in each direction. Each minute cost a dollar and the two winners would get $60.00 each. I was busy on the bus, and when someone bought a "minute," I'd stuff the dollar in my pocket. When we got to Reno, nothing could be left on the bus, so I had the bellman take everything to my room. On one of the trips, I was given a room with two queen size beds and the maid was still making up the room, when the bellman came in with my suitcase and a big box of liquor and glasses. I sat down and pulled the one-dollar bills from my pocket, smoothing and stacking them. "Oh," I said, "I'm so tired, I've been working all day!" I could see the maid from the reflection in the mirror with her mouth hanging open, just staring at me, and I could tell exactly what she was thinking. "If I were you,

Honey, I'd charge more than a dollar!" Rather than explain, it was more fun to just let her think…whatever. Perhaps, like the couple in San Francisco, she's somewhere telling her version of the story.

The Cruise

I was manager of the travel agency where I worked, and one day a sales rep came in from the Prudential Grace Line. They had just relocated from the east coast and needed passengers for an upcoming cruise. The ship was a cargo liner and carried eighty-five passengers, but they only had about fifteen booked. They offered the owner a free cruise. She said she couldn't go, but could her manager go? The cruise was sixty days long and was leaving in ten days. I didn't even have a passport, and said there was no way I could go. After going home that evening, the kids and I went to my parents' house and I told my mom, "I got the craziest offer today." When she heard what it was, she just stared at me. "Why can't you go? This is the trip of a lifetime." Well, ten days later, there I was, throwing serpentine off the side of the *Santa Mariana*. We had moved from my rented house and stored all of our stuff in my parents' garage, had a yard sale, got a passport and all the necessary shots. I was able to take Jade-Lynn, who was now eight, with me and Michael stayed with my parents. So off we sailed, under the Golden Gate Bridge, on what was truly the trip of a lifetime. My mother had made the impossible possible.

I always say that being a mother is the only job I have ever taken seriously, wanting to be able to say at the end of my life that the world is a better place for my children having been born. People used to say to me, "Oh, you're so lucky to have such good kids." Well, let me tell you, luck had nothing to do with it! It's hard work raising kids. Even though I was a single mom for eleven years and always worked, sometimes long hours, I al-

ways knew where my kids were and with whom they were playing. They knew I said what I meant and I meant what I said, and
they were taught manners and respect for others. We never had
much money, and they never complained.

It always irks me when the excuse for bad kids is said to be
single parents. Of course it's better to have a two-parent home,
but pretty much, the excuse for bad kids is bad parents, single
or otherwise. I had no apprehensions leaving my three-year-old
son with my sixty-two-year-old mother or taking my eight-year-
old daughter on a cruise where she was the only child. I never
could raise one eyebrow like my mother did, but I did have the
"look" — the secret weapon of mothers everywhere.

We stopped in Long Beach to pick up passengers, bypassed
Mexico, stopped in Columbia, went through the Panama Canal,
stopped in Aruba and Trinidad, sailed down the east coast of
South America, through the Straits of Magellan, up the west
coast, and back to San Francisco. I'm not going to write about
the trip, because it's a book unto itself, and besides, there were
no trains involved. I will say, however, that my guardian angel
went into overdrive!

I do want to tell you about Jade-Lynn, as the trip had a terrific
impact on her life. My daughter was an extremely timid and shy
child (really easy to discipline). She used to spend summers on
a ranch in Oregon with her father's parents, and a lot of time
with mine, so she was very comfortable around adults. On the
ship she became everyone's pet. She would sit on the Captain's
knee, slap him on the back and say, "Well, hello, old Captain!"
(I think she had seen one too many Shirley Temple films.) One
night, we retired to our cabin and there was this tray with hot
chocolate, cookies, and strawberries on the table. "Did you order
these?" "No, Mommy," she said, "But Blackie (the head purser)
did ask me if I liked hot chocolate."

About the middle of the cruise, we picked up two new passengers. One evening before dinner, I was in the main lounge,

sitting at the bar having a cocktail with one of the other passengers. Our new arrivals were sitting a couple of seats away. In skipped Jade-Lynn. She was quite petite, always perfectly neat and coordinately dressed (quite unlike her scruffy, little tomboy of a mother). Her hair was up in pigtails with pink ribbons that matched her pink dress. She wore white knee socks and white Mary-Jane shoes. She skipped over to the bar, hopped up on the empty stool next to me, slapped the bar and said, "Bartender, give me a scotch and soda." "Yes, Miss," he replied and turned to make her nightly Shirley Temple that he had her sign for. This was a game she and Everett, the bartender and one of her new great friends, played. How she knew the names of all the drinks she ordered was a mystery, but every night It was something new. By the way, just as I used to play with cap pistols as a kid (we all did), yet have never shot a gun in my life, Jade now only drinks an occasional glass of wine. Anyway, used to her game with Everett, I didn't even turn around, but I could see in the mirror the gaping faces of our new passengers. I think they were trying to figure out if Jade-Lynn was a midget. Finally, I turned to them and said, "I think I'd better explain. This is my eight-year-old daughter and that (pointing to the drink) is a Shirley Temple."

As our ship was half cargo, we stopped at ports never frequented by regular cruise ships. In Buena Ventura, Columbia, we stopped to load coffee. Our crew referred to this port as "the hell-hole of the Pacific". A mini-bus took us to a local orphanage, where we delivered apples (a rare treat for the kids). Passengers were not allowed in the rest of the town, where the TB and VD rates were about 80%, and the best hotel in town had a little boy in front renting cats to take care of the rats in your room! Even one of our ship's officers had his wristwatch swiped off his arm by a "wharf rat"—a little boy around ten years old, who proceeded to jump in the water through about six inches of muck and oil (In comparison, the San Francisco Bay was pristine!), and there was a stench permeating the town. The source turned out to be a huge mound of rotting potatoes, dumped when they were going bad. (I always wondered why they weren't dumped in the water where they would have been consumed by marine life.) With no comparisons, the locals seemed to accept these conditions as normal. I was watching from the deck of our ship and said to one of the crew "I wonder how far I'd get if I walked into town?" "Oh, you'd be perfectly safe. They know you're a mother and they, being devout Catholics, revere and respect the Madonna—and mothers."

Jade-Lynn saw the terrible disparity of the mansions right next to the hovels in Lima, Peru, and the unbelievable poverty in Ecuador. As a single-mom family, we often didn't have two nickels to rub together, but we were broke, not poor, and Jade-Lynn knew the difference. She came back from that trip with wisdom, confidence and compassion and she was just eight years old!

Amtrak

On the cruise, I had plenty of time to take inventory of my life. I had come to a point where I couldn't really afford renting a house, but that problem had been solved. I would have to find a new place to live when I got home, preferring to stay in Burlingame. I was very close to my mother, and she had a terrific impact on my kids. It was a safe community, and the schools were excellent. Jade-Lynn actually attended the same grammar school as Henry and I had. One time, there was a school function—a potluck dinner—and as I walked in with my dish, my old sixth-grade teacher spotted me. He was now the principal and was visibly shaken seeing me, "What are you doing here?" You see, I was always in trouble in school—not because I was a bad kid, but I gave mischievous new meaning. It all stemmed from my need to make the other kids laugh. Anyway, I told him that I now had a child attending Coolidge School. "Oh, no! Who is it?" he cried with dismay. When I told him it was Jade-Lynn, he couldn't believe it. "But she's so good!" I attended a parent-teacher conference, where the teacher said how she enjoyed having Jade-Lynn in her class, as she was so delightful, and she wished all the other students were like her (music to a mother's ears). She then looked at her papers and said, "I see she's from a broken home!" That really upset me. Why did she even bring it up? So I let her know, "There is nothing broken about my home!"

I like to say there are three stupid things in life. (Stupid things are things you can change, and don't.) One is to stay in a bad job, the second is to stay in a bad marriage, and the third is to have a bad mattress! Why the mattress? Because if you don't get a good night's sleep, the first two are in jeopardy! Most things in your life are by choice. Unfortunately, the wisdom to make good choices often only comes with age and experience. The best we can do is accept and take responsibility for the bad choices we make and turn negatives into positives. The best choice I ever made was having my children.

People often say that I love children. I say, "I love good children!" When my kids were little, I'd have so many kids playing at my house, people thought it was a day care. One neighbor told me, "We can't understand it. You're the strictest mother around, yet all the kids want to play at your place." "Hello!!!" All the kids had to abide by six rules: no fighting, no name-calling (I know I called Henry names, but I would have been in big trouble if my mother had heard me!), no tattle-taleing, no screaming, no running in the house, and no whining. If any one of these rules were broken, the perpetrator was either put on a naughty chair or sent home. Some of the worst brats I've seen are from two-parent homes, where there is a bad marriage. Don't get me wrong. I love marriage and abhor divorce. But like raising kids, marriage takes a lot of hard work, and if it becomes absolutely unfixable, get out, and give yourself and your kids a shot at happiness.

The downside of living in Burlingame was that it was full of snobs. I grew up with very little money in a rich community, and now my kids were in the same boat. Actually, I learned a very valuable lesson at a very young age. (I think most people never do learn this lesson.) Money has absolutely no correlation to happiness or class. I've known some very rich people who were wonderful—compassionate, caring, and not snobby at all—and others who were miserable and wouldn't give you the time of day. I've known college graduates who were rather stupid, and high school dropouts who were smart. Class has a lot more to do with character than money, and education is more about curiosity and reading than getting a degree. Just as prejudice can be found in all races, snobbism can be found in all social classes, and the root causes of both are ignorance and insecurity.

So, I needed to find a new place to live in Burlingame. Even as manager of the travel agency, plus my side trips to Reno, I wasn't making enough money to live on. I figured I had three options to make it financially: get a second job, get married, or find a better paying job. I couldn't justify leaving my kids for a second job—I was all they had. When I did my bus trips to Reno it wasn't every weekend, but it was still hard leaving them so often. Henry was a confirmed bachelor, and we only dated sporadically, so I didn't see marriage in my future. The agency was managing just fine without me. (Your indispensability can be measured by the hole that is left when withdrawing your fist from a bucket of water!) Option number three remained my only choice.

When we got back home I found a place to live, a block off Broadway. There was a large house on a corner that had been built in 1907. It had been converted into two flats, and we moved into the upstairs one. The flat had three bedrooms, so the kids each got their own room. It was like a giant dollhouse with dormer windows, window seats, built-in bookshelves, and slanted ceilings. We just loved that place and lived there for eight years. There was a lawn and small garden in front, and I did all of the garden maintenance, having always loved gardening (my therapy). I built a picket fence around the lawn and pulled a "Tom Sawyer". After rounding up a bunch of old, used men's shirts, I outfitted all of the kids in the neighborhood and let them paint the fence. They were so proud of their feat and I never had to worry about anyone marring the paint.

Amtrak was new and hiring, and with my travel-agent background I had no trouble getting a job in the reservation department. The "res" bureau was located in the Ferry Building at the foot of Market Street in San Francisco. So here I was again, commuting by train to The City. The streetcars from Burlingame to The City were long gone, ending service in 1949 when the City of San Francisco took over the Market Street Railway and suspended service to other counties.

Amtrak inherited a reservation system from Southern Pacific—the famous "wheel". SP had made a large round table, and placed an actual train wheel horizontally on the top of it, creating a large lazy-Susan. Built on the wheel was a round wooden cabinet, full of cubbyholes. Each cubbyhole contained some bound-together cards. Each card represented a train car, with diagrams of either a coach car or a sleeper. The agents would sit around the table with telephones on the counter in front of the wheel. When a reservation was taken the agent would spin the wheel to extract the appropriate "train" from a cubbyhole, and the passenger's name would be written in pencil in the coach seat or the bedroom. If there was a cancellation, the name was erased and the space opened up. When all of the spaces were filled, the train was sold out. Our computer generation today would scoff at such a primitive system, but considering it was used when there were many more trains and passengers, and one always talked to a "live" agent, I think it worked pretty darn well! When you call Amtrak today, you get "Julie"—an auto-mated answering system. Just to get an arrival time, you have to go through a menu, then "Julie" asks you to say the name of the arrival city. "Oakland, California." "Did you say Denver, Colorado?" "No, Oakland, California." "Did you say Albany, New York?" "No, you idiot, Oakland, California, Oakland, California!" "Please state the arrival city." It's a good thing there isn't a real person at Amtrak doing this or she would be hunted down and tied to the tracks!

As automobile and airplane traffic became more prevalent, fewer and fewer people traveled by train. Before Amtrak, rail-roads made their money with freight trains and most of them wanted to get out of the passenger service. They had to show the government low ridership to be allowed to drop the passen-ger trains, so there was a concerted effort to discourage train travel. Schedules were devised so trains would miss connec-tions, equipment was not maintained, reservationists were rude and not helpful, and "sold out" trains would leave half empty. There were exceptions, of course. Southern Railway took great pride in their passenger trains and was one of the last to give them up. In 1970, Congress passed the Rail Passenger Service Act establishing the National Railroad Passenger Corporation— Amtrak. Service began May 1, 1971, serving forty-three states with twenty-one routes.

In the beginning all the equipment was left over from the rail-roads. Although it would probably be denied, we were pretty sure the best equipment was used back east, where most of the train services operated. The problems were so bad—no heat, no air conditioning, broken seats, engine failures—and Amtrak was running on tracks owned by railroads who didn't want passen-ger trains interfering with their freight traffic. There were so many complaints that all the res agents had to attend a special class on how to handle irate phone calls. When I worked at Am-trak, if the train came in the same day we called it on time!—

well, almost. I knew Amtrak was going to make it when, at the end of one call, regarding an especially harrowing experience on the *California Zephyr*, I said, "Is there anything else I can help you with, Sir?" "Yes," he said, "I want to book another trip." What a lot of people just don't understand is that train travel is so much more than transportation. It's a life experience and train travelers love it, warts and all.

We used to have a contest in the res bureau on who would get the most outlandish call, and one day I won, hands down, when taking a call for a roomette—a tiny room with a single chair for day use that would open to make a bed that was the width of the chair and the length of the room. The woman calling asked me if she could bring her dog. In those early days, dogs were allowed if you had sleeping accommodations. "Yes, you can bring a dog." "How many?" "Did you say how many?" "Yes." "Well, how many do you have?" "Three." "Three! What kind of dogs are they?" "A Great Dane and two German Shepherds." "Please hold while I check with my supervisor." At first, we all thought it was a joke, but after the supervisor talked with her, we realized she was dead serious. We looked it up in the rulebook, and there was no mention of the quantity or size of the dog allowed, so a new rule was created for that situation. One small dog was allowed. I would have loved to see the look on the porter's face had we granted her request.

With my travel agent background, I convinced my manager that travel agents needed special handling, apart from the general public, and was given my own desk. It was so successful that another agent was added, then two more, and the Amtrak Travel Agency Department was born.

When Amtrak started, they had to offer jobs to all the displaced employees from the railroads. Most assimilated very well, but there were a few that just didn't get it. One res agent from SP was so rude on the phone, she had to be constantly reminded that her job now was to actually put people on the train—not to discourage them. To make us more familiar with the product, we were encouraged to ride the trains ourselves (for free). I took my kids to Portland on the *Coast Starlight*. We had coach seats, and the one thing I made sure of (recalling those nuns on my trip to the World's Fair) was that we brought blankets. I had a little Amtrak employee pin, but didn't wear it, and never mentioned working for Amtrak. We were riding in old SP equipment and the cars on the train lost power. We had just gone to the dining car where the waiters had put candles on all the tables. The chefs were able to keep on cooking (I'm not sure whether it was propane gas or presto logs fueling the stove), and I enjoyed one of the finest steak dinners I've ever eaten. Candlelight on a train is so romantic, and there I was with my two kids!

The conductor on the train was a very disgruntled leftover from SP. He obviously hated Amtrak and was very vocal about it with the passengers, blaming Amtrak for all of the problems on the train. Never saying a word, I put my Amtrak pin on and made sure he saw it. He blanched and suddenly got very quiet. I never reported his behavior, but he didn't know that, and I hoped he changed his ways. It was almost impossible for Amtrak to fire anyone, but most of the bad ones either left on their own or retired.

When Amtrak finally went to computer reservations, they moved their reservation center to a big facility in Riverside in Southern California. That move didn't appeal to this San Francisco native, so I ended my career with Amtrak. I really loved that job, and learned so much about trains.

The Reno Fun Train

The *Reno Fun Train* was started in 1963 by the Southern Pacific Railroad and the Reno Chamber of Commerce. It ran in the winter when it was dangerous and sometimes impossible to drive to Reno, the railroad had spare equipment and Reno needed the business. When SP got out of the passenger business the handling of the train was awarded to a private tour company—American Rail Tours. Before leaving Amtrak, I was approached to be the manager of the *Fun Train*, so I didn't have to look for a new job. Their office was also in The City, and I started work there handling reservations. The train operated January through March, and was truly a party all the way to Reno. The train consisted of coaches, a dance car with live music, and a diner. Meals were included on the train, and several hotels and motels were used in Reno. It left after work on Friday evening and returned on Sunday.

Before January I sometimes worked on the weekends when the office was closed, and would take my kids with me. Their favorite memory of that was making hot chocolate from the water cooler. I would give them little jobs to do, and Jade-Lynn was so serious and efficient. Michael, my "little man", was quite protective of his big sister and "little mommy". One night, we left rather late and needed to get to the train station. Michael, now four years old, suddenly stepped to the curb on Market Street and hailed a cab. The driver was so startled, he stopped to pick us up and laughed all the way to the station.

As manager, when the *Fun Train* started running I had to go on the train. It was hard being gone every weekend, but I only had to do it for two months. My mom watched the kids, but wouldn't accept any payment from me. Mom always had a thing for silver dollars. They were more common then, and when we were little she would save them, only spending them when she had enough for a savings bond for one of us kids, but other than that she just couldn't spend them. I wasn't much of a gambler, but after watching people playing blackjack in Reno where silver dollars were used, I noticed that at some point almost everyone was $25.00 ahead so each trip I would play blackjack until I was $25.00 ahead, cash out, and take the silver dollars home to Mom.

The train was eighteen cars long and carried around seven

hundred passengers, and oh boy, did it ever get wild. The trip from Oakland to Reno was scheduled to take seven hours but was most often delayed due to the snow conditions in the high Sierras. Although meals were served, people brought their own food and drinks too—lots of drinks! The train started in Oakland after work and picked up passengers on the way to Reno. By the time we got to Sacramento, the people waiting for the train had been partying at the station and were looped before they even boarded. To this day, I still feel a little anxiety when pulling into the Sacramento station. I had never seen so much drinking and craziness in my life, and here I was, thirty years old, in charge of the train. One time, I had to find a replacement band for one of the trips and I found one in Sacramento. They were told which car to board on the train, and when we pulled into the Sacramento station, there, sitting on the platform, was a full-sized, upright piano. It's still hard to believe it got maneuvered up the stairs and through the vestibule to the dance car.

On one trip on the way home, we were slowly winding our way through the high Sierra Nevada Mountains when I got a page requesting me to go to a car for a medical emergency. Running through about ten cars to get there, I asked two passengers along the way, who had "Dr." in front of their names, if they would go with me. When we arrived, we found an older woman lying on her back in the vestibule. She was part of an Italian senior group from San Francisco. Her husband was kneeling beside her, rosary in hand, crying and praying in Italian. She had had a heart attack, and the conductor had called for an ambulance to meet the train at the first possible juncture, quite a distance from our present location. The train normally went very slowly around the multiple curves cut into the sides of the high mountains. In this situation, the engineer pushed the train up to the maximum speed it could safely go. That alone was both exciting and frightening. The doctors were on the floor working on her, and my job was to hold up her legs to elevate them. There was so little room and the doorway where she would be taken off was piled high with luggage. I had one of the attendants step over me to the luggage to clear the space. I now had to hold her legs with one arm and pass luggage with the other. At one point, the doctors were yelling her name and beating on her chest. Her legs shuddered and then went limp, then they moved again. We finally reached the rendezvous point and had to wait in the eerie silence of the snow for the ambulance. Finally, we saw two figures running down a hill through the snow carrying a stretcher and an oxygen tank. When they tried to use the tank, it had a faulty valve and didn't work. They finally got her off, and we were on our way. When thanking the doctors, I told them that I thought she had died when her legs went limp. They looked at each other and said they weren't going to tell me, but she had technically died three times! I found out later that one doctor was a psychiatrist and the other a dentist.

When the train arrived in Oakland, I called the hospital and was told she had survived. The group she was with had boarded a bus for the transfer to San Francisco and I was able to give them the good news before they left, to many cheers and tears. Emotionally and physically spent, I went into work the next day and told my boss I didn't mind handling the drunks, breaking up the fights, and all the other problems, but if those doctors hadn't been onboard, the woman would have died. I said I wouldn't go on another train unless there were at least a nurse and an oxygen tank onboard. He thought I was bluffing and said no, so I quit. I'd had it with trains! (or so I thought.)

Railtown 1897

Henry had gone to work at Great Western Tours (GWT) in San Francisco. They owned and operated an entire excursion train and ran it in Mexico. Because of GWT's vast experience in running trains, Sierra Railroad, located in the foothills of the

Sierra Nevada Mountains in the heart of California gold country, asked GWT to show them how to run tourist trains, and Henry was tapped for the job.

Sierra Railroad was originally built in 1897 to carry freight and passengers from Oakdale to a point in Calaveras County near the town of Angels. The roundhouse, turntable, machine shop, and large depot were located at Jamestown. Over the years, the passenger service was dropped, but, besides the freight business, Sierra RR had become a famous movie locale. Many westerns were filmed in Jamestown, including *High Noon* with Gary Cooper and Grace Kelly. The coach is still there where W.C. fields and Mae West filmed *My Little Chickadee*. Both *Back to the Future* movies and the TV show *Petticoat Junction* were also filmed there. The water tower used in the opening shots of *Petticoat Junction* can be seen from the depot.

The new tourist operation was called Railtown 1897, with Henry as its first manager. He lived in Twain Harte, near Jamestown, for two years. One of the first employees he hired was a local seventeen-year-old kid, Dave Sell. He started in the ticket office and ended up thirteen years later as an engineer and master mechanic. Dick Reynolds, who owned GWT, started the first dinner trains in the world at Jamestown on Sierra Railroad. I was working at Amtrak at the time and our entire reservation department was invited to Jamestown. In addition to the train where you dined onboard, they also had the *Twilight Limited*, a train ride followed by a barbecue in their park at the depot—our invitation was for the latter.

Jamestown (Jimtown to the locals) was an old Mother Lode mining town, frequented by miners, cowboys, and railroad men. The town was small, and a lot of the original buildings were still there. The Willows was a popular hotel, with a dining room and saloon that was a favorite hangout for the locals, who would get dressed up for Saturday night (which meant putting on a clean tee shirt!). The Willows has since then been "gussied up," but when we were there it was still pretty close to the original. After the train ride and barbecue, a bunch of us decided to continue the party at the Willows. Henry's parents had come up for the weekend, so he was off with them, missing all the fun. There was a door to the street on the corner and another at the other end of a long bar. A jukebox was playing and a local couple, she being quite a bit older than he, was dancing a kind of a Texas two-step. They would shuffle down the length of the bar, go out the corner door, shuffle back up on the outside past all the windows, and come back in through the door at the other end of the bar. Every time they came back in, everyone would laugh and cheer. It was so crazy and so much fun. Our friend, Chuck, who worked with Henry at GWT, asked me to dance. Chuck was a big guy, about 6'2", but was very light on his feet and a terrific dancer. We danced, and started a tradition that lasted over forty years—our yearly dance.

I didn't drive then, and my ride up there had to leave early, so I needed a ride back. Rick, one of my co-workers in the res bureau, offered to drive me home. He had lived with a companion for years, and really wasn't much interested in girls. On the long drive home he started to get sleepy, and said he needed to stop somewhere and take a nap. He pulled off the road, put his head against his window and I put my head against my window, and we both fell asleep. It became a running joke that we had slept together, but he came to me one day and said we couldn't joke about it anymore, because it was just ruining his reputation

The Gilroy Garlic Festival and the Pacifics

One of Chuck's and my most memorable yearly dances was in Gilroy. A group of us decided to take the special train from San Francisco to Gilroy, south of San Jose, for the annual Garlic Festival (Gilroy being the garlic capital of the world). It's quite an event, with music and dancing and cook-offs—everything garlic, even wine and ice cream. We had seen just about everything at the festival and it was hot, so we all decided to go back to town and wait for the train to leave. Someone said how a cold gin and tonic would hit the spot, and we went in search of an accommodating establishment. The first two bars we went to only served beer and wine, and the bartenders only spoke Spanish (none of us even knew how to say gin and tonic in Spanish). We finally found an establishment that served mixed drinks. There was a large seating area with a dance floor across the room from the bar. As it was the middle of the afternoon, the area was dark and the chairs were all on top of the tables. Someone started playing the jukebox, and Chuck put out his hand, saying, "Shall we?" We were the only ones dancing on that darkened dance floor, and the bartender got so excited he lit up the mirror ball over our heads. I felt like a princess with her Prince Charming!

The Garlic Festival Special was pulled by SP #2472—a big 4-6-2 Pacific, built by the Baldwin Locomotive works in 1921. "Pacific" is a term designating the 4-6-2 wheel configuration. The first true Pacific was built from a design of the New Zealand Railway in 1901, and was produced by Baldwin. Because the design featured a large firebox, this big, powerful engine became a mainstay of railroads running long-distance trains. The #2472 originally ran from Ogden, Utah, to Oakland, California, on the Overland Route, and was eventually used to pull commute trains between San Francisco and San Jose, ending in 1957. In 1959, the engine was put on static display at the San Mateo County Fairgrounds. In 1976, The Golden Gate Railway Museum (GGRM) relocated the #2472 to their facility at Hunters Point in San Francisco (site of Candlestick Park and the decommissioned Hunters Point naval Shipyard). After a thorough restoration, #2472 pulled several excursions in the 1990s and early 2000s, even double heading with the #4449.

In 2006, the GGRM was evicted from Hunters Point due to a

massive redevelopment of the area. Along with the #2472, they had a large assortment of rolling stock and no place to go. PLA to the rescue! After GGRM sold off or scrapped their excess equipment, they moved to the Niles Canyon Railway.

There are only three Pacifics left (all built by Baldwin), and the PLA has one of them—#2467. This engine was also built in 1921, and was donated to the City of Oakland. It ended up in Harrison Square Railroad Park, along with business car #121 (named the *Western*), a baggage car, and a coach, watched over by a group of volunteers including several engineers who worked for the SP. The PLA acquired the engine, along with the *Western* in 1990. The business car had been built by Pullman in 1903 for the Chicago, Indianapolis and Louisville Railway. In 1926 it was rebuilt by the SP, when it became #121 *Western*. The baggage car and coach went to the Western Railway Museum in Rio Vista, California.

The #2467 was moved to a side track at the Oakland Army Terminal, where it was painstakingly restored by PLA volunteers, including some new members—the same SP volunteers who had so diligently watched over it in the park. Most of them had full-time jobs and could only work on the engine on their days off, so the restoration spanned a nine-year period. Those dedicated, mechanical magicians brought the #2467 back to life and it was returned to operation, steaming from Oakland to Sacramento and making a glorious appearance at Rail Fair 1999. At the throttle was Errol Ohman—one of the dedicated SP engineers. Rail Fair was a double feature for Errol as he took this occasion to propose to his lady love, Carol. (Two years later, Henry and I were guests at their wedding in Jamestown where they repeated their vows standing in front of the Sierra Railroad engine #28.) The 2467 is currently on loan to the California State Railroad Museum as a prominent, static display and has been seen by thousands of people.

The third remaining Pacific engine was built in 1923, and cur-

rently resides at the San Jose Fairgrounds, where it is being restored by the California Trolley Railroad Corporation. Henry
and I would have seen all three of these engines in operation as
children, as they transported our fathers to and from work.

The New Year's Eve Rescue

Every year, Henry would take the kids and me out to chop
down our Christmas Tree. I would always make a big pot of
stew to eat when we got home. We'd take a thermos of hot
chocolate to drink, only after we had procured our perfect tree.
When we got home, we would have our first hot buttered rum,
sans the rum for the kids of course. While Jade and I prepared
dinner (a teacher had started calling her simply Jade, and it
stuck), Michael and Henry would put the lights on the tree. After
dinner, Jade and I would finish decorating the tree. It was exactly the same procedure year after year. I love tradition, and I
think it's important for children, giving them a sense of antici-
pation and security. Henry's dad had passed away, and he was
living in his childhood home with his mother. He would always
spend Christmas Eve with us at my home, where we would
open up our gifts to each other.

It was 1975, and there was going to be a special New Year's
Eve train up on the Sierra Railroad. I rarely ask for anything, but
I really wanted to go on that train. Henry said he didn't like New
Year's Eve parties, and he didn't want to go. The more I asked,
the more adamant he got about not going, until we were barely
speaking. Well, I wasn't about to sit at home, so I took the kids,
including Jade's best friend, Jeannette, to San Juan Bautista. It
seemed like Jeanette spent more time with us than at her own
home, and I thought of her as my second daughter. To this day,
she calls me Matahara.

San Juan Bautista is special to me, as it was the site of my
great, great grandfather's land grant. His name was Don Manuel

Larios. My mother used to take us kids there at least once a year and I did the same with my children. He's buried there in the cemetery—land he donated to the town. Some of his things are in the town's museum, located near the Mission San Juan Bautista, one of the original 21 California Missions. It's a great town to visit. Besides the historic square by the Mission, there are terrific Mexican restaurants, antique stores, and a bakery on Main Street that was there when I was a little girl. It's a family tradition that whoever goes to San Juan Bautista has to bring back Portuguese orange nut bread from the bakery for everyone in the family. (I've never found that delicious bread anywhere else.)

Michael had to make a model of a California Mission for school, so it was a perfect excuse for us to go. Off we went in my old Ford Fairline stick shift, singing our old songs all the way down. Henry and I never, ever fought, and I decided to bring him back a little "I'm sorry" gift, finding the perfect offering at an antique store. It was this little cast metal cable car that cost $6.00. After paying for it, I turned it over and a tiny little stamp declared it was "Made in Occupied Japan". It would have cost a whole lot more if the store had seen that first, so it was quite a find.

By the time we were headed home it was dark, but we would be back home way before midnight. To get on the freeway we had to drive down a dark, country road in Morgan Hill. I stepped on the clutch, and the pedal went straight to the floor. So there I was on New Year's Eve, in a broken down car with three kids and, of course, in those days no cell phone. It was a pretty desolate stretch of road, but we could see a farmhouse in the distance. I locked the girls in the car and took Michael, then about seven, with me. As we approached the house, we saw these large, dark shapes in the front yard rising up and growling. "Michael, turn around and slowly walk back to the car. Don't look back, and don't run!" I put the hood up and there we sat. A car finally came down the road and stopped. In it was a very nice couple, and the man walked with me back to the farmhouse. When we approached the yard this time, the three big dogs there were all wagging their tails! It was a small farm owned by an older Mexican couple, and they couldn't have been nicer. After calling AAA, I went back and got the kids and we waited at the house. Being New Year's Eve, it was quite a wait, and the couple made us feel so welcome. I've always believed there is so much more good than bad in the world, but good doesn't sell, so bad gets more attention by the press.

When the tow truck came we all crammed into the front seat. There was no rail or bus line the driver could take us to, so, after dropping off the car at a garage, he took us to Cindy's, a restaurant open twenty-four house. There was a phone booth in front of the restaurant, and I called Henry. He wasn't home, so I left a message with his mother and gave her the telephone number in the phone booth. When asked to repeat the number, she gave me her own. His mother was very, very confused, and after giving her the number again I worried about him getting the message at all. We were in our backgammon stage then and took the game with us everywhere, so we spent the time drinking hot chocolate and playing backgammon, taking turns waiting in the phone booth.

After our little tiff, Henry, who also had a bus driver's license and did occasional charters, had agreed to take a group to Monterey. While he was there, he picked up some champagne and a stalk of Brussels sprouts as an "I'm sorry" gift to me (just because he knew I was quirky enough to enjoy getting it), and he went over to my place when he got home. We weren't there, of course, and when he asked my neighbor where we had gone, she said she couldn't remember, but it started with an "S". Henry thought I had gone to Sonora, near Jamestown, to ride the New Year's Eve train by myself. He had been invited to another party, across the Bay, and was so upset with me he decided to go. It was raining hard that night, and while he was driving on the freeway, a highway patrol car in front of him spun out. Seeing that, he decided it wasn't that great of an idea to be out driving in such a storm on New Year's Eve, so he turned around and went home. His mother had forgotten about my message, but he saw the note by the phone and called. He had a little brown Toyota, and drove all the way to Morgan Hill in that storm to rescue us, so happy I hadn't gone to Jamestown. We got to my place in time to greet the New Year. The kids were dancing and singing, and said it was the best New Year's Eve ever.

Cross Country Amtrak

In the summer of 1979, I had a week's vacation and decided to visit my sister, Letty, and her family in Boone, North Carolina. The kids and I flew after work on Friday to Los Angeles. A friend of ours picked us up and took us grocery shopping, as we were going coach on the train, and I didn't have enough money for us to eat all of our meals in the diner.

I never thought much of the idea of being a best friend and buddy to your own child. I think children need parents to be parents. I did, however, really enjoy the company of my children. They were a delight to be with and we had a lot of fun. It was inconceivable to me to talk back to my own mother and my kids didn't talk back to me and they never fought with each other. The train, The *Sunset Limited*, left Los Angeles at 10:30 pm, and we got seats at the end of the car, where there was extra room. There was a young man in the seat behind us. He was a cute, charming, eighteen-year-old Oxford student from England, named Harry. Jade, who was fifteen at the time, didn't mind it at all that we made his acquaintance. Since we had more food than we needed, it was shared with our new traveling companion. We had brought our backgammon game with us too, and nearly wore it out on the trip.

When we got to El Paso, Texas, we could see Mexico out of one side of the train and the U.S. out of the other. It was like night and day. It reminded me of the mansions and hovels in Peru, but at least here, it was two different countries. When we got to San Antonio there was time to go into the station and stretch our legs. It had been nice weather, but while we were in the station we heard this booming sound of thunder and ran to the train in a deluge of rain. Even on the train, the thunder was so loud it seemed like the train was going to be knocked off the tracks. We didn't get summer thunders storms like that in California, and it was frightening and exhilarating at the same time. I had never traveled cross country before and had always seen maps of the United States that showed Texas in yellow, brown, or orange. I guess in my mind the whole state was desert and cactus, and I was amazed to see east Texas so lush and green.

When we got to New Orleans, we had lodgings at the Hansel and Gretel Hotel in the French Quarter. Harry was staying at the local YMCA, and we made plans to sight-see New Orleans together. There was a very peculiar, mustached man on the train, who wore a light gray suit. He certainly didn't look "American", so we decided he just might be a spy. At night we saw him on Bourbon Street , strangely darting from one place to another, and he so intrigued us that we decided to follow him. It became quite a game, and at the time it was great fun. Looking back on it, I wonder if he had noticed he was being dogged by a woman and three kids, enough to give anyone trepidations. If he really was a spy (which was highly unlikely), he may have changed his profession after that evening! If he wasn't a spy, he just may have ended up in therapy!

Everyone was out walking in the middle of Bourbon Street, which was closed off to traffic, and the fronts to the jazz clubs were open so you could see and hear the musicians playing from the street. When we walked back to our hotel, we were amazed at all the cockroaches running across the sidewalk and up the buildings. That night at the hotel we were so cold. Outside was hot and humid, but it seemed everybody kept their air conditioners cranked all the way up.

The next day we took streetcars through beautiful neighborhoods, visited an above ground cemetery and walked down these little stairs to the water. We took off our shoes and stuck our feet in the Mississippi River. Looking back, I can't imagine why we did that, but at the time it seemed appropriate! We also ate beignets at the *Café Du Monde* and dinner at Tujagues. Tujagues was a bar on a corner with an adjacent dining room, dating back to 1856—the second oldest restaurant in New Orleans. When we were there, the dinner price was very reasonable and included about seven courses of small portions—wonderful French-Creole food. The dining room was plain with long wooden tables, and the place probably hadn't changed for fifty years. Henry and I went to New Orleans years later and I said we had to eat at Tujagues. When we walked in, there were these little round tables with white tablecloths and flowers on them. It, like the Willows in Jamestown, had been all "gussied" up and was more expensive. But for me it had lost so much of its historical charm.

The next day we left on the train for Tuscaloosa, Alabama. Unlike shy Jade, Michael was a very gregarious child. Like Jade, he was very comfortable around adults and made friends with everybody. Before we got to Tuscaloosa, Jade and I were playing backgammon in the lounge car and Michael had returned to our coach seats. We left the lounge to go get our suitcase from the coach, and Michael wasn't there. The train had stopped and I thought he might have gotten off the train. Well, he wasn't on the platform either. I found the conductor and told him the train couldn't go, as I was missing my eleven-year-old son. A search ensued, and Michael was found in the men's lounge, regaling passengers with a story. I can't imagine where he got that from!

We stopped at Tuscaloosa to visit my nephew, Greg, who was

attending a swim camp at the University of Alabama. He was five months older than Jade, but we hadn't seen Greg for years and didn't know if we would recognize him. We were sitting on some stairs where we were told the swimming students would pass by. This one darling boy appeared and I told the kids, "Oh, I hope that's him," but he walked on by. We were disappointed and turned to watch him go. He got about twenty feet away, turned around, stared at us, and said in this heavy southern accent, "Aunt Connie?" What a lovely visit we had. The hotel room here was actually colder than our room in New Orleans, and even though it was hot outside, we had to ask for extra blankets, as there was no thermostat in the room.

We only spent one night in Tuscaloosa, taking the train the next day to Charlotte, North Carolina. Letty had to come quite a distance from Boone to pick us up, giving me a new appreciation of the proximity I had always had to trains. We had a nice three-day visit, including a visit to the *Tweetsie Railroad*, located in Blowing Rock, NC. Opened as a family-oriented tourist train in 1957, the three-mile run featured the 1917 coal-fired *Engine #12*, the only surviving narrow gauge engine on the East Tennessee and Western North Carolina Railroad. Michael especially enjoyed spending time with Letty's other son, Patrick. They were not only about the same age, but people thought they were twins.

When we got back on the train on our way to Washington D.C., it was after one in the morning and the train was totally dark. We went through car after car, dragging our heavy suitcase, looking for three seats together. Seeing our plight, a passenger was nice enough to move his seat, so the kids could sit together. I was in the same car, but at the other end. What I found annoying were all of the people stretched out, taking up seats they hadn't paid for. As the conductor knew how many people were boarding at each station, he really should have saved seats together for new passengers, and directed them to the available car, as was the procedure on the *Coast Starlight*.

We had never been to Washington D.C. before, and the high-light was seeing Lincoln's memorial. Opened in 1922, the 19-foot sculpture of a seated Abraham Lincoln, our 16th president, seemed to embody the very essence of his soul. I had seen lots of pictures of the monument, but it was overwhelmingly mag-nificent in person. I remember looking up in awed silence, as tears streamed down my face.

We had a map of the city, but didn't realize that the streets were laid out like spokes of a wheel and there were identical ad-dresses for south and north, and for east and west. I was trying to get to the Smithsonian, and had walked in the opposite direc-tion. There was a cab and bus strike going on, so there was no public transportation. Well, we walked and walked and walked. The neighborhood we found ourselves in was pretty rough. Let's say, we really, really didn't fit in, and people were starting to come out of their houses to look at us. Oh boy, what had I gotten us into? Just then, an older black man came driving up in a cab and said, "I think you had better get in, now!" He took us to the train station, and I gave him almost all the rest of my money as a tip. I guess angels have striking cab drivers on speed dial!

We had arrived in Washington in the morning, and were catching an afternoon train to New York. On arrival in New York we didn't have time to see the city and took a subway straight to the airport. We were lugging this big, old, heavy Samsonite suitcase (no wheels then) through the subway tunnels and we weren't sure which way to go. We asked three different people, commuters rushing by, and no one would even talk to us. I may be a bit prejudiced, but that wouldn't have happened in San Francisco.

We finally found the right subway train to the airport and took a red-eye flight home. It turned out to be a red eye in more ways than one. Onboard, they were showing a movie, "The Champ", with Jon Voight and Ricky Schroeder. That was the biggest tearjerker movie I had ever seen. All of the passengers were crying. Grown men were actually audibly sobbing. I can't imagine why they would ever show that movie on a plane. The plane was late, and in those days people could meet you right at the gate. Henry was waiting with several other people, and when they saw our faces they thought something horrible had happened onboard! I had to go to work later that day and my eyes were still puffy and red.

The Engagement

Also in 1975, I went to work for I. Magnin—a high-scale department store based in San Francisco. I worked at the distribution center in the town of Brisbane, south of The City. It was a warehouse, so we didn't have to dress up, which suited me just fine.

With my scruffy little tomboy demeanor and lack of interest in high fashion, it's a wonder I wasn't fired on principle alone! I admire and appreciate fashionable clothes on other people, but give me a hundred dollars and I make a beeline for a nursery or the Home Depot. Building things is in my blood. My dad's uncle, Charlie Weeks, was the first developer of East Palo Alto. He named it Runnymede and envisioned independent living by each resident, raising chickens and selling the eggs through a community co-op. His brother-in-law, my grandfather was a contractor and built many of the homes in the development, including his own house that is still there. He employed my dad as a carpenter when he was a young man, and Dad in turn taught my siblings and me how to use tools when we were little kids (before power tools). To this day, I love building things and I actually owned my own cement mixer, which came in mighty handy when I laid over 3,000 bricks in my back yard! I always get asked how I know how to lay bricks, and I say "If you can ice a cake, you can lay a brick!" Of course garden bricks are a different skill than bricks on a building.

Henry was working in the office of Great Western Tours, located on the ninth floor of the elegant Palace Hotel in San Francisco. I drove to work from Burlingame and Henry commuted by train. Once in a while, I'd go to The City after work and give him a ride home. Henry and I were like the odd couple. I was Oscar and he was Felix. Even in kindergarten he was clean and neat, and at Great Western Tours he always wore a three-piece suit and tie to work. One afternoon, I had driven to The City to pick him up and I parked in an alley across the street from the hotel. I felt so conspicuous going up in the elevator with some very well-heeled guests, and as Henry and I were walking toward my car I said, "Gee, I wonder what people must think. Here you are, a well-dressed businessman, and I look like some sort of bag lady!" Just then, with no warning, he looked at me and yelled really loud, "FIFTY DOLLARS?" All the people in the alley were looking at me, and there wasn't even a manhole to dive into! The maid in Reno would have been happy to know my rates had gone up!

By 1979, Henry and I had dated for ten years (steadily since that New Year's Eve rescue in 1975). I had accepted the fact that he was a confirmed bachelor. If we were ever to marry, it would be after his mother and my two little dogs had died and my children were grown. I still remember Michael, at about ten years of age, putting his hands on his hips and saying to Henry, "When are you going to marry my mother?" It was funny watching Henry squirm out of that one.

So here we were on another Christmas Eve, opening up our gifts to each other. My gift to Henry was a beautiful collectors' carafe of Jack Daniels. He opened it and poured himself a double (I now know it was for courage). My present from him was in a tiny box. When I opened it, there inside was a small birthstone ring. I was really confused, as my birthstone is amethyst and this was a garnet. When my kids saw that ring, they thought it was an engagement ring and jumped on Henry, screaming and laughing. I thought, "Oh, poor Henry," and I started to laugh. I could hardly wait to hear how he was going to get out of it and explain the mistake to them. The more excited they got, the harder I laughed. I was doubled over and my sides hurt. Tears were running down my face.

Suddenly, I heard Henry say to the kids, "I've never done this before, but I didn't think she'd act like this." What? Wait! What? What was he talking about? It seemed that he had been down to Morro Bay and gone Christmas shopping with Anne, the manager of Great Western Tours' Hearst Castle package. He saw these little birthstone rings and asked Anne if she thought one could work as an engagement ring. All of our friends thought Henry was never going to get married, so when he said that, she said, "Yes, yes, it certainly could!" Why a garnet? Henry had my birthday off by one day. The next morning I called his house and asked, "Remember last night, did you really mean it?" After dating for ten years, I was in shock. Henry always says he thought it was sweet of me to give him an out like that. He also tells everyone he doesn't like to rush into things. Really?

That year, Henry had put together an excursion for the New Year's weekend up on the Sierra Railroad. It was supposed to be the last of the passenger train runs on that railroad, so there was a dinner train in the evening of the 30th and a trip to Oakdale on the 31st. (It wasn't the last passenger run—the Sierra railroad has had four of these "last runs" and the train is still running today,) Henry still wasn't about to celebrate New Years Eve on the Sierra Railroad and we went home after the train on the 31st!. Karl Koenig (a classmate of ours from seventh grade and fellow charter member of the Pacific Locomotive Association) and his wife, Bonnie, went, as did our dear friends, Dan and Rose-Marie. I worked with Rose-Marie at I. Magnin. (We later got married in her beautiful garden at her home in Redwood City.)

One of my favorite railroad stories features Karl. He had

quite an illustrious history with trains, starting with engine service for the Southern Pacific. He was also editor of Pacific News magazine and the author of several railroad books, and his career culminated in ownership of his own short line, Hardin Southern Railroad in Kentucky. At one point he went to work for Amtrak as a conductor on the San Joaquin trains in California. On one of his first trips, a passenger complained about the heat in the car. Karl officiously said he would remedy the problem and with great authority, opened a cabinet at the end of the car. Expecting to find an air conditioning panel inside, he was dismayed to find it was a broom closet. With every eye upon him, he reached in with great flourish and rattled the brooms. After closing the door, he put his hand up under the air conditioner and loudly announced "There, that's better!" and walked to the next car. Everyone was satisfied and he received no more complaints about the heat.

We announced our engagement on the dinner train. There was a combine car on the train, built in 1911 for the Arizona and Eastern Railroad. It was a combination of freight, passenger, and mail service, hence, a combine. (This same car is now part of the Niles Canyon Railway collection.) There was an old upright piano on the car, and everybody was singing. The piano player kept playing, *The bells are ringing for me and my gal.* What a night! We stayed with our friends that night at a motel in Sonora. The next morning, we all went to the coffee shop for breakfast. We got horrible service and after finally putting in our order, we waited and waited to be served. Finally, Henry said he had to go, since he was in charge of the train, but for us to come after we had eaten breakfast. We finally got served and everybody kept saying that it was a good thing I was with them, as the train wouldn't leave without me. We drove to Jamestown to catch the train and it was gone! No one could believe it. Dan and Rose-Marie were going home that day and not riding the train to Oakdale, so Karl and Bonnie and I piled into their car and off we went to catch up with the train. We drove to a juncture where the train would pass by and stood by the tracks. Here came the train...and there went the train! It didn't even slow down. We piled back in the car and headed this time for a place where dozens of rail fans were lining the route to take pictures. Bonnie and I, who were both wearing skirts, stood beside the tracks and showed our legs! Here came the train, and this time it stopped! It turned out that Henry was planning on stopping there anyway, but all those rail fans didn't know that. As far as they knew, it was our gorgeous gams that stopped that train! I was so humiliated that he had left without me and said this was about to be the shortest engagement ever!

When we got to Oakdale, the train stopped next to a big park. All the passengers detrained and Henry gave a speech from the platform of the rear car. Bonnie and I were standing in the park and I said (loudly), "Well, I don't know who that guy is, but I'm certainly not going to vote for him!"

I guess I did vote for him after all, as we married in June of 1980. As a couple, over a span of ten years, we had attended quite a few weddings, so we drew on our joint experiences when planning our own, collaborating on everything, even picking out our wedding china together. Rose-Marie and Dan lived in a lovely home in Redwood City with a large old-fashioned garden and we repeated our vows there under a flower-strewn arch in front of a magnificent five-hundred-year-old oak tree. The personnel director from I. Magnin's, Linda, did all of the flowers, Dick Reynolds and Chuck Vercelli catered the affair and three friends and fellow rail fans from Rio Vista were part of the wedding party—Bill Kluver, Henry's best man, The Reverend Don McGinnis who married us, and John Plytnick who played the piano.

We had scheduled a wedding rehearsal the evening before followed by a dinner at the Lanai Restaurant in San Mateo. We were all in the garden waiting for Henry to arrive with his mother and aunt. He was going to pick up the wedding cake in The City after work and bring it with him. He was late and everyone started to make jokes about him getting cold feet (a runaway groom!). We had reservations at the restaurant and the time was getting later and later! Pretty soon the jokes stopped and everyone started to avoid looking at me or gave me sympathetic, sad glances. Suddenly, over the fence we saw the top of a bus that had stopped in front of the house—an odd sight in an elegant residential neighborhood. We all ran out to see Henry in the driver's seat. The bus door opened and his little aunt and his mother emerged. When Henry had gone to the bakery to pick up the three-layered wedding cake, there was no way it could fit in his little Toyota. One of his San Simeon Stages buses, used for his Hearst Castle tour, was in San Francisco for a new paint job and he had commandeered it to transport the cake in the luggage bin. We went through the rehearsal in double-time and then we all piled into the bus for the ride to the restaurant, singing all the way. Considering the rest of our life, this crazy episode was a pretty appropriate way to start.

Joyce, my matron of Honor lived in Oregon and almost didn't make it to the wedding. On May 18th Mt. St. Helens erupted. (It still seems bizarre that there was an active volcano in Oregon.) There was so much ash in the atmosphere that it prevented flights from leaving Portland. I think she managed to get on a flight just in time for the rehearsal on June 13th. Twenty years later we threw an anniversary party. Our invitation read: "20 years ago two unbelievable events occurred. The first was Mt. St. Helens erupting. The second was Henry married Connie!" The saying "When pigs fly" comes to mind and I don't think until Don got to the "I now pronounce you…….." that anyone (including me) really believed it. I do believe that every single person who came to our wedding brought a camera for proof. Don turned to our guests after the ceremony and said, "Ladies and gentlemen, may I introduce Mr. And Mrs. Henry

Luna." The first time someone called me Loony Bird, I swear I could hear God saying, "Gotcha!"

Henry moved into my place and we lived there the first year of our marriage. In 1981 we bought a house in Walnut Creek, about twenty miles east of San Francisco, and commuted by car together for two years. We had to drive through the Caldecott Tunnel and across the Bay Bridge, to where Henry would go to work in San Francisco. I would continue on to Brisbane—a twenty four mile trip from Walnut Creek. I knew there had been a few catty remarks by some of my co-workers regarding my rather modest engagement ring, but the talk stopped when Henry bought me a house!

After Jade graduated from high school, she worked with Henry at Great Western Tours and in 1983 when Henry started his own business, Key Tours, in Walnut Creek, Jade worked there with him. I continued commuting to Brisbane by myself for two more years.

My mother had a massive stroke in 1979 and was in a wheelchair after that. She had further medical complications and by the end of 1984 I was going to Burlingame after work every day to help her before heading on home. Mom always worried about me driving so much and was happy when I retired from I. Magnin on my birthday, February 1, 1985. It's almost like she knew, now that I was safe, she could leave. My mother passed away fifteen days later on February 16. That's also the day I grew up.

Coolidge Elementary School 1947. Henry, top row, 3rd from right. Harriet 2nd row, 2nd from left. Me, bottom row, 4th from the right.

Burlingame High School 50th Reunion. Left to right: Henry, me, Paul, and Harriet.

6th grade class at Coolidge Elementary. Paul, front row. Me (kneeling) and Henry, 2nd row. Harriet, top row, 2nd from left.

Ellis Crawford, the first airline stewardess.

Just engaged!

Just married!

Chapter II My Destiny

My Life as a Cook

Another memory of my third year on this earth is of standing on a chair with an eggbeater, helping to make bread pudding. My mother taught me basic cooking. When shopping in grocery stores now, I think how simple cooking used to be. There were very few choices and no prepared food. TV dinners were a big thing when they came out, but again, simple. The good thing was, there was very little added to the food. Bread wasn't full of preservatives, so it went stale. We had a bin in our kitchen and we saved all the stale bread to make bread pudding.

My father's parents lived in Palo Alto, where they had a big garden and raised chickens and rabbits. During WWII, millions of people had "Victory Gardens" growing food for themselves, even in containers on fire escapes in the cities. Most of our neighbors had fruit trees and when the fruit was ripe it was shared with all of the neighbors. Our big crop was apricots and walnuts and every year Mom preserved jars of apricots and jam. What a shock it was when I tasted my first store-bought apricot. Nothing can compare to tree-ripened fruit. After the war, we still had a vegetable garden. We also had chickens and rabbits until Burlingame passed an ordinance banning them inside the city limit and we had to get rid of them.

We kids were included in planning the garden and my dad used to say that every child should plant radishes, because they sprout in three days. No one in their right mind put poison on the food they were growing and there was no talk about organic vegetables—we all just grew them. I remember going into the garden with a saltshaker and eating lettuce leaves and radishes right there after hosing them off. My favorite thing was dipping a stalk of rhubarb in my palm full of sugar. We all knew rhubarb leaves were poisonous and not to eat them. I don't know if kids just used to have more common sense, but it seems now, if some kids are told something is poisonous they try to either sniff it or smoke it to try to get high.

It seems that the more food has been altered, the more allergies have occurred. When I was young, every kid in my class ate peanut butter and jelly sandwiches, and I can't remember anyone who was lactose or gluten intolerant. Mostly, diabetes was something that old, overweight people got, and in a class of thirty, there might have been three overweight (but not obese) kids. We had the freedom to be kids, without all of the over-protective measures of today. If kids today lost their electronic gadgets, would they know how to play? It's something I often wonder. Would they know how to build forts and climb trees, play hide and go seek, and dig holes? Would they dare to ride a bike without a helmet and would they spend only the money they had earned? We learned to read from "Dick and Jane" books in school and honed that skill with stacks of comic books. Dealing with bullies as kids taught us how to cope as adults with unfair bosses and corrupt politicians. Life is not always fair and the sooner you learn that truth the better off you are. Choosing not to be a victim actually frees you to get along with your life and making it the best it can be.

I honestly believe every school should have a vegetable garden, where students are taught how to grow food. A lot of vegetables ripen in the summer, but there could be an extended summer program allowing students to harvest what they had grown and sell it at a farmers' market. The profits could go back to the school, giving the kids a little practical business education as well. I also think kids should be taught the fundamentals of cooking and nutrition.

Our little grammar school in Burlingame went from kindergarten to the sixth grade, and we had a cafeteria. The food was inexpensive and nutritious. The cook, who I remember as a warm and patient woman, worked alone and children could help in the kitchen and receive a free lunch. I loved doing this. The job I remember the most is drying the silverware and the most memorable food was the apple crisp (the best I've ever had). Good cooks know that nutritious food can also be delicious. I think school cafeterias have pretty much become a thing of the past. I suppose it was deemed too expensive, but considering that, in many cases, it may have been the best meal of the day for many students, it's a shame the program was stopped. In the Intermediate School in Burlingame that Henry and I attended for our seventh and eighth grades, we had a homemaking class and a shop class teaching valuable skills. The boys went part of the year to homemaking while the girls took shop, and it was the other way around the rest of the year. Now, it seems that kids only know how to shop—at the mall!

When we were in grammar school Harriet's mother worked and her grandmother did the cooking and didn't teach Harriett how to cook. I, on the other hand, cooked all of the time. My sister Pat was six years older than me and cooked more than I did, but mostly I remember our kitchen was a family affair. I remember teaching Harriet how to make a cherry pie, and in high school I made spaghetti for both my church group and my YWCA group. In my senior year in high school Pat was married and Letty worked so I bought all the food for our family and cooked dinner, as my mom, who was a registered nurse, worked nights.

When I moved out of home at eighteen I had to support myself while I attended the College of San Mateo during the day. I had two jobs, one in the early morning and one at night. In the early mornings I worked as a board-marker at a stock exchange. The stock activity used to be displayed on a ticker-tape, and my job was to run back and forth on an elevated platform and write down all the updated figures on a big chalkboard. At night I washed dishes by hand at the Denmark House Restaurant in Burlingame. It was owned and run by a widow who had a thirteen-year-old daughter. The restaurant was in a large house and the restaurant's dining section was the house's living and dining rooms. The dishwashing area was in the large back porch. The mother and daughter lived in the rest of the house. The mother (who was from Denmark) did all of the cooking, and it was some of the best food I have ever eaten. The prices were very reasonable and a lot of her customers were there every night. It was there that the seed was planted for me to one day have my own little café.

I didn't drive—I rode a bicycle. At that time only young kids rode bicycles. Even high school kids considered themselves too old for such a childish activity. For me, it was transportation. I took drama in college and my friends, who all had cars, teased me about the bike. One day my friend, Dick, asked if he could ride my bike. He liked it so much he went out and bought one for himself. He was a natural leader and pretty soon most of the other kids in the class had bought bikes as well. One of our classmates, Mike, lived across the San Francisco Bay in Hayward. Today, the San Mateo-Hayward Bridge has been rebuilt and is higher and wider, but back then it was just two lanes built close to the water. Dick and I put our bikes in the back of his convertible and drove across the bridge, parking about two blocks away, out of sight of Mike's house. We rode our bikes to his house and stopped, gasping for breath (we were actors, after all), and convinced Mike we had just ridden over the bridge. Of course, that wasn't allowed so Dick told Mike, "You wouldn't believe what Connie had to promise the toll-keeper to let us on the bridge!" After sufficiently recuperating from our "marathon", we took our leave and rode back to Dick's car to load our bikes. On our way out of Hayward, laughing all the way, we passed Mike in his convertible. He was so worried that he was out looking for us, to give us a ride home. Busted! I've always thought bicycle companies should pay me a commission for being such a pioneer!

Ever since I can remember I've never followed the crowd, and I taught my kids to do the same. It amuses me that many of the people who claim to be such non-conformists are often the biggest conformists of them all. Back then it was beatniks and hippies, now it's tattoos, rainbow colored hair and body piercings. There will always be innovators and leaders who introduce new trends and those who go along because they really like and enjoy the trend, but many followers just want to fit in. Since time began, every new generation wants to disassociate from their predecessors and this is normal. Things were pretty wild and crazy in the 1920s when my parents were teenagers—certainly shocking to their elders. For my generation, it was rock and roll. I think now what has changed is the obsession adults have with staying young and youngsters have with acting older. The innocence of children and the serenity and wisdom that comes with age have been compromised and bought off by the fashion, cosmetic and drug industries. Perhaps now, the true non-conformist is one who is comfortable in his or her own skin, accepting and enjoying whatever age they are.

My drama class friends used to bring me bags of apples and I would bake them apple pies. It wasn't work, it was fun, but little did I know I was honing my skills for a future career. Everyone in my family was a good cook, including my brother. One time Pat and Bill both brought chicken liver pate to a family party. I wisely abstained from voicing an opinion as to the best one, but I've always said my sister Pat is the most talented cook in the family. She became a chemist-engineer (We always like to say she really is a rocket scientist, as she worked on the star-wars program!) and when dining out, she is able to analyze all the dishes. She's also very creative and can improve almost any

recipe she tries. Letty was busy in high school, being both cute
and popular, and she didn't do much cooking then. After her
kids were born she went back to college, got straight As and became a CPA. In any case, today she is a terrific cook. Both my
kids were taught to cook and they are both very good at it. I've
never understood mothers who don't teach their kids to cook,
although nowadays a lot of mothers (and grandmothers) don't
know how themselves. I have a friend who says the favorite
thing she likes to make for dinner is reservations!

Even after I was married and had children, I always worked
and I always cooked dinner. Eating out was a treat, but that was
expensive and also often a disappointment. I didn't see why I
should pay for food that I could make better at home at a fraction
of the cost.

When I worked at I. Magnin, every Friday was "Dip Day". I
worked with a very diverse bunch of people and everyone
would bring their best dishes. We comprised all kinds of nation-
alities and races and "Dip Day" was an international smorgas-
bord! Some of the best recipes I have now are from those days.
(I would kill for a good lumpia!) A cookbook was even created.
One of the best cooks was my friend, Rose-Marie, and I learned
so much from her.

I became known as the "Pie Lady." I would take orders for
pies and bring them to work. When I left I. Magnin, it was my
intention to open a little café around Walnut Creek. With a name,
menus and recipes, I started looking for a location. Henry, who
is normally a very positive guy, started to criticize everything I
planned. Finally, he admitted the source of his negativity. He
figured if he owned his own business and I owned mine, we
would never see each other. Of course, this was true. So, my
dream went onto the back burner.

Key Tours

Henry and I work so differently that we never thought we could work together. He is very methodical and conservative. I am very creative and erratic. He can't even watch me work! Even at home, he would plan a project, lay out all his tools, wear the proper clothing, then proceed with a start, middle, and finish, before even considering another task. I, on the other hand, would have five or six projects going at the same time. I've always had the ability to envision things, sometimes sketching them out, but most of the time just working with my mind. One time, I was putting up individual lattice on the fence in our back yard. It was a custom design, so the prefab lattices couldn't be used. From the top of the ladder, our covered patio was seen in a new light. It was a dirty white and every time I looked down, it bugged me more and more. Finally, standing it no longer, I climbed down the ladder, went to the paint store, came home, moved all the furniture, painted the patio a light mint green with white trim, moved everything back, and went back to putting up the lattice. Actually, I think most men work like Henry and most women are multi-taskers. If they weren't, no children would ever live!

Henry came to appreciate what I did, as I never had a "Honeydo" list for him. I was the Honey that did! When we first moved into our house there was a broken window. Henry said we would have to call a glazier. I didn't even know what a glazier was. Growing up in Burlingame, we used to play baseball in the street. Our house had a glassed-in front porch with all these little windowpanes. Every time we hit a ball through a window, the perpetrator had to replace the window (my dad had cleverly taught us how). Henry was amazed when I fixed the window and I was amazed that he didn't know how! I never spent money on clothes, hair, make-up, nails, shoes, and jewelry. I built things and gardened and cooked. Henry's favorite sight of me, though, was in the kitchen. It was the closest I came to being a traditional wife! One time, he bought me a pink sweatshirt. On it was a picture of a ruler and a saying— "Every inch a woman!" I think he wanted the neighbors to know I was a little bit more than just a handy(wo)man!

I went to work at Key Tours on a temporary basis. We were a tour operator specializing in Amtrak tours and cruises. Jade was in the cruise department—my shy, timid daughter no more! At age nineteen she led a group tour on the *Fairsky* cruise ship, looked like a little model, and was so poised. People didn't even think we were related! I took reservations, and my temporary status stretched out over twenty years. Eventually, I handled all the Amtrak groups, and did the bookkeeping. The department I worked with at Amtrak was the Travel Agent Desk, my contribution to Amtrak so many years before.

The Virginia City

Besides Amtrak tours and cruises, for a while Key Tours managed the *Virginia City* private railcar. It was a 1928 Pullman car that had been owned by Lucius Beebe. His first railcar, called *The Gold Coast* had been built in 1905 and was retired (it is on display today at the California State Railroad Museum, located in Old Sacramento.) The 1928 version was decorated by a Hollywood set designer and is over the top ornate. The car features a working marble fireplace, Venetian side lamps, a crystal chandelier, French provincial furniture, and silk curtains. (It's often referred to as a "bordello on wheels".) Lucius Beebe was a society man-about-town in San Francisco, an author of many books about railroads and, at one time, was editor of the *Territorial Enterprise* in Virginia City, Nevada (whose most illustrious reporter in the 1800s was Mark Twain). Beebe traveled and entertained on the *Virginia City* with his companion and co-author, Charles Clegg, and also with a St. Bernard dog, T. Bone Towser, who, incidentally, was assigned to bedroom C.

My Inspiration—Joe

Key Tours also used other private railcars for some of our packages. One car was the *Yerba Buena*. It was a Pullman sleeper, built in 1942 and converted to a business car in 1965. It was quite elegant, with its teak and mahogany interior, two drawing rooms, two bedrooms, dining room, rear lounge, and open platform. We used it for our Glacier Park package tour, leaving out of Oakland. On one of our departures we had no guests booked from Oakland to Seattle, so Henry and I decided to take a little vacation on our own tour.

We boarded the train in Martinez and since the train left in the late evening, ate dinner at a restaurant across from the depot. We were already full when the waiter suggested bread pudding for dessert. Against our better judgment, we justified getting just one and splitting it. The pudding came and I think the portion could have easily fed three people. It was so delicious that we devoured the whole thing and waddled our way to the depot. When the train came we were greeted by Joe, our car attendant and chef. Sitting on the table in the rear lounge was a plate full of club sandwiches. I couldn't even look at them, but, somehow, Henry (not wanting to hurt Joe's feelings) managed to eat half of one. Joe looked to be in his eighties. He was an old black chef from the heydays of the trains from the forties and fifties. There were just the three of us on the car, and we asked Joe to sit with us in the rear lounge. "Oh, no, ma'am, I can't do that." "Joe, that's silly. Of course you can, it's just us." "On, no, I can't." After a while, I said "Oh, Joe, John (the owner of the car) said you would give us anything we wanted. Is this true?" "Oh, yes, ma'am. What would you like?" "What I would like is for you to sit with us!" We had him!

After Henry went to bed, Joe and I sat in the dining room. He said it was his favorite time, when all the passengers had retired for the evening and he could enjoy a cold bottle of beer. That night, he told me wonderful stories about his life on the trains. In the Northwest, sometimes the trains would stop and the cooks would get off and pick fresh blueberries for pies that night. One chef, Joe told me, was so jealous of his recipes that he would hang a blanket in the kitchen, so the other cooks couldn't see him cooking. In the old days, tables in the dining car had to be set so that each one was a mirror image of the one across the aisle. To remember where to place the salt and pepper, since the pepper was hot and the engine was hot, the pepper was always toward the engine and this was referred to as "hot to hot".

I was entranced, and it was this evening with Joe that changed my life and pointed my way down a new path: as a private railcar chef. Joe's cooking was "old school" railroad—never fancy-schmancy, French, or California Cuisine. It was just basic, down to earth, fresh, and delicious (and lots of it!). This was also the style of Fred Harvey (the father of railroad cuisine), and it was my inspiration to emulate this style of cooking my entire career as a chef which was to cover a span of twenty-five years.

The Native Son

The *Native Son* was a Union Pacific dome lounge built in 1955. It's even possible this was the very same car I had ridden in so many years before when I went to the Seattle World's Fair. A bedroom under the dome had been removed to make space for a kitchen, but at first there was just a sink and a small electric stove. Later, a refrigerator/freezer unit was added, and also plates, glasses, and flatware, but there were no cooking utensils. My very first job cooking for private railcars was for the *Native Son*. Another employee at Key Tours had chartered the car for a group and asked me if I would cater a lunch for them. I prepared the food ahead of time and planned to load it on the train when it stopped in Martinez. It had been raining and raining, and when I got to the station I had to wade through a foot of muddy,

cold water to get to the train. Martinez is located on the Carquinez Straits, an extension of the San Francisco Bay. With a
combination of heavy rainfall and a high tide, the low level areas
of the town had flooded. But the "show must go on", and the
food got delivered to the train. The next day, I went to the Martinez station and found the floor covered with a thick layer of
gooey mud. A new station in Martinez has since been built,
wisely at a little higher elevation.

At this time I was working full time in the office taking reservations for our Amtrak tours. Henry had put together an excursion for the PLA using the *Native Son* and asked me if I would
like to come along and do the cooking. I guess I figured if he had
enough faith in me that I could do it, then I believed it too. So
that's how it started.

In the office, I was put in charge of booking groups on Amtrak and some of them started going by private car. In the beginning, I just chartered the *Native Son*. I can't remember when I
started using other cars, but when one car is not available, you
look around for another one. Other railroad chefs are hired to
do just the shopping and cooking. I did it all, putting together
the whole package—booking the group, reserving the car and
the hotel space, hiring waiters, arranging flowers, washing and
ironing the jackets and linens, stocking the bar, shopping, loading the train, and cooking.

The *Native Son* was based in Fullerton, located in Southern
California, and its owner, Dave Rohr, was one of the nicest guys
in the business. He had a young kid go along on the trips to take
care of the car, Will Walters. Will was one of the hardest workers
I've ever seen. He was thin and wiry, and unbelievably strong
for his size. When we were stopped at a station with a little lay-
over (like Sacramento), it was nothing to see Will outside the car
cleaning windows. When he wasn't working on the car, he'd be
hunkered down in the crew room, writing about trains (such a
rail fan!).

After we'd run quite a few trips using the *Native Son*, the car really needed a paint job on the outside, but Dave couldn't spare the five thousand dollars it would cost to get it done. Telling me something can't be done is like waving a red flag at a bull. Key Holidays ran a package tour to Reno all year long, using the *California Zephyr* and ten different hotels in Reno. I contacted all of these hotels, and also the Reno/Sparks Convention and Visitors' Authority, and pitched the idea of a "moving billboard". Five of the hotels and the RSCVA put up a thousand dollars each and provided their logos, which were then made into giant decals. I contacted a mobile paint company in Southern California and one weekend the *Native Son*, parked on a siding surrounded by large warehouses, got a makeover. The paint company was used to painting trucks and had never painted anything so large as a dome car for a train. The hardest part was masking off the dome windows with paper. Standing on the top of a tall ladder with the wind whipping the paper around was quite a challenge. We had perfectly matched the Union Pacific yellow color, and when the car was painted it looked terrific. The decals were affixed to the sides of the *Native Son* and it ran in service around six months with them before they were removed. The largest decal was the Reno Arch, with lettering that read "Reno Railcar." There was also a decal for Key Holidays, so we all got some terrific publicity, and the *Native Son* got a spiffy new paint job.

Jim Ramos was from Southern California and used to come on the *Native Son* as it's mechanic as well as work for me as a waiter. On one trip to Reno he had to fly home the evening we arrived, so he was showing the other waiters (Michael, Tom, and Darrel) how to work the car. The electrical cabinet was located at the bottom of the stairs to the dome and he had it open showing his attentive "students" what they needed to know for the return trip. When he finished, he closed the cabinet door and the car went dark! A wire had gotten crimped in the door and shorted out the electrical system. When we got to Sparks, the switcher put us on a siding where the ground power wasn't working. It was winter and cold outside and I remember trying to heat some hot chocolate with candles. We had some leftover fried chicken and apple pie, so we offered it, along with tepid hot chocolate to the yard crew in Sparks. They must have liked it, as they ended up moving us several times before finding a working ground power location. Jim said he had never seen a yard crew so accommodating before. It was routine for us to always offer food to the yard crews and sometimes we even got food up to the engineers on Amtrak. We didn't do it for favors, but when we needed one, it certainly didn't hurt. We still like to tease Jim about ending his lesson with a blackout!

Whenever I make an apple pie, I think about one of the funniest things that happened on the *Native Son*. We had a weekend trip to Reno for a group of thirty-two. On Saturday, I went to the car in Sparks and baked six apple pies for the trip home on Sunday. As the kitchen was under the dome, the large window was at street level and there was a long table in front of the window. I always used large glass pie plates and piled the apples high so the final product looked pretty scrumptious. The six pies were on racks on the table and could be seen from the outside. When the *Zephyr* stopped in Sparks, the *Native Son* was attached to the end of the train right next to the Amtrak dining car. Before the train left, one of the Amtrak cooks walked past our car and spotted the pies. He dropped to his knees and, rolling his eyes, he alternately pointed to his open mouth and to the pies and then clasped his hands in prayer. When we stopped in Reno to pick up our group, there he was on his knees repeating his enthusiastic plea for a piece of pie. This very funny performance was repeated at every Amtrak stop on the way to Oakland to the delight of a very amused audience on the train. Needless to say, when we arrived in the yards in Oakland, he was rewarded with the object of his desire.

The owner of the *Native Son*, Dave Rohr, used to bring a

group from Los Angeles to San Francisco every Thanksgiving and the car would be in Oakland long enough for me to use it for an overnight trip up to Reno. On one of my trips, I turned on the oven to prepare lunch and the kitchen filled with smoke. I think I may have turned the air a little blue myself when I discovered the source of the problem. Apparently, on the way up from LA, the chef decided to bake some pumpkin pies. It can be tricky putting a pumpkin pie in the oven at home without sloshing the mix up on the crusts, but on a moving train!!! I can't imagine what he was thinking, but the worst part was that none of it was cleaned up. (He was probably too busy trying to come up with an alternate dessert.) I can't remember how I managed to cook lunch, but I do remember soaking and cleaning oven parts the rest of the trip.

I used to say that I was the only chef who could bake a soufflé on a moving train, but when I served them, I called them pancakes! When I baked pies on the train I felt such a connection to history, influenced by Joe's story of those blueberry pies.

Doubling the Hill

Henry had arranged an excursion for the Pacific Locomotive Association (PLA). With thirty-two guests, we took Amtrak's *San Joaquin* from Oakland to Bakersfield, with a bus transfer to Los Angeles. Our overnight stay was at the Biltmore Hotel, a Los Angeles Historical Landmark built in 1923. Everyone else on the trip had a small overnight bag. I had a huge, heavy suitcase, as I had to bring all of my pots and pans, bowls, and cooking utensils with me. In the morning, Henry and I took a cab to a grocery store, leaving my suitcase at the bell desk. (We should have put it in the cab.) My menu that day included my famous fried chicken. The cab dropped me off in the rail yard, where I loaded the supplies onto the *Native Son*, and stayed to start getting ready. Henry returned to the hotel to escort the group to the

Union Station. The *Native Son* was attached to the rear of the *Coast Starlight*—Amtrak's long-distance train running between Los Angeles and Seattle. Our train pulled into the station and our group boarded. After all of the luggage was put onboard, I asked Henry for my suitcase. He had this stricken look on his face, and I don't know what I looked like, but the entire group has always referred to it as "the look"! (Probably it was the infamous "mother look" that strikes fear in hapless souls throughout the world!) A rail fan friend was seeing us off and offered to drive Henry back to the hotel to retrieve my suitcase. Off they ran. When it was time for the train to depart, he hadn't returned and I asked the conductor to hold the train. At this point, I was the one who got "the look", as he called out, "all aboard". Our next stop was Glendale. I opened the vestibule door and—no Henry. I had been desperately trying to figure out a way to cook chicken with no pan, no tin foil, nothing. (I really didn't think chicken sushi was a good idea!) Finally, as the whistle blew, here came Henry, dragging my very heavy suitcase. He jumped onboard, to the cheers of the entire group. We were going to serve an early dinner past San Luis Obispo, so I started frying my chicken in batches. The sink drains off beneath the train, onto the ties, so I was dumping the oil between batches. With thirty-two guests, a lot of chicken was getting fried.

North of San Luis Obispo there is quite a long grade—the Cuesta Grade. It's kind of funny, but in Spanish the word cuesta means grade, so we were ascending the "grade grade". The tracks ran right through the Cal Poly College campus. The school specialized in engineering and architecture, but they also had a large agriculture and husbandry program. Pens of pigs and horses were located adjacent to the tracks. As we were a group of rail fans, there were quite a few scanners onboard and we could hear the crew and dispatchers talking. A member of our group, Dick Murdock, was a retired SP engineer, and the author of many railroads books, so we had our own expert onboard.

Our train was quite long, and halfway up the grade it stopped. Trains gain traction from the sanders—a device that literally shoots sand onto the tracks in front of the engine wheels. Well, the story we heard later was that someone forgot to put sand in the sanders. The train stopped on a curve and from our vantage point, we could see the wheels of the engine sending out sparks as they spun in place. We heard a voice on the scanners say, "Back up, and make a run for the hill." Now, we had just passed by all these pigs and horses, and they watched us as we reversed our course. The train picked up speed, passed the livestock again, and this time came to a halt a little further up the hill. We heard on the scanners a repeat of the first order so again the train backed up, this time further, and made another valiant attempt, to no avail. On the third try we backed almost all the way to "San Louie", and went as fast and as far as we could ("I think I can, I think I can, I think I can!"), putting on quite a show for what I imagine were very amused and entertained livestock. I've always pictured them in my mind as pigs and horses watching a tennis match! Finally, we could go no farther. Here was the train in the middle of nowhere, in complete darkness—stuck. Almost all freight trains between northern and southern California go down the middle of the state through the San Joaquin Valley and the Tehachapi Pass, so we were pretty much alone on the coastline. A decision was made to "double the hill"—a railroad maneuver that involves splitting the train in half. The engine would take the first half of the train over the hill, place it in a siding, leave it, return to take the second half up, and put the train back together. This procedure is not normally used on a passenger train, probably because the rear car would be vulnerable with no power to provide a rear light, especially at night. In our case, we were on the end of the train, the *Native* Son powered by its own generator. So, the first half of our train left and we were sitting there with about six coaches. As the power to those coaches came from the engine, they were completely in the dark with no heat and no food. We, on the other hand, had light, music, heat, open bar, and a fried chicken dinner and being rail fans, our group was ecstatic to be involved in such a rare maneuver for a passenger train. From one of the passenger cars, sitting there in the dark, came a plaintiff cry, "Hey, are you guys back there eating fried chicken?" It's a wonder they didn't storm our car!

And the rumor that it was my chicken grease on the rails that made them slippery and prevented traction is simply not true!

Our adventure wasn't over yet. We were north of San Jose, going through the marshland of San Francisco Bay, when our crew "died". This is railroad speak for when the engine crew and conductor run out of legal operating time. The train had to stop and take on a new crew. This is a safety precaution and quite serious. It sometimes can take quite a while to find a new crew, and get them to the train, which it did. I think we arrived in Oakland around 1:30 a.m., where the *Native Son* was taken off the train.

To me, the real hero of the trip was the conductor, who made the decision to "double the hill". We heard later that he was reprimanded for his actions, but if we had waited for a relief engine from San Luis Obispo, we probably would have been another two hours late. This happened over twenty-five years ago, and people are still talking about the *Coast Starlight* that "doubled the hill" on the Cuesta Grade.

The PLA and the Niles Canyon Railway

Six college students started the Pacific Locomotive Association (PLA) in 1961, in Henry's backyard in Burlingame. At first, they visited and participated in every remaining steam operation they could find. In 1962 they purchased a 2-6-2-tank engine, #6, from Howard Terminal in Oakland, with the provision that it would never be scrapped. The locomotive was originally built

by Baldwin in 1922 for the Sierra Railway and ran as #30. The
PLA eventually acquired more equipment and operated the Castro Point Railway at Point Molate in Richmond, California, as a
living museum. The railway was on Navy property, and in 1985
the Navy told the PLA that they would have to vacate the property. By this time, the collection of cars and engines was extensive and had to be put into storage until a new home was found.

That new home was to be located in Niles Canyon—one of
the most historic routes of the Transcontinental Railroad, com-
missioned by Abraham Lincoln at the start of the Civil War.

Today, there are parallel tracks that run though Niles Canyon
between Niles and the tiny town of Sunol. The convoluted history of these two lines started In 1862 when the Western Pacific
Railroad was formed to build a railroad from San Jose to Sacramento. A connection from San Jose to San Francisco was to complete the final phase of the Transcontinental Railroad connecting
the country from ocean to ocean. In 1865, construction started
north from San Jose and got as far as two and a half miles into
Niles Canyon where construction was halted due to a lack of
funds. In 1868 The Central Pacific Railroad purchased the bank-
rupt Western Pacific and resumed construction, completing the
line in 1869. In 1885 the Central Pacific reorganized with the
Southern Pacific Railroad (SP) which became the dominant railroad. In 1909, a second transcontinental railroad company built
a line through Niles Canyon on the southern side of Alameda
Creek which flows through the canyon. It was also called the
Western Pacific, but was not related to the earlier railroad. The
most famous train to traverse the canyon was Western Pacific's
California Zephyr. It was run by three different railroads—Western Pacific from Oakland to Salt Lake City, Utah, via Niles
Canyon, Pleasanton, Stockton, and the Feather River Canyon—
the Denver and Rio Grande from Salt Lake City to Denver, Colorado, and the Chicago, Burlington and Quincy Railroad from
Denver to Chicago, Illinois. The *California Zephyr* was the first

train to feature vista-dome cars and on-board hostesses called Zephyrettes. For the inaugural run in 1949, each woman passenger received a silver and orange orchid corsage (matching the color scheme of the train) that was flown in from Hilo, Hawaii for the occasion. Known as the *"Silver Lady"*, the elegance and level of service found on the original *California Zephyr* can only be emulated in our country today on private railcars. The *"Silver Lady's"* last run was in 1970. Today, Amtrak runs a train from Oakland to Chicago called the *California Zephyr*. The route is more direct and the trackage is now completely owned by the Union Pacific Railroad.

In 1981 the Union Pacific Railroad acquired the Western Pacific Railroad and continued to run freight trains through the canyon. in 1984, the Southern Pacific abandoned their line on the north side of the canyon and removed all the rail. Any good ties left were removed by the local farmers. Alameda County became the new owners of the line and in 1984 the county leased the historic last link of the transcontinental railroad to the PLA, who established the Niles Canyon Railway (NCRy). In 1998, a new train began service in the canyon on the Union Pacific tracks—the Altamont Corridor Express (ACE). This heavily used commute train goes between San Jose and Stockton and has four trains a day in each direction.

The PLA organization is one hundred percent volunteer, so it took three years to replace enough of the track to run our trains. The SP said they would leave in the switch that connected our line to their main line, but they went ahead and removed it, so the only way we could get our equipment in was by truck. Almost all of the rail that was replaced was donated to us from the Union Pacific Railroad and they eventually put in a switch to our tracks that enabled us to move in the rest of our stored equipment.

After more than twenty-eight years, the facilities are almost unrecognizable and the membership that started with those first

six is now about a thousand strong. I started going to Castro
Point Railway with Henry, and finally joined the PLA. When the
museum was moved to Niles Canyon, I was in charge of the
Commissary Department—a position I held for twenty years.

The biggest event (and most successful money maker) is the
Train of Lights. An entire train (sometimes there have been two
sets) is decorated with thousands of lights and runs in December. Every year, it gets bigger and better, and it is truly spectacular.

Each Spring, hundreds of school children visit Niles Canyon
for an educational train ride. PLA docents explain the importance our line played in the development of the Bay Area and
the West from the first trains to the present day, as well as teaching about railroad safety—a living history lesson that is much
more memorable than sitting in a classroom!

Over the years more special trains have been added and get
more popular with each run. In April and May, the *Wildflower
Special* trains are featured. Our past president, Jim Evans, made
it his mission to sow hundreds of thousands of California poppy
seeds along the right-of-way, and the spectacular sight every
Spring will be his lasting legacy. Summer time features the *Wine
Tasting Specials* show-casing wines from the area's local wineries,
and *Beer on the Rails*—also using local breweries. The highlight
of Mother's Day is high tea served onboard, in August we have
Hot August Nights on the Rails, and *Romance on the Rails* is a reality
on our Valentine's Train. My successor managing the Commissary Dept., Bob Bradley, initiated the *Cancer Train* that runs
every April to benefit the *Relay for Life*. One of our more noisy
events occurs when dozens of speeders (motorized motor cars)
descend on our line and rides for the public are offered as they
putt-putt through the Canyon. Most of our special trains run on
Saturday, as Sunday is reserved for our public runs, which orig-
inate out of both Niles and Sunol.

The most amazing thing about all of this activity is that it is run by volunteers! The membership includes a wide range of social and economic status. The catalyst for all of us is simply a love of trains. Two of our finest mechanics are women (one of them used to work on an oil rig!), and the various talents of our members is immeasurable. The inclusion of people of all ages and from all walks of life has been paramount in making the PLA and the Niles Canyon Railway the success they are.

Our lease with Alameda County included a horse pasture next to the tracks in Sunol. A group was formed in Sunol, called the Friends of the Park, and they transformed that pasture into the most wonderful park. It is private, and can be used by the NCRy, their passengers, and the citizens of Sunol. Our big picnic every year is on the Fourth of July, with a barbecue in the park and a train ride.

I started the *Harvest Moon Train*, with a prime rib dinner (sometimes eaten in the park and sometimes on the train). The yearly Harvest Moon event is still happening (the prime-rib dinner has been replaced with a pot-luck dinner in the park before the train ride.) It's really an experience to travel through the canyon beautifully lit by a full moon. The ride from Sunol to Niles is six miles and crosses two historic bridges over the Alameda Creek. Although there is a winding highway through the canyon, most of it is unchanged and when riding the NCRy's vintage trains, it's easy to imagine the travel experience of the past.

I really enjoyed catering weddings on the train. One time I was just providing hors d'oeuvres and drinks (their dinner was going to be at Elliston—a local winery located up the road from the depot). Before we stopped the train for the ceremony, the bride was at the end of the train in a caboose and the groom was at the other end of the train standing behind the engine in an open car. I was in the next car working at the bar in the combine and could see him right behind the engine. I went out and suggested he come inside. The bride was actually the rail fan and I

think this was the first steam train ride for the groom. I didn't
think the bride would be too happy with him looking like a dal-
matian in all the wedding pictures coved with black spots from
the exhaust of the engine. The train stopped at a picturesque
stop and the bride and bridesmaids got off the caboose and
boarded the train making their way to the covered open car.
They were all elegantly dressed and I can still picture the bride
in her long white satin gown carrying red roses. I think the most
fun wedding was that of the PLA's president at the time, Jim
Evans. This time we had a caboose on both ends of the train—
Jim in one and Kathy in the other. They owned two dogs that
were more like children than pets. One was black and the other
was white and to me they looked like the little Scottie dog from
Monopoly or a set of salt and pepper shakers. They had a girl to
take care of the dogs on the train as they were part of the wedding party—the ring bearers. They were even wearing little bow
ties that bore the rings. A decorated flat car had been parked on
a siding and, upon reaching it, the train stopped and Jim and
Kathy emerged from their cabooses (or is that cabeese?). They
walked to the middle of the train where they crossed over on a
ramp to the flat car to be married while all of the guests watched
from open cars on the train. I was working in the "Bones"—an
open sightseeing car that had a covered section in the middle.
Drinks and hors d' oeuvres were served before the ceremony.
Afterwards, while the train remained stationary, a buffet featuring a full prime rib dinner was set up. We had trays so the guests
could take their meals back to their seats. I kept the pre-cooked
prime ribs in a hot box and carved them on the train. To divert
the bees away from the train, I threw the juice and unusable
pieces of meat off the side. I didn't normally throw garbage off
the train, but there were so many critters in the canyon, I knew
there wouldn't be a trace of it the next day. The girl handling
the dogs took them for a walk down the side of the train and
when they discovered the discarded meat, they were the happi-

est participants at the wedding—duly rewarded for a stellar performance!

My daughter, Jade, got married at the historic Little Brown
Church in Sunol and had her reception on the train. I prepared
all of the food, but as Mother of the Bride, I didn't work on the
train. It seemed so odd to have my waiters serve me my own
food.

The best thing about the weddings on the train was that the
guests had so much fun. Weddings can be rather predictable and
boring (and terribly expensive) with guests sitting at a table and
not much socializing with the other guests. On a train, people
not only enjoy the ride and the scenery, but there is also a lot of
visiting, Guests walk the train and the experience is not easily
forgotten, plus the cost is a fraction of a traditional wedding.

I also catered many celebrations in the park. Golden Rail
Videos produced a terrific video called *The Secret of Niles Canyon*.
In it is a shot of Cliff, in his waiter's outfit standing on the train
steps looking at his watch. I know it was taken on one of the
wedding trains as you can see paper wedding bells hanging
from the top of a covered open car. Cliff looked so official, like
he was checking whether the train was leaving on time. Only he
and I knew he was looking at his watch and thinking "Isn't this
almost over? I want to go home!"

By the time I left the Commissary Department there were
sixty-one members in it because we always had so much fun.
Every July 3rd we'd meet at our house to prepare for the July 4th
picnic. (Sometimes for up to 300.) Henry's job was to barbecue
dinner for everyone while the rest of us prepared the food, table
decorations and baggies that contained a plate, utensils, napkin,
toothpick, hand-wipe and tootsie pop. We would serve green
salad, fruit salad, chili beans and cold "picnic chicken" plus
dessert. It was quite an assembly line and every year PLA member, Dave Burla, ended up frying all the chicken. In the park we
barbecued hamburgers, cheeseburgers and hot dogs. Every year,

we would have a "Members' Train" on the Train of Lights. For that, we would assemble the night before at our house for 'The night of the thousand sandwiches". We would make 500 chicken salad croissant sandwiches, cut them in half and wrap them. On the train they were served on the train along with Costco cookies. The "Santa Servers" wore the white, private car waiters' jackets and Santa hats. The cutest "Santa Servers" were definitely my own granddaughters, Katie and Sarah!

But remember the saying about a person's indispensability? The PLA's Commissary Department is better than ever and doing just fine without me.

Sitting in the rail yards in Sparks, Nevada, was an old 1928 SP diner. It had been used as a maintenance away car for several years, but now sat unused, idle, and empty. It was occupied by bums and had been trashed. Many of the windows were broken, the floor was a foot thick with refuse, and any fixture that could be removed was missing. Henry, who has a genius to recognize potential (he married me, didn't he?), wanted that car for our museum. He asked the SP if they would donate it to the PLA and they said, "No!". Over a period of three years he asked several more times. The last time it was not only "No!", it was "Hell, No!". It wasn't long afterwards that the PLA received a letter stating that we could have the car but we would have to remove it from their property in thirty days or they were going to scrap it on the spot. It was in good enough condition to send it to Niles Canyon by rail, but the SP wouldn't approve the move, so we had to truck it from Sparks to Niles Canyon (not cheap!). It was put on a specially built truck trailer that made it too high to go under many overpasses, so it had to go all the way to Barstow in southern California, then back through Bakersfield and up the San Joaquin Valley to finally reach our yard at Brightside in Niles Canyon. After cleaning up the car we had planned to give the interior a fresh coat of paint. Some of the approximately nine coats of paint applied by the SP over the years had chipped off, revealing wood underneath. The paneling in that car turned out to be rare Cuban mahogany. What a find! Volunteers, led by PLA member, Bud Barlow, painstakingly stripped the paint and restored the wood to its original state, working endless hours on that project for at least eight years. Stripping the ceiling revealed silk-screened California poppies, which we restored and replicated as closely as possible.

On one of my trips on the *Tamalpais* to Denver, a guest rode with us between Denver and Glenwood Springs. His name was Richard Luckin. He had written the definitive book on railroad china — *Dining on Rails: an encyclopedia of railroad china* as well as producing various videos under Luckin Productions. He had an enormous, fantastic collection of old railway china, and he created almost all of the new railroad china, including the china for the *Tamalpais* and the poppy pattern sold at the California Railroad Museum in Sacramento. I worked with him to design china for the NCRy, duplicating the California poppy from the ceiling of the diner. When the restoration of this diner has been completed and the NCRy starts running dinner trains in the Canyon, this china will be used. We were surprised to get an order for a complete set of our china from the Smithsonian Museum in Washington, D.C. and individual pieces as well as full sets of it are available for purchase through our gift store.

The restoration has been completed at the time of this writing. Although the dinner trains have not yet commenced, the car has been used (sans the tables) in lounge service on some of our special trains. Along with a triple unit diner in our collection, one day the NCRy will probably run the most authentic, historical dinner train in the country.

Sadly, Bud passed away before the completion of the project. He was such a gentle, sweet man and I think his spirit will always be part of the car.

My First Crew

When my son was in high school he hung around with five other kids. They were best friends and did everything together. There were five boys and one girl, and they all called me Mom. Five of the six of them ended up working for me on the private railcars. Michael (my son), Darrel, and Tom were my first crew on the *Native Son*, when they were just eighteen years old. Henry also worked on one of my first trips, but refused to go again after one of the guests asked me how much to tip "my boy". I thought it was funny, but Henry failed to see the humor in it. He definitely did not want to be "my boy"!

The kids looked so sharp in their waiters' outfits. It was hard work, but we all had such fun that it didn't seem like work at all. We even had a theme song. I played it the night before while preparing for the trip, in the yards before we left, during the trip, and always after the trip, when we would sit down and count and divide up the tips. The song was Bobby McFerrin's *Don't Worry, Be Happy*.

The boys are all married now, with children of their own. Over the years, Tom (and then Michael) got burned out. Darrel never did, and would go on a trip tomorrow if I asked him. We all have such wonderful memories, which will stay with us always.

Over the years I hired a lot of different waiters. Some were recommended to me by the car owners and some I found on my own. I was always on the lookout for potential waiters. Experience was not necessarily a prerequisite with me. What was more important was personality and attitude. One time, Darrel's younger brother Shawn came on a trip. He was bigger and stronger than Darrel and I think he thought if Darrel could do it, he could too. We were serving tall glasses of the Luna Fizz, my signature drink, and Shawn picked up a tray full. We told him that was too many, but he had seen the other waiters do it and thought he could manage as well. Anyone who works on a train knows that balancing takes muscles not normally used and experience matters. Well, Shawn went out with the tray, lost his balance and the whole tray got dumped. What a mess! We teased Shawn all week-end and when we went to the yards in the morning on the day we left, the boys were all prepping the car. "Where's Shawn?" I asked. We found him asleep in one of the bedrooms, completely worn out. It takes a lot more than strength to have the stamina be a waiter on a train!

Before I ever started cooking on trains, I was a guest during a trip onboard the *Virginia City*. The waiter was a young man by the name of William. He was in the rear lounge carrying a loaded tray of drinks when the train lurched. William responded with what looked like a finely honed choreographed ballet move and not a drop was spilled! I immediately dubbed the move "The William Shuffle" and over the years whenever a similar feat was performed by one of my waiters, we would always say he had done "The William Shuffle". How my waiters did what they did was beyond me. I could cook on a train, but there was no way I could do their job.

The Group from St. Kevin's

One of my first groups was from Saint Kevin's Catholic Church in San Francisco. Quite a few of them had grown up together in the City, fought in WWII, and been friends for many years. They went every year to Reno and they often chartered the car for trips to other places. They became one of our favorite groups.

One year they took the *Native Son* to Bakersfield, a charter bus to Las Vegas and Laughlin, a bus to Long Beach, where they stayed on the *Queen Mary* where it is permanently docked, and then took the *Native Son* back to Oakland from Los Angeles. Another time they did almost the same trip, but after Las Vegas they went by a private charter bus to Branson and New Orleans before returning to Long Beach. That was the hardest trip to plan, as I had to book places to stay often enough for the bus driver to get enough rest. I also needed to put them up in nice places with access to a restaurant and a bar (they were Catholics, not Mormons!) In California, there are hotels and motels everywhere—not the case in many other states. I printed up itineraries for each member of the group with space for notes. A nun was going along, and I said she could grade the papers at the end of the trip! Two brothers were part of that group, Mel and Pete Annuzzi, together with their wives, Marie and Linda. Marie always organized the trips and it was such a pleasure to work with her.

Another member of the group was Al Scoma, owner of Scoma's Restaurant at Fisherman's Wharf in San Francisco. We always had an open bar onboard and, because of limited space, I would ask the group ahead of time their individual drink preferences. One year, for their yearly trip to Reno, Al Scoma asked for *Amer Picone*. I went to six liquor stores looking for it, to no avail. The last store told me it was imported, but thought it might not still be available. He sold me a "knock-off" assuring me that no one would know the difference. On the trip, my waiter informed me that Mr. Scoma had asked for his *Amer Picone* on the rocks. He was served his drink, and about twenty seconds later came to the kitchen. "What is this?" he said scowling, as he tossed it down the sink. "Oh, Mr. Scoma, I'm so sorry, I looked everywhere for *Amer Picone* and no one had it." When he saw I was on the verge of tears, he said, "It's okay, little girl, don't cry, it's all right."

Well, the next year, I was determined to find the real stuff. Certainly, it could be found in North Beach (traditionally an Italian section of San Francisco), so that's where I went. One of the most amusing things in television shows and movies filmed in San Francisco is the availability of parking places. Actors always find parking right in front of wherever they go. The truth is there are rarely any parking places, and when you do find one it's blocks away from your destination! So Henry drove, and he double-parked while I ran into the little Mom and Pop liquor stores all over North Beach. But instead of Italians, it turned out the stores were all being run by Chinese now who didn't know what I was talking about. Ready to give up, I spotted one more little store on a corner. It was run by a little old Chinese lady and her son. She told me she didn't know *Amer Picone*. About to admit defeat, I glanced up to the top of a high shelf. There were some small, dusty bottles with faded labels. "Look, look I think that's *Amer Picone!*" I cried. Her son had to climb a ladder to get the bottles down. I bought all six of them, and after dusting them off and ringing me up, she hunched over a piece of paper, licked her pencil, and wrote in Chinese, muttering, "Vely slow sella, vely slow sella." That had to be the understatement of the year, as the bottles looked like they had been up there for thirty years!

I was so ready for Al Scoma. The group always stayed at the Eldorado Hotel in Reno, owned by the Italian Carano family. When I was booking the rooms for the group, I related my *Amer Picone* story to our contact in the sales department. She said Mr. Scoma always asked them for it, too, so I gave one of my bottles to her, and now we were both ready for him. The trip came, the drink was ordered, over the rocks it went, and out with the waiter. About twenty seconds later, there stood Al Scoma in the doorway of the kitchen, glass in hand, eyes shining, shaking with excitement. "Where did you get this? I own a bar and I can't get this!"

Amer Picone is imported from France and, apparently, over the years it's changed. (I can only imagine finding a <u>real</u> coke from my youth.) In the forties and fifties *Amer Picone* was used in a popular drink, called Picone Punch, and is still served in Basque restaurants, but I think I bought the last of the "real stuff" there in North Beach. My waiters and I thought it must be wonderful, so we all had a little taste of it. It was awful (must be better in the punch drink). Al Scoma wasn't in good health and when he could no longer go on the trips I gave the rest of my supply to him (no one else ever requested it).

At Scoma's Restaurant there is an Annuzzi room. Henry, Michael and I went to dinner there and on the wall above our table was a picture of Mel and Pete sitting on the rear platform of the business car *Tamalpais* (their favorite spot).

The Cars' Mascots

The mascot on the *Native Son* was a rubber chicken. It stayed in the kitchen—most of the time. The car had a large rear lounge, with four dining tables, two on each side, each table seating four people. There was more chair seating at the rear of the car, as well as upstairs in the dome. The kitchen was located under the dome. The crew/luggage room and a bedroom were at the front end. The essence of the *Native Son* was its openness and friendliness. It was not formal, and our guests would board and feel right at home.

My waiters got to pick the recipient of the rubber chicken, usually the group leader, group character, or pretty girl they had all been flirting with. We would have two sittings for lunch and would arrange for the "chosen one" to be on the second seating. I would put the chicken on a silver platter, tuck its little legs under, put a cherry in its beak, and garnish on the sides. It would be served last, with great ceremony. The waiters would go out in a line, with the lead waiter carrying the platter up high. I followed in the rear, carrying the real meal. It always brought down the house, and the only problem was getting the chicken back. (Everyone always wanted to keep it!)

We did so many trips with the rubber chicken that, with the movement of the train and the heat in the kitchen, our chicken wore out and had to be replaced three times. Once in a while, we would get a serious group, where the chicken wasn't appropriate. But most of the time it became one of the highlights of the trip, with much laughter by both the guests and the crew. We never used the chicken on any other car. It just seemed to fit the *Native Son*.

The mascot on the business car, *Tamalpais*, was a leprechaun. One year, I had a charter over St, Patrick's Day, and part of the decoration was a little felt leprechaun with long, floppy legs. On the trip, when no one was looking, the waiters kept putting him in different locations (like he was jumping around the car on his own). We named him Tammy Boy, and he ended up going on all our trips. My guys used to put him in crazy places for my benefit—the freezer, the blender, the coffee pot. You never knew where he was going to appear. The trick was to never be caught moving Tammy Boy around.

The Tamalpais

The *Tamalpais* was a 1923 Santa Fe executive car. During the fifties a lot of the railroads installed air conditioning, and dramatically altered the looks of the business cars with formica and lowered, paneled ceilings. The *Tamalpais* escaped the formica, but did have the low, flat ceilings installed in the rear lounge and dining room to cover the air conditioning ducts. The car sat in the Sacramento rail yard for years and years. I understand it had been owned by someone in the witness protection system, which made its purchase quite complicated. When it was finally bought and opened, it was a treasure trove. The car was full of cabinets in every nook and cranny, and they were filled with old railroad china and silver—all sorts of goodies. Many of the new owners lived in Marin County and they named the car *Tamalpais* after Mount Tamalpais (which is located in that county) and also the ferryboat *Tamalpais* (located in Seattle). Pictures of both the mountain and the ferryboat graced the wall in the rear lounge of the car.

When I first started working on the car, bedroom C (the secretary's room) had one lower bed and a cabinet on the wall for dispatches. The cabinet was removed and an upper bunk was added to give the car three double bedrooms. Bedroom A was the largest and featured a double bed. It had a door to bedroom B so they could be made into a suite. All of the bedrooms had a toilet and sink, and there was a full bathroom between bedrooms B and C, which had a large, glassed-in shower. There was a brass fixture on the wall in the bathroom that intrigued me. I finally found out it was a resting place for a cigar! The couch in the rear lounge could also be converted into upper and lower beds for night-time use. The dining room had a heavy oak table that seated eight, and a sideboard with drawers and cupboards. Down the hall, toward the kitchen was the crew room, with its own shower and upper and lower berths. I used this room for storage for my day trips, but slept in it for cross-country trips.

When the car attendant and I went out on long trips we would take sleeping bags, so we didn't have to use the car linen or bother making our beds. The chef and waiter are the last to bed and the first up, and when I traveled with my waiter, Cliff, we had our routine down to a science. After everything was done for the night and the guests had all gone to bed, I would go to the crew room, take a shower, brush my teeth, and change for bed. I always wore something to bed that I could wear in public (like a jogging outfit), as you never knew if an emergency was going to have you up and running around in the middle of the night. I'd then snuggle into the lower bunk (so cozy!). Cliff would prepare for bed in the kitchen, which could be closed off. He would then come in and climb up to the upper berth. Someone asked me one time if Cliff snored. To tell the truth, after working all day for such long hours, I was out like a light and rarely woke during the night. In the morning, I would get up early (before the guests were up), take my clothes and toilet kit to the kitchen where I'd turn on the coffee, and get dressed there.

Cliff would get up, take his shower, and get dressed in the crew room. We were happy to have it. Some private cars don't have enough beds for the crew, and sleeping accommodations can end up being in the lounge or in a booked room on Amtrak.

One time we had a group booked from Oakland to Los Angeles. *The Coast Starlight* was delayed by a freight derailment north of San Francisco and arrived in Oakland twelve hours late. Most of the group cancelled, but six of them went on what was now an overnight trip. The crew room was packed with supplies, but we managed to clear off the upper bunk for my bed. My waiters, Michael and Cliff, slept on the floor in the dining room. I had never slept in the upper bunk before and was terrified of falling out. The bed was parallel to the side of the train and there were no safety straps to keep you from falling. I finally tucked the sheet under me so if I rolled, the sheet would keep me from falling. It was such a long day, we were just exhausted. In the middle of the night, I was awakened by a crashing sound and then a kind of whirring. The train was still running and I was so tired that I just went back to sleep. In the morning, I found out that the latch to the dish cabinet in the dining room hadn't been secured, and a jolt of the train sent some of the dishes (heavy railroad china) flying out and down on Michael's legs. The whirring sound was the vacuum cleaner picking up the broken china. Michael was pretty sore but carried on as if nothing was wrong.

In the hall between the dining room and the kitchen was a beautiful door with a leaded glass window. The craftsmanship on these old cars was unbelievable. There was a tiny pantry between the crew room and the kitchen where the waiter would make all the drinks. It had an opening to the kitchen over its counter, so the plates of food could be picked up from the pantry side. The floor space in the kitchen was about two feet by three feet, and the chef really didn't have to do any walking, just turn around. Every inch of space was utilized, and there certainly wasn't any room for either a microwave or a dishwasher. I used to tell people that I had ten dishwashers, then hold up my two hands. I don't know how many times I heard, "How does all that food come out of such a little kitchen?" Although it was tiny, the stove had a huge oven. It was large enough to accommodate large pans of prime rib, racks of lamb, and chicken all at the same time. I once had eighty people on a trip using three private cars, and did all of the cooking in the *Tamalpais* kitchen. When asked how I did it I couldn't explain. It amazed me too!

I'm a Civil War buff, and when reading about the thousands of soldiers fighting in just one battle I always wonder how in the world the camp cooks fed that many people, with no modern equipment. Compared to that, whatever I've done is nothing!

The rear lounge at the end of the *Tamalpais* was so comfortable. On one side of the rear door was a desk with gauges, including two speedometers: one for going forward and one for going backward. An old-fashioned, upright, black telephone (that worked) was on the desk. On the other side of the door was a low cabinet with doors that housed a television set and a tape/CD player. I always put a brass tray on top of the cabinet with a glass humidor for cigars, liquors (sherry, port, cognac, and Gentleman Jack's Sipping Whiskey), and cordial glasses. We had four folding chairs and lap blankets for the rear platform (always a popular spot), as well as a brass receptacle full of sand for cigarette and cigar butts.

There were three strictly enforced rules: no smoking in the car, no sitting on the railing, and no standing backwards on the platform. On one trip we had a couple in the group who kept sitting on the railing. The waiters kept telling them not to do that, but as soon as they were out of sight, the couple went right back to it. The boys finally came and got me. I think it was because of my age, but I seemed to have the "mother" effect on people. I went to the rear of the car and told our misbehaving guests how dangerous it was to sit on the railing and not to do it again. After

I went back to the kitchen, Darrel said to them "You'd better not do that again. We had a group last week, and she locked the door and no one could sit outside!" Of course I hadn't done that, but it intimidated them enough to behave!

It was fun to see guys (and sometimes gals) sitting outside, a cigar in one hand and a glass of cognac in the other, playing "railroad baron". They thought they'd died and gone to heaven! We had a red carpet that we rolled out on the platform for boarding. I always thought this would be the first clue to the group as to what to expect on the trip. It was fun to watch the other people at the stations, witnessing the "celebrities" boarding the private car. The waiters wore black shoes and pants, white shirts, white Eton jackets, and black bow ties. When boarding passengers, they donned white gloves and a "conductor's" hat. They were classy, but not pretentious. (I have a life-long abhorrence of snobbery.)

The authenticity made the *Tamalpais* quite unique. The original oak paneling and beautiful brass fixtures required a lot of polishing, but it was well worth it. As fond as I was of the *Native Son*, the *Tam* was my favorite car, and I cooked on it more than any other.

My nephew, Greg Magdanz, lived in North Carolina and worked for a large international company. One day he called me and said his company was having a conference in San Francisco. They were going to book a room at their hotel for a breakfast/lunch meeting for eight people and wondered if I could recommend an alternate meeting space. He wasn't expecting my suggestion of a stationary private railcar that just happened to have a dining room table that coincidentally seated eight people. The *Tamalpais* used to be stored between trips adjacent to the Oakland Army Base (just down the track from where the #2467 was being restored). A huge pile of recycled asphalt was between the car and the public road and shielded it from view. When the van arrived with the group from San Francisco and was making it's way down the service road, Greg's boss said, "Magdanz, what the hell have you gotten us into?" His apprehension was alleviated as soon as he boarded the car. One of my favorite things is witnessing first time visitors to a private car. Most people have no idea that such wonderful relics from history even exist. After examining the car, the eight attendees settled around the dining table with their laptops. I knew my food was going to be a lot better than the usual commercial fare at the hotel. As Greg's boss also heralded from North Carolina, I even included grits in the breakfast menu. They told me later that this was not only the most enjoyable meeting they had ever had, but also the most productive, and their only regret was that the train wasn't moving.

A consortium of about sixteen investors owned the *Tamalpais*. I worked with one of the owners, Jon Kirchanski, who was an Amtrak engineer. He booked all the trips I did with Amtrak, and worked tirelessly to keep the car running, often going along as the car mechanic. He restored the ceiling in the rear lounge to its original height (a monumental task), and I can't praise him enough for his dedication and friendship. Henry had known Jon since he was a teen-ager and he participated as a bartender at our wedding. Before the wedding, Henry was helping set up everything in the garden and when he went to change into his light gray tuxedo for the ceremony, he found he had forgotten his black shoes. He went around to all of the guys there until he found someone wearing his shoe size and traded his brown shoes with him. So Henry married me wearing Jon Kirchanski's shoes!

My Rules

I was always very particular how my private cars were to be run. A lot of my waiters worked on other cars too, with other standards, so I needed to make it clear what I expected of them on my trips. I didn't have the time or inclination to be telling them what and how to do things, so I came up with:

Key Holidays' Guideline — Private Railcar Waiters:

The private railcar experience is so unique that every effort should be made to make it an unparalleled one. The onboard staff is critical in this endeavor.

GROOMING

Waiters should be clean-shaven and have a tidy appearance.

ATTIRE

Black shoes (polished), black pants — pressed (no jeans), two white long-sleeve dress shirts — pressed. Eton jackets and bow ties will be provided. The Key pin and name badge should be worn on the left side of jacket. While on the trip, maintain a neat appearance. If uniform gets soiled, attempt to remove the spot with club soda. If unsuccessful, change into second jacket.

BEFORE THE PASSENGERS BOARD

The cars should be clean and polished. If necessary, vacuum, polish the wood and brass. Wipe down rear platform. Make sure the bathroom is spotless and that paper hand towels and a full roll of toilet paper are provided.

BOARDING THE PASSENGERS

Wear Car Attendant hat and white gloves to board and off-board passengers.

Put out the red carpet and the step box.

Board the passengers first and ask them to go directly to the dining room or the bedrooms where they will stay until the luggage is put away. Food and drinks will be waiting for them in the dining room.

An attendant should always be by the step box to assist with boarding.

The guests should *never* handle their own luggage.

Put all the luggage on the vestibule before transferring it to the bedroom.

Offer to take coats and hang them up in the luggage room.

Point out the two enforced rules on the car. (1) No smoking inside the car. (2) No sitting or standing backwards on the rear platform (except on provided chairs).

DUTIES

The key to a smooth trip is teamwork. There is no room on-board for prima-donnas (including the chef). If something needs doing, just do it. The following is a list of general duties.

Keep a fresh carafe of regular and decaf coffee. Make a new pot as needed.

Fill the nut bowls and refill as necessary. They should never be empty.

Make sure the candles are lit. Replace if they get too low.

Keep an eye on the flowers. If any are wilted or broken, remove.

Try to pick up and keep the carpet clean.

On every pass through the car, pick up dirty glasses, napkins and plates.

On the *Tamalpais*, Keep the bathroom sink wiped dry with cloth (under the sink).

Keep the music playing. Ask if anyone wants to hear something special.

SERVICE

Our guests' comfort and satisfaction is our number 1 priority. Treat everyone as you would like to be treated.

Never refer to the guests as "you guys".

Maintain a relaxed, cheerful attitude. Enjoy your job, have fun, and the group will have fun too. However, remember you are not a guest. Don't talk about your personal life unless specifically asked. Never complain or be negative.

Check often if anyone needs anything.

Even if the group is not a good one, never stoop to their level.

Always provide first class service. (They just won't be welcome back.)

Never sit down and join the group—even if they ask.

Never solicit gratuities in anyway.

SERVING

Never serve a drink, including coffee, filled to the top (it will spill).

Unless black, serve coffee with a small creamer and sugar. Let the guests fix their own.

For tea, offer the selection first and bring the tea back to the galley. Serve the tea in an individual pot already brewed, cup and saucer (not a mug), small pitcher of milk, sugar bowl, and lemon wedge.

Serve all drinks, including coffee and tea, with a cocktail napkin.

Serve all water (bottled) in a goblet with ice and half a slice of lemon.

BAR SERVICE

Check list before the trip to see what brands are available and offer choices.

Prepare garnishes ahead of time—lime and lemon wedges, lemon and orange slices, and celery stalks.

Use marinated asparagus for Bloody Marys.

Put cherry in soft drinks.

Always ask up or over (ice) for Manhattans.

Use a fresh glass for each drink.

For beer, ask if they would like a glass. Use water goblet for beer.

Be cognizant of guests' ability to handle liquor. Serve less or lighten drinks as necessary.

MEAL SERVICE

See diagram for preferred place setting. Put napkin in wine glass. Salad forks and plates to be chilled in kitchen.

Put full water goblets and butterballs on table before ringing for dinner.

Use dinner chimes to announce meals.

Put out wine (cabernet, merlot, white, and white zin), champagne, and Martinelli's on sideboard before the meal.

Take orders and serve ladies first.

Whenever possible, serve from the left and take off from the right.

Take salad orders—offer both choices or half and half.

Serve rolls.

Serve salad.

Serve wine (watch wine and water, and offer refills as necessary).

Never remove dishes until everyone has finished that course.

Take main course orders—offer choices—may have multiple choices.

Don't forget the guests on other sitting. Check to see if they need anything.

After main course, offer choice of desserts (if available). Offer coffee or tea (both served in cup and saucer (not mug).

Offer mint before leaving table.

If first sitting is dawdling, diplomatically suggest they be served dessert and coffee in rear lounge.

Set the table for second sitting. Change cloth if soiled.

Crew meals and breaks are taken when all service is covered.

OFFLOADING

Allow ample time to move luggage before arrival.

Clear the rear platform. Ask the guests to remain in their seats or in the dining room. Transfer luggage to platform.

Pass out coats to guests.

When train stops, one attendant should get off the train. With the trap up, the bags are handed down and placed on the platform.

Put step box down and assist the guests off the train.

GRATUITIES

All gratuities are pooled and split evenly among the crew.
Put gratuities in tip jar in the pantry.
Never count $$ in front of guests.
AT THE END OF THE TRIP
Vacuum, polish the wood and brass, empty the wastebaskets, help offload supplies, clean the kitchen mats, put down the runner. With everyone working, this can be done fairly fast.

NEVER harass or give a bad time to the chef!!!

My First Trip on the *Tamalpais*

Looking back to my first experience cooking on the *Tamalpais*, it's a wonder I ever used her again. Luckily, the group was from the PLA and was understanding about mechanical difficulties, as the car still needed a lot of work. On the return trip something went wrong with the propane stove. There were no burners on the stove. The whole top surface was a grill. I used one side for cooking and the other side to keep things warm. The grill plates (there were two of them) could be lifted off, but I never could do it, as they were really, really heavy. Well, apparently, a flap was stuck and not enough air was mixing with the propane, so instead of heat, I got soot. There was a leak in the roof in the kitchen, directly over my head. On the return trip, it was raining hard, and wet soot was dripping on my head. The kitchen was so small and there was only one deep sink and no room for anyone else, so the chef had to wash dishes, pots, and pans, everything by hand. One of our group fixed the stove, but every time I washed dishes they'd be covered with soot in minutes. My white chef's hat was black, and plastered to my head, and my white dress and shoes were covered with soot. I looked like I was cooking in "blackface"! One of the owners of the car, Lou, was also a member of the PLA and had come along as the car mechanic. Every time he saw me he broke out laughing and then apologized. To this day, the memory of that trip amuses him.

Somehow, everyone got fed, but what a mess! Over the years, I came to love that kitchen.

The Explosion

To turn the stove on in the *Tamalpais* you had to turn a "faucet" handle on the floor and light the pilot lights with a long match through tiny holes on the grill. To light the oven a button at the base of the stove had to be depressed and held, while you lit the pilot light inside the oven. If the button was released too early, the flame would go out. I found the time it took to sing an entire verse of Zippity Doo Dah was perfect for keeping the flame lit. The pilot light unit for the hot water heater was too high for me to reach, so I needed to do that using a step ladder.

I had a group going to Reno to celebrate a birthday. For birthdays the waiters would greet the guests on the platform with helium balloons. We also put balloons in the dining room for decoration. My waiters for this trip were Darrel Saunders and Cliff McDaniel. We were in the Oakland yards, preparing for the trip. Cliff was setting the table for the buffet and blowing up the helium balloons in the dining room. Darrel was doing some last minute cleaning, and I was in the kitchen cooking. I had lit all the pilot lights when I first got onboard, and the stove was working just fine. Then the pilot light on the stove went out, which had never happened before. I thought, "Well, I'll just have to re-light it." Darrel came to the kitchen, saw me reach for the matches, and said, "I wouldn't do that if I were you." "Oh, it's OK, the pilot light just went out." He had just come from the dining room and could smell the gas. I, being in the kitchen the whole time, had acclimated to it. When he realized that I was about to light the stove despite his warning, he ran down the hallway toward the dining room where Cliff had just put up the balloons. I lit the match and KABOOM! The concussion literally lifted Darrel into the air and propelled him horizontally into the dining room, to the amazement of Cliff. The car was eighty-two feet long and the balloons from the dining room ended up in the rear lounge. The big, heavy steel grills on the stove were lifted up and were lying at crazy angles. The hair on my arms was gone, and the hair around my face and my eyebrows was singed. Darrel and Cliff thought I must be dead and were greatly relieved when I emerged from the kitchen, shaken, but miraculously unharmed (My angel on duty!).

I could see how worried the guys were, so I thought I'd better do something to ease the tension and make them laugh. I glanced in the mirror on the sideboard and said, "Darrel, go get your camera and take my picture." I did look funny with my singed hair. The funny thing is, when that picture was developed, I looked normal. That could only happen to me. Anyway, we got the stove relit and the car in order, and I changed into my Chef's attire. When the train arrived at the station, the guys were waiting for the guests outside on the platform and I had gone to the rear lounge to greet them. I glanced down to see the doily on the brass tray with the cigars and liquors was covered with black specks. I quickly turned it over before the group boarded, and was amazed that the soot had come all the way from the kitchen at the other end of the car. Both Darrel and Cliff complained of ringing in their ears all day long and discreetly cleaned up miscellaneous soot throughout the car. I, on the other hand, felt perfectly OK. I got off with the group in Reno, where their hotel was, and caught a cab to the airport, where I rented a van for the weekend. The guys rode the *Tamalpais* to Sparks, where it would be switched off in the yard and where I would pick them up to go to our hotel in Reno. Feeling just fine, I got into the van, put my hands on the steering wheel, and then I started to shake. I remember saying out loud, very slowly, "I really shouldn't be driving this car." I felt so strange, and my ears were ringing as I slowly drove to Sparks, where Cliff took over and drove to Reno. I think what had happened was that when I thought I was OK on the train, I was actually in shock. As soon as I wasn't working, reality set in. After that trip, whenever I lit the pilot lights, my waiters would nervously stay in the rear lounge until it was done!

Hopping the Freight

One of the funniest trips we did was to Reno on the *Tamalpais*, when Darrel was my waiter. After our passengers got off the train in Reno, we rode on the car to Sparks, where it was taken off the *California Zephyr*, which was on its way to Chicago. The car was put on ground power in the yard, and we finished cleaning up. We had booked hotel rooms in Reno and Darrel called for a cab on his cell phone. It was wintertime and had been raining a lot, so the yard was full of big puddles. There was a mountain of dirt where the Union Pacific had been preparing a spot for container truck parking, so the yard was a big mess. It was freezing cold, windy and wet, and we were both exhausted. The cab never came and after multiple calls we decided to walk down the tracks in the yard, where there were lights, to a spot across from the Nugget Hotel. Our plan was to walk across the street and catch a cab from the hotel. We each had a suitcase on wheels, and it was quite a long, miserable walk.

When we finally reached the spot across from the hotel, we discovered a very long freight train was parked on a track between us and the hotel blocking our way. I almost started to cry. I was too tired to walk back, and the cab wasn't coming anyway. One thing you knew, working around railroad yards, was that you never, ever go underneath a train, even one that is parked. There was a flat car with rungs on the side, and we decided to go over the top. It was so cold we were shivering and I asked Darrel what would we do if the train started moving. He said he would call his wife and say, "Sh Sh Sh Shari, w w w we're in S S S S Salt La La Lake C C City!" We were so tired, and that struck us so funny, we started to laugh. We threw our suitcases on top of the car and I went up first. I got laughing so hard, I could hardly make it. Tears were streaming down my face and my side hurt. I got to the top and climbed safely down the other side. When Darrel was on top he threw down our suitcases. I was facing him and said, "Well, that wasn't so bad." "Oh, yeah," he said, pointing over my shoulder, "Turn around." I couldn't believe it! Another freight train was parked between us and the hotel. This one had a flat car, but no rungs on its side, so we had to climb up a slippery wheel. I told you my birth date, so you know I was no spring chicken! We finally managed to get over that second train.

Nugget Avenue runs between the hotel and the rail yards in Sparks. Next to the street is a short, grassy slope and thick bushes, to block the view of the yards from the hotel. The large valet entrance is located here, so we knew there would be cabs. It was Friday night, and there were a lot of cars and people. We parted the bushes and walked across the street, to the amazement of quite a few people. I can't imagine what they thought. Here was this kid and old lady, suitcases in tow, emerging through the bushes from a rail yard, in the dead of winter. I don't know if we had anything to do with it, but there is now a fence along that whole area. One thing about Darrel—he has asthma, and we always laugh so much, he's sure to bring extra inhalers with him.

The Oakland Hills Fire

Henry put an excursion together for the PLA, taking the *Native Son* from Oakland to Hanford through the San Joaquin Valley. After the group got off in Hanford I stayed with the car to Bakersfield where it stayed overnight. The next morning it left Bakersfield for Oakland and picked up the group for the trip home. In Hanford, Henry had arranged for an antique fire engine (in retrospect, an omen of the events to come later in the trip) to take the group on a tour of the town and to shuttle them to and from the hotel. The trip home Sunday was uneventful, and I had been in the kitchen the whole time. As we approached the Bay Area the evening sky was an odd color. Someone said that must be Oakland on fire. I thought it was an odd remark, but I didn't have a radio on the car and was oblivious to the news. Most of the group was up in the dome, and as we neared Oakland we could see the Oakland hills. We had returned the evening of the great Oakland Hills firestorm—October 20, 1991. What we first thought were streetlights turned out to be whole houses on fire. The extent of the fire was unbelievable. Considered the worst fire in the history of the state of California, It covered 1,520 square acres. The fire destroyed 3,354 homes, 437 apartments and condominiums, and killed 25 people. After the group got off at the Oakland station, the car went to the yards. The ground was thick with burnt material that had blown there from the fire. Normally, the winds blow eastward from the ocean. On this rare occasion, the strong winds blew in a westerly direction. Sooty chunks were found on the ocean beaches in San Francisco, over fifteen miles away from the fire. The route from the rail yards in Oakland to our home in Walnut Creek included traversing the Caldecott Tunnel, right through the middle of the conflagration, so we had to drive miles in a detour to get home.

One of the biggest problems contributing to the extent of the Oakland fire was the abundance of eucalyptus trees in the area. These trees are not native to California but were introduced and cultivated here as a fast-growing wood supply for construction and making railroad ties. There are still some old stands of eucalyptus where you can see them growing in carefully planted rows. They love the California weather and grow and spread like weeds. Unfortunately, the wood splits, twists as it dries, and isn't good for anything, and the trees are highly inflammable. The bark peels and litters the ground below and the oil from the trees discourages growth beneath them.

Almost twenty five years after the fire, homes and apartments have been rebuilt and there is little evidence of the massive devastation of the area. What is rather shocking is the abundance of new growth eucalyptus trees there. Sometimes I wonder if a chip is missing in the human brain, preventing us to learn from the past.

The Chapel Hill

I had an upcoming charter using the *Virginia City* to Los Angeles. Before my trip, the car was back east on someone else's charter and it incurred mechanical difficulties. It was replaced by the *Chapel Hill*, which continued the charter back to California and I ended up using that car for my trip to LA. It was a car I wasn't familiar with and I only got to work on it this one time, as it primarily is used on the east coast.

The *Chapel Hill* is the only private car I worked on that actually originated as a private car. Where the *Tamalpais* was paneled in masculine oak wood, he *Chapel Hill* had beautiful dark mahogany and an understated elegance. It was built in 1922 for Marjorie Merriweather Post (the Post Cereal heiress) and E.F. Hutton (a stockbroker and investment banker). Its original name was the *Hussar*. The car was sold to the Chesapeake and Ohio Railway in 1937, and later sold in 1971 to its present owner, DeWitt Chapel. He renamed it the *Chapel Hill*, after his alma mater in North Carolina. There is a lovely, small oval photograph of Marjorie Merriweather Post that sits in the rear lounge

I don't think any of the cars I worked on had air conditioning in the kitchen, but for some reason the heat in this kitchen was really intense. My waiter on the trip to LA was my son, Michael. He came into the kitchen and couldn't believe my looks. I had perspired so much I looked like I'd taken a shower with my clothes on. My chef's hat was plastered down on my head and my shoes squished when I walked. There was a thermometer hanging in the kitchen. "My God, Mom, it's 118 degrees in here!" Actually, the waiters would feel the heat in the kitchen a lot more than the chef, because they went in and out of it. The chef would acclimate to it and not notice it as much. When they say, "If you can't stand the heat, stay out of the kitchen", on a private railcar that's has literal meaning!

Clara's 80th Birthday

I did a lot of birthday trips over the years. One of my favorites was an eightieth birthday celebration for a lovely lady, Clara. The group included family members and old friends. They brought a montage of pictures that we put on display in the dining room. She had been a beautiful young woman, and had worked in a factory building airplanes during WWII. I remember her sitting in the dining room, regaling us with stories about her experiences. I think seniors have so much valuable wisdom, just from having lived through so much. It's rather a sad state of our society that youngsters and senior are often so isolated from each other. They each have so much to offer the other.

One of my favorite memories from riding on Amtrak was on the *Coast Starlight*. Seated in the observation lounge car was a smiling black teenage boy with headphones on, obviously animated by the music to which he was listening. Seated right next to him was an elderly white woman, wearing a light pink sweater and earphones over her snowy white hair, also smiling and obviously animated by the music to which she was listening. If I had to guess by their movements, he was listening to rap and her choice was classical. It would have made a great hit on YouTube. What great equalizers trains and music are.

Finding a Cousin

Another private car trip I did was for an elderly couple going
to Reno. Every year, they celebrated their birthdays together by
treating their friends to a unique event. They didn't have any
children and enjoyed coming up with something new and unusual every year. They thought of everything, including a roll of
quarters for every guest, meals, side trips in Reno, and souvenirs
of the trip. When talking with the wife before the trip to work
out all the details, I mentioned that my husband was currently
in Cuba. He had put together a trip for the PLA to take medical
supplies to Cuba. (of course, the fact that he distributed those
supplies to all the sugar cane steam train locations was a happy
coincidence for our train enthusiasts). She told me how her
grandfather had been like the George Washington of Cuba, and
that there was a statue of him at the Havana Airport. I said it was
fun to see your ancestors written about in books, and that my
great, great grandfather had a land grant in San Juan Bautista,
and was the last California Don. She said one of her guests, Katie
Orban, had a great, great grandfather who also had a land grant
in San Juan Bautista. Well, Don Manuel Larios turned out to be
a mutual ancestor, and I got to meet a distant cousin on the train.
What a small world

The Coldest Trip Ever

One winter a group took the *Tamalpais* to Glenwood Springs,
Colorado, for skiing. Private cars can only be taken off the train
at major stations, where there are switch engines and a place to
park the car. Ron was my waiter on that trip. He had come to
me from Southern California and had become one of my regular
waiters. We lost our heat on that trip and the car was so cold.
The only heat we had was from the propane stove in the kitchen.
It was an exceptionally cold winter and the group had to bundle

up in the car. After the group got off in Glenwood Springs, the car went on to Denver, where it was taken off The *California Zephyr* on it's way to Chicago. When sleeping on the car the waiter and I would bring sleeping bags for ourselves. Ron and I had planned to watch a movie in the rear lounge. Fully dressed, we zipped ourselves into our sleeping bags to watch our movie, but it was still too cold. I always kept a large supply of candles onboard, so Ron hung a blanket across the entrance to the hallway from the dining room and I put every candle on the dining room table and lit them all, trying to generate some heat. Anyone seeing us through the dining room windows probably thought we had some weird, satanic ritual going on! With the stove and oven turned on and those candles burning, we survived. I don't think I've ever been so cold in my life. Those old cars are wonderful, but they take a lot of maintenance to keep them running.

My Friend Milton

I think my favorite birthday trip of all was for Milton's ninety-fourth. I had done quite a few trips for Milton's son, Skip, and his friend David (and their wives and friends). The first trip for them was to Reno on the *Tamalpais*. After that, they went to Truckee a couple of times for skiing. They were UC alumni, and one time they took the *Tam* to Los Angeles for a football game between UC Berkeley and USC. The whole car was decorated in yellow and blue, with pennants on the wall and UC shot glasses. All of the flower arrangements on the car were yellow and blue as well. The car didn't have a drumhead, so I made one up with styrofoam that read "Go Bears". It looked pretty authentic (from a distance)! After the trip, they got to keep the pennants and glasses. It was a tradition to give the flowers to the group leader at the end of the trip. I usually had enough flowers left over to give to my waiters, too, for their wives or girlfriends to make up for me stealing away their men.

Back to Milton. I hadn't met Skip's father before and was rather concerned as the birthday trip was an overnight to Denver on the Sierra Hotel, a dome car. All the meals were served upstairs and I wondered if a ninety-four-year-old would be able to climb the stairs. Before the trip, Milton and his wife, Bette, came to the office. They looked like they were in their seventies, and they were both sharp as a tack. We had no trouble on that trip at all. In addition to Skip, Milton had another son, Mike, and they, along with their wives, both came along. Also, there was a third "son" Tom, informally adopted by the family, having once been engaged to Bette's daughter.

Tom was from Washington D.C. , and he asked me if I could cook venison and duck on the train. "Oh, of course!" I said. It's not in my nature to say I can't do something, but the truth was, I had never cooked either one before. Tom was a hunter, and he mailed me frozen venison before the trip. The ducks were brought onboard by Skip's brother, Mike, who had shot them. I started looking up recipes for venison and duck. I read that it helps to know the age of the deer. I could hardly know that, so I played it safe and made stew. I marinated the venison and took my hydrator on board to make jerky with the leftover scraps of meat. To my relief, Mike was very hands-on in advising me how to cook the ducks. They were quite tiny teal ducks, and didn't take much cooking. Tom's girlfriend, whom he had brought on the trip, said it was the best venison stew she had ever eaten. It seems the angel on my shoulder also gave culinary advice! On long trips, I like to offer choices for dessert, so, along with other goodies; I had made a large mango bread pudding, to serve as requested. This was one of my signature dishes and was always a big hit with all of my groups.

My waiter was Cliff (all the groups loved him). When we got to Denver, the group stayed at the Brown Hotel. Cliff and I stayed on the car, parked adjacent to the station. It was Cliff's

birthday, and I said I was going to treat him to dinner. Years before, when Ron and I had gone to Denver, we ate at a grill across
the street from the station. I thought that's where I was taking
Cliff, but we crossed the wrong street and walked into a restaurant called Morton's. We were both wearing jeans and sweatshirts and knew something wasn't right when the maitre d'
greeted us dressed in a tuxedo. Cliff said, "Oh, we're not prop-
erly dressed," and we started to leave, but the maitre d' said,
"No problem, Sir. Do you have reservations?" Of course we did-
n't, but he took us anyway. There was no room in the non-smok-
ing section, but we said we wouldn't mind sitting in the smoking
section, so he seated us right away.

It was quite a large restaurant and was packed, but the service was extraordinary. There was no menu. They just brought
out sample selections of meat, and you just chose what you
wanted. One steak was so thick it looked like a roast! When we
found out what the price was, Cliff wanted to leave, but I told
him I was treating him to his birthday dinner and we were going
to stay. Cliff had a glass of wine (I didn't drink alcohol then),
and we ordered dinner. The meal was one of the finest I've ever
eaten and well worth the price! They even brought a selection
of liquors at the end of the meal. When it came time to order
dessert, Cliff asked if they offered bread pudding. The waitress
said no, but she wished the chef made it because so many people
asked for it. Cliff then said, "Well, this is a famous private- rail-
car-chef, and she makes the best bread pudding in the world!"
(Anyone who knew Cliff can just hear him saying this.) I think
I kicked him under the table.

We had so many leftovers, we both took "doggie bags,"
which in this case were aluminum heat bags, back to the car. I
got an idea on the way back. I had a lot of mango bread pudding,
so I emptied my doggie bag, heated up some bread pudding,
topped it with bourbon sauce, and took it back to the restaurant.
When I brought it in, the maitre d' said, "Is that what I think it

is?" They had all heard about my bread pudding. I said, "Yes, it is, and it should be enough to share with the staff, small bites, of course."

For Milton's 97th birthday, I was the event planner/caterer for the affair. The Niles Canyon Railway runs a Christmas train, decorated inside and out with thousands of lights. As Milton's birthday was in the first part of January, the NCRy agreed to leave the train decorated for his charter. My splendidly attired waiters served drinks and hors d'oeuvres on the train while it ran slowly through Niles Canyon. When the train returned to Sunol, the group of about 130 guests walked across the street to the events center, where they had a sit-down dinner. After dinner, there was dancing to a live band.

For Milton's 99th birthday, he celebrated on the *Tamalpais*. The car was being repaired at Wayne Yetter's facility in Salinas, where he kept his own private cars as well. The *Tamalpais* had been bought by Tom (Milton's and Bette's "adopted son") and had been out of commission for some time, undergoing extensive restoration. Cliff and I drove down and prepared dinner on the car in the yard. It was a small dinner party, and then Milton and Bette stayed overnight on the car. After a family get- together for breakfast on the *Tamalpais*, we drove home. Of course, as we drove near San Juan Bautista, Cliff and I stopped at our favorite Mexican restaurant for lunch and picked up a supply of Portuguese orange nut bread at the bakery.

For Milton's 100th birthday I didn't have to cook! He had a big party at a country club and Henry and I were guests. They requested no presents, but I thought such a grand occasion warranted more than a birthday card, so I wrote a poem that was read by Skip at the party.

My Friend Milton

My friend Milton is one hundred years old.

He is quite amazing, and it needs to be told;

He's a better driver than most, 'specially me.

He is witty and charming, with a great memory,
With his Bette, right there at his side,
He traveled the world, making friends far and wide.
It's a privilege to know such a person as he,
And an honor to be at this great jubilee.
Just one error to fix since this missive's begun;
My friend Milton is one hundred years young!

When Milton turned 101, I think he was partied out—but
how could I just send him a plain card now? So, I wrote:
My friend Milton – Part II
2011 is finally done
And my friend Milton is one hundred and one.
With the speed of a train and a blink of an eye,
Since last year's big gala, this year has flown by.
With his Bette still there at his side,
Her love and devotion, as sure as the tide.
I'm already thinking of rhymes to write when
My friend Milton turns one hundred and ten.
But as for now at one hundred and one,
My friend Milton is still growing young!

Bad Groups – Good Groups

I tried to make the private rail car experience something special and unforgettable for everyone. There were flowers and candles and music. (Usually the music was from the forties and
fifties, and I always tried to match the music to the group.) The
Tamalpais was a "time-machine" that transported my passengers
back to a gentler, simpler time. Most of my groups went year
after year as once they took the private car, they didn't want to
travel any other way.

One of my favorite groups was a black church group. The
leader of that group was more affluent than the rest. She was an

opera singer and was very cultured and charming. The rest of
the group were low to middle income, hard-working, unpretentious people, who had more class in their little fingers than all
my bad groups combined! After all the blacks had contributed
to the success of the railroads, I thought it was poetic justice that
they were now enjoying the amenities of a private railcar and
being waited on themselves.

Reservations were taken over the phone, and once in a while
we would get a baaaad group. I usually don't like to generalize,
but the worst groups tended to be liquor distributors, car sales-
men, and bachelor parties. My criteria, which had to be met in
order to book a second trip, were to respect and appreciate the
car and to respect and appreciate the crew. If one or the other
wasn't done, I'd never take them again. Here's a truth for you:
money does not equate to class or happiness. I did trips for a lot
of very affluent groups who were very classy, but it was due
more to their character than their money.

Once, I had a "yuppie" group going to Reno. They were on
a dome car, going through some of the most spectacular scenery
in the Sierra Nevada Mountains and they were all on a laptop
or using a cell phone. It saddened me to think of all that they
were missing. They were also upset that the train took so long.
The train on the return trip was 45 minutes late and most of them
rented a van and drove home. (In my mind, 45 minutes late on
the *California Zephyr* was on time!) With most of my groups, we
had to pry their little fingers off the handrails to get them off the
train at the end of the trip. This group may have been considered
successful, but I don't think they were successfully living.

The advice to "stop and smell the roses." is not new but the
wisdom of it seems more needed now than ever. The accelera-
tion of technical advances seems to have played havoc with our
priorities. We are surrounded with an over-abundance of beauty
(food for our souls) but our eyes need to be open to see it.

I think this "yuppie" group was one of my crew's favorites.

On the return trip, there were three waiters to take care of six passengers. At the end of every trip I lined up empty grocery bags, wrote the crew names on them, and divvied up the leftovers. On this trip they got a ton of food to take home!

Meals on the Train

I used to serve an all-day buffet on the way to Reno and a sit down luncheon on the way home. On one trip, a passenger was standing at the buffet table in the dining room, scarfing down coconut prawns. "We're here in Reno. You have to get off." "I can't stop," he replied, "These are so good, I can't stop!" Well, he had to get off, so I quickly fixed a doggie bag of prawns for him.

The buffet would start with breakfast items — Grand Marnier French toast, artichoke frittata, homemade corned beef hash, fresh fruit, ambrosia, banana bread, pumpkin bread and breakfast meats. As the day progressed, I'd add a vegetable platter with a curry dip, an antipasto platter, meatballs, chicken wings, deviled eggs, ham rolls, smoked salmon, chicken salad croissants, cheese and grapes, and more. I would save the best for last, either coconut prawns or rack of lamb. For the latter, I would roast several racks of lamb, cut them into individual pieces, and place those, bone side up, on a silver platter. A frill would be placed on each rib so they could be picked up. The waiter would pass the platter, and when those bones came back to the kitchen they were so clean they looked like they had been dipped in acid.

The private rail car community was not large. The chefs in a region either knew each other or knew about each other, and we all had our own styles. I always tried to be true to railroad tradition. Some of the chefs' menus read like they came from a French Restaurant, but I always figure, if what you are serving is a green bean, call it a green bean, not some name that not everyone can pronounce, or know what it is. My unpretentious attitude earned me criticism sometimes. I was even chastised for not being a "real" chef, as I didn't go to culinary school. But that didn't faze me. I was told that the difference between a chef and a cook was that the chef created the recipe and the cook followed the recipe. Well, if this was the case, I was certainly a chef!

With an outlook like mine and a silly sense of humor, I named my rack of lamb dish lambsickles. They were a hit with the passengers and the name stuck.

I would always go through the menu with the group leader before the trip, and try to accommodate any special dietary requests. When I first started cooking on the cars, out of a group of thirty-two maybe three or four were diabetic and allergies seemed rare. After twenty-five years it seemed like half of my group were either diabetic or had some kind of food allergies. I've come to believe that diabetes is an epidemic. It used to be mainly a disease of older, overweight people. Now, it includes young, skinny people, even kids. Something is very, very wrong. It's terrible to serve everyone dessert except those with diabetes so I always tried to have a sugar- free cake available. One time, I had someone who was allergic to garlic. I never realized before just how much garlic I used in my cooking.

On the outbound trip to Reno groups were more sociable and wanted to spend time together. Sometimes, it was a case of family and friends getting together once a year. After spending time together in Reno and staying up late, the trip home was generally a lot more subdued. That's why I started doing an all-day buffet for the outbound trip and a sit-down luncheon for the way back (served in two sittings) on the *Tamalpais*. The buffet was also easier on my crew. The big dining room table would be pushed against one side of the dining room and the eight chairs placed along the outside edge of the room with one at each end. I'd place a large flower arrangement on the table at the back, with candles on either side. In the morning, as the passengers arrived and boarded, they were directed to the dining room and the drink and food-ladened table. This gave the crew a clear way to load the luggage and bring it down the hall to Bedroom A, a large room with a double bed. Bedrooms B and C were sitting rooms during the day, with long couches, so we always kept them open for seating.

In the morning we always provided fresh coffee, bloody Mary's and mimosas. For years, I had been asked for Ramos fizzes, but declined the request because of the raw egg ingredient. Finally, I made up my own version (sans raw egg) and dubbed it the *Luna Fizz*, which became a favorite on the car. With the omission of gin it also became a delicious offering for non-drinkers. It wasn't long before I heard the *Luna Fizz* was being offered on other private cars. I also made a Brandy Alexander that I only served when the train was stopped for a long time. While the Amtrak passengers were complaining about the delay my groups would be happy because they knew what was coming.

The exceptional waiters, like Cliff, were in demand and worked on many different cars. They were my source (spies) for relaying to me how other cars were run and what other chefs were doing. I've often thought that one of the advantages of not going to a culinary school is that I never had anyone telling me what and how I should cook, which enabled me to think "outside the box". I wanted the dining experience to be unique, and so many of my recipes were my own creation.

Probably the most elaborate dish I prepared was my smoked salmon tray. I knew other chefs offered lox and bagels on their private cars, but I wanted to offer something different and special. I have a metal tray that has clamps on the underside that hold four pre-frozen cans that keep the surface cold for hours. I would slather cream cheese on the entire surface and then score an outline of a fish. into the cheese. The smoked salmon was layered and mounded until it looked like the scales of this fish. A slice of green olive with pimento was used for the eye. Chopped red onions and capers were in the corners of the "sea bed" and my "coral" was a row of small tomato slices. Cream cheese was piped on top in the shape of waves, and the finishing touch was fresh dill placed upright as my "sea weed". Next to the platter was a basket of sliced mini-bagels. It looked like a picture and everyone wanted to take a photograph before it got devoured. It was fun to make and I got quite fast at putting it together. I also knew that no other chef would take the time and effort to copy it, so it remained a unique original.

It was fun being creative and personalizing the trip for each group. In going over the menu and beverage selection with the group before the trip, I'd try to ascertain personal preferences of not only food, but colors, flowers, music, etc. so the trip could be customized for them.

Because of the size of the kitchen and the added work and expense, most other chefs offered only one entree. With so many people not eating red meat, pork and seafood, a lot of chicken was served. I felt, for the price they were paying, the guests should be offered choices. I also didn't want to make people choose ahead of time, so the waiters took orders at the table. My typical menu included Caesar salad, spinach salad, rack of lamb, prime rib, chicken picatta or some kind of fish, parsley potatoes and squash medley. I usually made just one dessert. They could have any combination of whatever they wanted. Sometimes I would make a salad with mango and avocado slices and chilled prawns and, of course, if they had requested any other menu I would accommodate them. On the sideboard were merlot, chardonnay, and white zinfandel wines, and Martinelli's apple cider. Beer and champagne were available on request.

I loved adding fun details to the experience for my groups. One of my charters to Reno was a group of police officers. All of my groups were given names, so they were "The Smokies". When they boarded the *Tamalpais*, the music playing was a jazzy version of *Dragnet*, and when they went to the buffet, besides the usual offerings, there was a large silver tray on the sideboard, stacked with doughnuts (which were gone in an hour!)

Butterballs and Caesar Salad

On my first trips, I cut butter into little squares for the table. That looked terrible to me, so I found some butter paddles and decided to make butterballs. These small, wooden paddles have grooves on one side. You place a butter square on the grooved side, roll it around with the other paddle, and make a pretty little butterball. And if you squeezed a little harder you could make the ball look like a butter seashell. The trick was to keep the paddles chilled in ice-water. I trained all of my waiters to make butterballs, and they got quite fast and competitive. I think they're still arguing over who's was the best. Pretty soon, the other private car chefs were asking me where to buy the paddles. Eventually, I went to creating "flower" butter pats using a pastry bag, as it was much faster and the result just as pretty.

When I think of butterballs, I am reminded of one of my New Year's Eve trips to Reno. For my New Year's package, I used a mixture of private cars and Amtrak coaches. It was the one trip I would sell to individuals, taking around 125 guests. I usually had three private cars and two Amtrak coaches. Every trip was unique and I offered the New Years trip for ten years. Some of the same people went year after year.

One year the *Tamalpais* was on the end of the train with Tom as the designated waiter. We had a party of eight friends and they had been assigned, along with eight other people, to the *Tam*. The eight friends were seniors and had been friends forever. These four couples often traveled together and were very close.

On the New Year's trips we always went up on the thirtieth and returned on the second, giving us three nights in Reno, and my hotel rooms were always at the Sands and the Circus Circus. New Year's in Reno is a lot of fun, where the countdown to midnight is on Virginia Street, under the famous arch proclaiming Reno "The Biggest Little City in the World".

On the night of January first, the four couples were having cocktails before dinner in one of the couple's hotel room, a corner suite at the Circus Circus. Henry and I were in the room directly below them. When it came time to go to dinner, one of the husbands seemed to have fallen asleep in his chair. Well, he wasn't asleep, he had quietly passed away, undetected. What a shock! They called our room to tell us, and the hotel moved the couple in whose room it occurred to other accommodations. We were scheduled to depart the next day and the group felt it best that the wife come back with them on the train (the husband's body was to be brought back later).

I put a sign on the dining room table in the *Tam* to reserve it for this group of friends and made one of the bedrooms available for the wife. When I had a chance, I came out of the kitchen and sat with them, and asked if the wife had been given any sedatives. They said no, but just then the wife emerged from the bedroom to join them. The woman next to me said, "See that glass of water she's holding? Well, it's not water, it's gin." I said, "Good!" When the wife sat down there was an awkward silence. What could one say? Someone started to talk about food and asked me how I made the butterballs. I glanced at my waiter, Tom, and without a word he left the car. A few minutes later, he came in carrying a chopping board with cubes of butter and the butter paddles in ice-water. After a demonstration by Tom, the board was passed around the table and everyone learned how to make butterballs. It was the perfect medicine for all of us. When we arrived in Oakland, her grown children met the wife. She asked if they could come on the car to see where their father had enjoyed himself. Of course they could! After the shock wore off, I thought, "What a great way to go." He had just experienced the private car, seen in the New Year in the company of his dear friends, and went quietly in his sleep, with no stress or pain. It was just a little bit hard on the rest of us, especially Tom, who had spent so much time with them on the way up. A couple of years later I ran into the wife, who was happily remarried, and she thanked me for the kindnesses shown to her on the train.

Another year, one of the private cars in the New Year's consist was the *Virginia City*. It was placed between the *Native Son* and Amtrak. It was supposed to be put on the train backwards with the rear platform next to the last Amtrak car, but it was attached the other way around. This meant that when going from the rear door of the *Native Son* to the *Virginia City* you were outside on the rear platform, which was windy and cold. I was cooking in the kitchen on the *Native Son* and the waiters were taking the food to the other cars. Michael was the waiter on the *Virginia City* and he took a tray of six Caesar Salads through the *Native Son* and out the rear door. He suddenly appeared back in the kitchen with the tray and six empty plates. When he had stepped outside, the salad went flying everywhere. I often wonder, did the people riding in the rear cars notice lettuce and croutons flying past their windows?

The Great Reno Flood

I was going up on my annual trip to Reno for New Years and was using the *Columbia River*, a Union Pacific dome diner (along with the *Tamalpais*), so I had a large kitchen in which to cook. Because I booked individuals over the phone, I had quite a few new guests I didn't know. One party of six was coming from Fresno, taking the *San Joaquin* to Stockton and the Amtrak bus to Sacramento, where they would board our train.

Had I known that the Amtrak bus driver almost threw them off his bus, I never would have allowed them on our car. They were drunk before they even got on. We had a very nice group of people onboard, and it was a challenge to my waiters to keep this new group in line. The leader of the group was the worst. He actually staggered with a drink in his hand and spilled some of it into an open purse that was on the floor next to a sweet, elderly lady. Instead of apologizing, he spewed profanities over the loss of his drink. The *Columbia River* had a serving station upstairs in the dome, where the waiters would prepare the drinks, and these jerks started helping themselves to the liquor. The car's kitchen was at the end of the car, accessed by a hallway. There was no reason for passengers to go down that hall, and I had opened the rear door to get some fresh air. The drunken leader of that obnoxious group staggered down the hall and was swaying in the open doorway. There wasn't even a bar across the opening, and he almost fell out. "Sir, you can't stand there. You're not allowed to stand there." He wheeled around and cursed me, using the most foul language you can imagine. Darrel (who is a little taller than I) saw this and ran to get my son (who is over six feet). Michael has always been my peacemaker, and he managed to calm the guy. We told the group to sit down and stay put, and not cause any more trouble. My other passengers said later, if I had pushed him off the train they would have all chipped in to pay for a top defense attorney!

Now, I'm not easily intimidated, and under other circumstances would have put that group off the train in Truckee. The reason I didn't, was because I was convinced that if I did, they would make their way to Reno, hunt down my crew, hurt them (or worse), and burn up the cars. We were definitely dealing with a criminal element. Thankfully, they had booked the trip only one way. Looking back, I think this was an omen of the troubles to come on that trip. When we arrived in Reno, I got off to take a cab to the airport to pick up a rental car. There was a mix-up with the reservation and I was only able to get a compact car instead of a van. When I got to Sparks to pick up the crew, I found they had no ground power and couldn't finish cleaning the cars.

Besides my private car waiters, I used Mike and Michele (classmates of my son, Michael's) to host the Amtrak coach passengers in our New Year's group. The two of them came every year and would pass out drinks and fried chicken during the trip. Michael had married Michelle (the daughter of a good friend of mine from high school), and we always referred to the two Michelles as one L and two Ls. Michael's wife (two Ls) was a massage therapist and had her own business in Walnut Creek— "Touch of Tranquility". She had come along to help me in the kitchen. Her business was located above a beauty salon, and one of the hairdressers, Francesco, wanted to come too. He was nice looking, very proper and presentable, and I needed another waiter for this trip, so I'd hired him. So that was the crew.

We decided to go back and finish cleaning the next day. We agreed to meet around 10:00 a.m. Henry didn't come on this trip, so I had a room to myself. In the morning, I decided to take a soothing, hot bath. The water was running in the tub and I went to put on the hotel shower cap. As I lifted it up in front of my face with two hands, the elastic snagged on my nose, lifted up my eyelashes, and smacked me right across my eyeballs. I literally could not open my eyes! There I was, alone, naked, in excruciating pain, groping around trying to shut off the water—blinded by a shower cap. Unbelievable! Finally, I managed to get one eye open, and then the other. It was very painful, but I was greatly relieved that I could see.

At 10:00 we all met, and how we all fit into that little rental car is beyond me. There were three in the front seat and five in the back - reminiscent of those little cars at the circus where a bevy of clowns would emerge. It had been raining continually since we'd arrived in Reno, and it was pouring so hard, the windshield wipers couldn't keep up. About half way to Sparks, I said, "The craziest thing happened to me this morning." When I told them about my misadventure with the shower cap, they all started laughing hysterically. Michele was sitting in the front seat next to me, laughing so hard she was crying and slapping the dashboard. Up to this time, I hadn't seen the humor in it (probably because of the pain), but then I started laughing too. I always cry when I laugh hard, but this time the tears were stinging my injured eyes. I was squished into the driver's seat, trying to drive in that pouring rain with my eyes stinging. That we didn't get into an accident was a miracle (more proof of my angel).

We got the cars cleaned up and then returned to our hotel. We all had rooms on the fourteenth floor of the Sands Hotel. That night, we were going to meet in the hall and go out to dinner. When I stepped into the hallway, all of the light fixtures on the wall around my room had been covered with shower caps. Michele then proceeded to perform a very melodramatic reenactment of my experience (except the naked part)—very, very funny.

The next morning we woke to the news that Reno was flooded. The Truckee River, which runs right through the middle of town, had overflowed her banks. The river's originating source is the sole outlet of Lake Tahoe and unseasonably warm winds and rain were melting the mountain snow, overwhelming the river's capacity to contain the torrential overflow from the lake.. The Reno Hilton, located halfway between Reno and Sparks, was now an island, the water at the airport was up to the bellies of the airplanes, and the highway to Reno from California was closed. Both Harrah's and the Fitzgerald's Hotels, near the river, were flooded.

We had a wonderful vantage point from the fourteenth floor of our hotel. We could see a traffic light over by the river blinking red, yellow, and green, but two of the lights were under water. Garage doors and whole trees were rushing down the river and crashing into cement bridges. I had never seen anything like it before (or since). The electricity to the city was turned off and the only power came from generators. There were no lights in the hotel rooms, and only one elevator was working. There were emergency lights in the hallways and telephones worked. Some of the slot machines were working (which gave off a surprising amount of light). I heard criticism of this, but what were people supposed to do, sit in their dark rooms? The restaurants also were partially closed down.

A couple of my waiters and I were able to drive on high ground to a shopping mall where we purchased sixty-four flashlights. (That's how many rooms we had for our group of 120). We also bought a dozen candles. We then drove to the private cars and took some leftover food, including racks of lamb and prime rib, back to the hotel. When we got back, I hand wrote an update for our group, explaining what was happening. The hotel copy machine was working, so I had sixty-four copies made. My crew split up and hand-delivered flashlights and an update to each room. My group were the only hotel guests to have flashlights for their darkened rooms.

That night, the crew and I met in one of our rooms. With all the candles lit and our feast from the cars, it was actually kind of fun—almost like camping. I remember looking over to a dark corner where Francesco was sitting. He was gnawing on a prime rib bone and had juice all over his face (it was easier to imaging him nibbling caviar). I think these primitive conditions brought out the animal in our fastidious and proper little hairdresser!

We were scheduled to leave the next morning, but a mudslide had blocked the rail line and the highway was still closed. We were trapped in Reno! I had ordered box lunches for the coach passengers for the trip home (and always ordered extras). I didn't cancel with the caterer, figuring they would know that no one would be leaving Reno, but the food was delivered to the hotel anyway. It turned out to be a fortunate and welcome mistake. My crew delivered the food to the rooms and my entire group got something to eat. I was trying to give everyone an update about every four hours via hand-delivered notices to their rooms. As soon as I knew we weren't going back by rail, I contacted the local bus company. Key Holidays (we'd changed our name from Key Tours) did a lot of business with them, so they knew who I was. I arranged for charter buses to leave as soon as the highway was opened. Even with the updates, it became usual to go to my room, see the blinking light on the telephone, and hear something like, "You have eighteen messages". When it looked like the highway would open soon, more lunches were ordered for the trip back.

Henry often escorted tours without me and would call home. I'd answer the phone to hear his attempt to mimic Stevie Wonder, singing *"I just called to say I love you."* Only once (after a derailment of a rail car occupied by his group) he called with a quiver in his voice—"I want to come home!" As a group leader, you have to maintain a calm demeanor on the surface no matter how stressed you are. This time it was my turn to call call Henry, crying "I want to come home!"

One lane was finally opened and we were on the first buses to leave Reno. Ron was left with the private cars, and he came back with them when the rail line opened. Financially, the trip was a disaster. We had to pay for an extra night at the hotel, flashlights, food, the bus charter home and refunds of a hundred dollars each for the private car passengers (we didn't have to refund anything, but Key Holidays had a policy to "make things right"). Overall, the passengers were very understanding. It's funny, when everything goes smoothly, events can be very forgettable, but when things go wrong memories are made, and time usually turns disasters into great experiences and fond memories.

When Ron returned with the private cars, Henry and I hosted a dinner at our home for my crew. What they had endured on that trip was so far beyond the call of duty. With their good humor, dedication and compassion, a disaster was turned into a great adventure and it was an honor to work with such a class act! They all got souvenir flashlights and they gave me a box of shower caps. For years, I would receive shower caps from all over the world.

I also got requests from many of the guests who were on that trip to do it again. But the reason this was the last of the New Year's Eve trips was that my entire crew said if I did it again I would be doing it alone!

Key Holidays' *Reno Fun Train*

Key Holidays was selected to be the tour operator for the *Reno Fun Train* around 1993. Over the years, the meals on the *Fun Train* had been dropped. With my experience, having been the manager of the *Fun Train* so many years before, I suggested to Henry that we include the meals again. There was so much drinking on the train, eating something substantial was really essential. Without meals, for some guys, dinner would be a six-pack and a bag of potato chips!

On board entertainment included a piano/lounge car—a private car (*The Royal Gorge)* owned by Wayne Yetter. It was also our souvenir shop. Shirley Tripoli, who worked in the office, ran the shop and even after she retired and lived In Oregon she still came down to work on the train. Shirley epitomized the saying, "charms the hide off an elephant." There was also a dance car with a live band—the "Funatics," who played every year on the train. They were just great and could play any kind of music. They even played outside on the platform, setting the mood for a fun time on the train. We also had a magician who walked the train performing as he went, a couple of folk singers, Peter and Paul (playing guitar and mandolin), and Chris (who played guitar and sang.

The *Fun Train* could get a little wild (that's putting it mildly!) and arrive in Reno late, so Henry started the *Snow Train*, going to Reno on Tuesday and coming back on Thursday (The *Fun*

Train went up on Friday and back on Sunday.) The *Snow Train* was designed more for seniors, and was suitable for youngsters as well. (You had to be over 21 to ride the *Fun Train*.) The *Snow Train* did have onboard entertainment, but there was no dance car. Two of the entertainers were quite famous. One was a world-renowned banjo player, Georgette Twain, and the other was John Fiore, accordionist.

I often had private car charters on the back of the *Fun* and *Snow Trains*. When Private cars were on the end of Amtrak trains, there was no access, because the door level on the newer Amtrak equipment was higher than the doors on the vintage private cars. But the *Fun Train* and *Snow Train* equipment was made up of older low-level coaches, so my private car groups had access to the rest of the train. The entertainers always came back to the private cars and John Fiore would always stop at my kitchen and sing "Someone's in the kitchen with Connie" (not Dinah). There was also a full-length dome car on the Fun Train, the last one in existence in Amtrak's fleet. Amtrak was going to scrap it but Henry talked them into keeping it. Coach seats on the rest of the train were assigned, but the dome was open seating and provided spectacular views through the mountains. The *Fun Train* equipment was a complete train consist and when the season was over it was used as a special train all over the country.

For many years a member of the PLA and outstanding railroad historian, Al Harvey, was the "Voice of the *Snow Train*." He sat in the dome and narrated a fascinating history of the train and surrounding area that was piped throughout the train. For a few years, my waiter Ron was the onboard manager of the *Fun Train*. Since he lived in Southern California, he stayed at our house for the season. I even had a brass nameplate that read "Ron's Room" that was put on the door of our guest room when he occupied it. Everyone working on the train became "family," and even a lot of the passengers who came year after year got to know everybody. There were beautiful, blonde, identical twin girls who booked every year, and when they arrived "the twins are onboard" was heard throughout the train! I especially remember that Wayne Yetter was completely smitten with them.

We still see two of the (retired) conductors, Bill Cotton and Bruce Adair and a frequent Amtrak engineer, Phil Gosney—all sharing the same wonderful memories.

The Spaghetti Train

Sometimes Harrah's Hotel in Reno would charter one of the *Fun Trains* to bring their preferred players to Reno. I was hired to provide hors d'oeuvres and wine for their guests on the train, and I used the *Plaza Santa Fe* dome car (also owned by Wayne). It would be placed on the end of the train and about twenty-five people at a time would come back and enjoy the amenities of a private railcar. The car had a bar underneath the dome, but no kitchen. There was a private dining room, in which I used to stage the food, and because there was no kitchen, enough food would be prepared ahead of time for the return trip as well. This private dining room was named the Turquoise Room, and when the car ran in public service on Santa Fe it was a favorite dining area for celebrities. I usually had three waiters, as we had to get people in and out fairly fast, to accommodate all the passengers. On this particular trip there were five hundred passengers and my waiters were Cliff McDaniel, Ollie Beaudry and Grant Stubblefield (my A Team).

There were snowstorms in the mountains and the freight trains ahead of us were backing up. The passengers had all been served outside-catered chicken pot pies in Sacramento, but, as the train became terribly delayed, they were getting hungry. Amtrak had two snack bars with limited food on the train, and they were soon sold out. The train got later and later, and people were getting more and more upset. Continued drinking, with no food compounded the situation. I finally told my waiters that we were going to serve all of the food I had prepared for the return trip. One of the items was a chicken salad croissant. By cutting them into thirds I had enough for the entire train, served along with the rest of the food and wine. That seemed to stave off any "mutiny" and we finally made it to Reno.

I think one of the most important qualities a rail chef must possess is a propensity for flexibility, as you never knew what was going to happen next. My waiters were fantastic at handling any situation thrown at them without complaint. Passengers were usually never aware that the game plan had changed, often more than once on the same trip.

Saturday morning, I went to Costco in Reno to buy the ingredients to replace the chicken salad croissants. At one end of the *Royal Gorge* is a curved bar which was used to sell souvenirs on the *Fun Train*. Adjacent to the bar was a kitchen. For the *Fun Train* trips it was used for storage and to prepare food for the crew. This is where I prepared the food to be served in the *Plaza Santa Fe* on the way home.

The weather report was pretty dismal. The snowfall in the mountains was so heavy and the storm so severe, I started to think the train on Sunday might be annulled. As I lay in bed on Saturday night, I thought about the train in the fifties that got stuck in the snow for three days. What if we were to get stuck in the mountains with nothing to eat? Knowing there was only one kitchen on board and one chef (namely me!), a plan formed in my mind.

Sunday morning arrived, and my waiters and I went to the rail yards in Sparks. The train was due to leave Reno at 10:00 am. We were told it wouldn't leave until 1:30. Not good. My scenario had started to look like a distinct reality, so I put my plan into action. Another car owner, Bob Klein, lived in Reno and was out seeing the train off. We borrowed his jeep and went to the local

Safeway in Sparks. Luckily, they had just stocked the shelves. We literally ran through the store and bought every loaf of French bread, every can of tomatoes, tomato paste, and mushrooms, and every package of spaghetti. We got bags of onions, jars of minced garlic, and all of their butter and ground beef. We had two shopping carts full, and amazed the checker with our purchase. We then went across the street to a party store and got a couple of dozen aluminum pans, and 500 plates, forks, and napkins. I can still picture my waiter, crunched in the back of the jeep, surrounded by bags of food. After loading the new supplies on the train, I started cooking in the kitchen of the *Royal Gorge* around 10:30.

Because the passengers had to be ready to board as soon as the train was given the orders to go, Harrah's made a banquet room available to them. The *Fun Train* band entertained them and the hotel provided some food. The train didn't actually depart Reno until 4:30 p.m.! When the passengers boarded the train, they received the catered deli lunch given to all our *Fun Train* riders for the return trip, and my marvelous waiters handled preparing and serving the hors d'oeuvres and wine in the *Plaza Santa Fe* without me.

By 4:30, I had made quite a few batches of spaghetti sauce, storing it in stacked aluminum pans, and any other receptacle I could find. I think one of the hardest things for me was opening up all those little cans with a small hand can opener. There was only room in the kitchen for one person, so I was on my own, but when I'm in "high gear", people who know me well know to leave me alone! I think the crew who did see me were concerned that I was having a break-down, not realizing my tears were the result of chopping bags of onions! The stove was a small electric one on its last legs, and only three burners were fully functional. I had three small skillets to brown the onions, garlic and meat that got added to the other ingredients in a soup pot. When the sauce was ready it was ladled into the aluminum pans and a new pot got started, After all of the sauce was cooked I put three large pots on the stove for the pasta and it seemed to take forever to get the water hot enough to cook it. I was lucky that the car was stationary in Sparks for so long, but once it started it became challenging to have those pans of sauce stacked around the kitchen!

I took a long chafing dish pan and placed it over one of the pots of hot water, opened the butter, and put it in the pan to melt Then I added the garlic. After slicing the bread lengthwise, each half loaf got dipped in the garlic butter and put in the oven, stacked in rows of alternate directions. They got cut into pieces when they were crisp. The train lurched and some melted butter spilled on the burners. Now the stove was on fire! I calmly grabbed the baking soda and sprinkled some on the burners, and the fire kept on burning. I dumped the whole box on it, and the fire still burned filling the kitchen with smoke. Wayne, the owner of the car, came to the rescue with a fire extinguisher and I remember, no longer calm, frantically yelling, "Don't hit the food! Don't hit the food!" He put the fire out and didn't hit the food.

One of the car attendants came to the kitchen to tell me she had some Hindus in her car, and ask if we had anything vegetarian for them. I found a can of olives in Wayne's cupboard, so, along with onions, garlic, tomatoes, and mushrooms, a vegetarian spaghetti sauce was created.

As each of the pots of pasta was cooked, I drained it, saving and recycling the hot water for the next pot as there was no time to boil completely new water. I can't tell you how many pots of spaghetti were cooked, but by the end the water was so starchy that a spoon could have stood up in it by itself. As soon as a batch of pasta was mixed with the sauce, I put it out on the souvenir counter along with slices of garlic bread. The wives and girlfriends of the band dished the spaghetti into bowls (bread on top) and the car attendants, along with some volunteer passengers, took trays of food back to their cars. All this, mind you, on a moving train. I remember saying that if anyone said it was Ragu or asked for parmesan, to throw them off the train! We started serving at 8:15 pm, and after all of the passengers were served, the crew and entertainers ate. I usually don't eat when I'm cooking, but I hadn't eaten all day. So after making sure everyone else was fed, I was able to sit down for the first time that day and enjoy the fruits of my labor. There was enough spaghetti left over for about four people! My greatest fear had been that there would not be enough food for everyone, which would have been a travesty and might have initiated a riot!. I had never made spaghetti for five hundred people before, so I really lucked out! (My shoulder-borne angel providing my "luck!")

My face looked like I had a severe sunburn, and I was exhausted. After eating, I just wanted to go sit quietly in the *Plaza Santa Fe*. The visits to the car were over and it was now empty. As I made my way through the coaches, I got applause, and a standing ovation, and people were grabbing and kissing my hands. Ah, the power of spaghetti!!!

The next *Fun Train* out had a private car group. I used to like to take a break when I could, and walk the train. I had just passed by one of the Amtrak coach attendants, when I heard her say to the passengers, "There she goes. Last week she fixed spaghetti on the train for 700 people." The story got repeated so many times, the number of people I fed reached a thousand (the train can't even carry that many). I finally decided to add to the tale myself. I tell people, that when we got to Truckee I got off, made may way to Lake Tahoe, and walked across the water!

Key Holidays and Harrah's received no complaints about that trip, and the *Royal Gorge* kitchen got a new stove! A week after the spaghetti train, I made a run to the same Safeway in Sparks to pick up supplies for the return trip. It was closed and empty! I couldn't believe it. Apparently the weight of the snow from that huge storm had collapsed the roof. My waiters said the cause was really the vacuum created by my purchase of so much food.

Overnight with Bubba

Two dome cars, the *Silver Solarium* and the *Plaza Santa Fe*, were attached to a *Fun Train* for a special promotion. Key Holidays had gotten Bubba Paris (who was a retired 49er) as an on-board celebrity. He walked the train, signed autographs, shook hands, and ended up in a lot of people's photographs. Bubba had brought his mother with him and they had seats in the *Silver Solarium*. It had been raining when they boarded the car and I took his raincoat from him. Just because I'm so silly, I slipped it on. I looked like Dopey from *Snow White*! I even got to try on his Superbowl ring. It was so heavy and big, I probably could have gotten three of my fingers in it. His mother was a very sweet lady.

We were following a long freight train, and it was snowing so hard the freight train got stuck. We couldn't get past it and the ground switch that would have enabled us to pass the train on an alternate track was frozen shut. I remember offering to boil water to get it open, but that couldn't work. Snow removal equipment was working ahead of the freight train to try to get the line open, but we were in for a long night. The coach passengers were the best off, as their chairs all had leg rests and reclined. The private car passengers had to sleep sitting up in their chairs. The problem was Bubba. He was just too big to sleep in a chair. He tried stretching across the aisle up in the dome, but that didn't work either. The owner of the *Solarium*, Roy, had a bedroom on board, so Bubba got the only bed on the train. My crew all went into the room where we had put the luggage, and slept on the floor. Roy had a room with a table and two bench seats. I took one and he took the other. What a night! I spent part of it trying to figure out what I had onboard that could be offered for breakfast.

When I woke up in the morning, the train was stopped. We had moved during the night, but were still about an hour out of Reno, at Donner Lake. Sunrise on the lake was so beautiful, truly breathtaking. People were waking up to a spectacular "good morning." Bubba's mother, who had just spent all night sitting up in a chair, was looking at the lake and praising God for its beauty. I've seen many wonderful things over the years on the trains, but that was one of the best.

Darrel's and My "New Look"

Darrel and I both worked in the office of Key Holidays. One day, we received in the mail an *S & H Uniform* magazine. Featured on the front cover were two male models, wearing the craziest uniforms for a chef and a waiter. The waiter's outfit had a blue tunic top with a stand up collar (like a Nehru jacket) and two rows of brass buttons, worn with white pants and white shoes. It looked like some kind of military uniform right out of a Gilbert and Sullivan production. The chef's hat and pants were printed with big, bright vegetables on a black background, with the same trim on the white chef's jacket. The shoes looked like black combat boots.

My waiters and I loved playing practical jokes on each other. Ron was one of the biggest jokesters and we were always trying to outdo each other. Darrel and I took pictures of our faces and put them over the models' faces. Our pictures looked so funny, especially mine, with a big, male hand protruding from the arm of the chef's jacket and those large, very masculine boots. We faxed the image to Ron in Southern California with the notation, "Hey, Ron! Darrel and I are going for a new look. What do you think?"

I got a request for a charter from Oakland to Santa Barbara

using the *Virginia City*. The car would be going on to Los Angeles, where it would stay until the trip home. Whenever we had a trip to LA, Ron would meet the car a take us shopping for supplies. When he found out the group was getting off in Santa Barbara he asked if he could bring his grandmother and ride the deadhead from Santa Barbara to LA. Of course he could. Darrel's wife, Shari also came and stayed in the crew room.

Darrel and I couldn't resist. We ordered those chef and waiter outfits from the catalog. Along with some black snow boots and new white sneakers we took them on our trip. The guests on the car were in on the joke, as we had to change into our outfits before we reached Santa Barbara.

The menu that day included Grand Mariner French toast for brunch, and beef rouladen, red cabbage with apples, carrots, and parsley potatoes for an early dinner. I have a deep pan with a basket to fry the French toast, but I had forgotten to bring it. The kitchen in the *Virginia City* still had the original set of pans, used during Beebe's time, and as his chef only cooked for two to six guests at a time the pans weren't very deep. I cooked the French toast in the largest pan without incident, but when the food was removed the hot oil was sloshing around. I crumpled up a paper bag and put it in the oil. That helped, but the oil was still coming up the sides. What I did next is admittedly incredibly stupid. I crumpled up a second bag and put it on top of the first one. The oil came right up the sides and washed over my left hand. The burns were severe, the pain excruciating, and I had dinner yet to prepare. I had a lot of peeling and chopping to do, and had to plunge my hand repeatedly into a bowl of ice water, to endure the pain. Somehow, that meal got made and served. Usually, the chef does all the dishes by hand, but there was no way I could put my hand in even warm water, so Shari got recruited to wash the dishes.

The group didn't know what had happened, but after the second seating I put my hand in my pocket and went to their leader and asked him if one of the guests might be a doctor. Luckily for me, one of them was. I asked him to come to the rear bedroom. When I showed him my hand he jumped up and ran back to the group. "Drugs, I need drugs! Does anyone have any drugs?" One of the passengers did have some powerful pain pills, and after taking one I had to sit down and elevate my hand. I was not deterred, however, from changing into my chef's outfit for Ron before Santa Barbara. The doctor wanted me to get off the train there and go to a hospital, but I promised him I would do that in LA.

After the group departed the train at Santa Barbara, Ron and his grandmother boarded the car. Ron's expression was priceless when he saw our outfits. We had him for about ten minutes before he cracked up laughing (he knew us too well).

When we arrived in LA, Ron drove me to a hospital in Glendora (where his mother worked as a nurse). The doctor did such a good job that my wedding ring didn't have to be cut off and I have no scarring at all. Ron called Henry and it was decided that he (Ron) would return with the car and do the cooking. I had planned multiple entrees on the way home. Ron wasn't happy about that, but he did an admirable job and the group was happy.

When I first started cooking on the trains I didn't have a uniform, just an apron over my street clothes. I was like the "little woman in the kitchen." Women passengers kept coming in and offering to do the dishes and share recipes, so I needed to give myself a more professional image. I didn't want to dress like the male chefs, so I came up with my own look: white dress, shoes and chef's hat, a red apron and railroad neckerchief and a red and white towel at my waist. I eventually replaced my dress with white pants and shirt, and this was my trademark look for twenty-five years.

The Friggin Shirt Company

One time we had a really bad group. Most of the people were nice enough, but the leader was totally obnoxious. A case where he mistakenly thought that because he had money he had class. Wrong!!! He got quite drunk and demanding and every other word out of his mouth started with an F. It was all we could do to get through that trip. Afterwards, when we were telling our cohorts about our experience, we substituted the word "friggin" in our narrative. It struck us funny and we started to say it for everything. Darrel, Ron and I, who were on that trip, came up with the idea of the Friggin Shirt Co. Because Darrel and I looked so funny in our crazy chef and waiter outfits, we were going to wear them and pose in different scenarios, print the picture on a tee shirt with a "Friggin" saying. Ron printed up some plain shirts with just the "Friggin Shirt Co" name. We gave one to the Amtrak bartender, Eddie, on the *Fun Train*. He wore it on every trip and people loved it. We were all so busy, we never followed up on it. Looking back, I wish we had.

Ozzie and Family

I had a group booked to go to Reno on the *Tamalpais*, traveling up on Friday and back on Sunday. On the Wednesday before the trip I received a call from a travel agent in Malibu, wanting to charter a private car one way from Los Angeles to Atlanta, Georgia. I suggested she check with the private cars located in the LA area. She said she'd done that and it looked like the *Tamalpais* was the only car that might be available. When I asked her the date she wanted the car, she said Wednesday. Most people charter private cars months in advance. I said, "What Wednesday?" She said, "Next Wednesday!" Most people would have immediately said no, but by this time you probably have realized I'm not like most people. It didn't seem feasible, as Amtrak required a ten-day notice to attach a car to the end of their trains. However, I said I'd see what I could do, and would call her back. I called Jon Kirchanski, who arranged the car movements for me with Amtrak. I said I knew it was less than ten days and Amtrak would decline the request, but to keep going up the ladder, trying to find someone who would say yes, and reminding them how much money they would get from the move. To his amazement and mine, someone up the Amtrak "food chain" did say yes.

I still had to do the shopping and preparation for my Reno trip, leaving in two days, and I needed to find a waiter/car attendant for the Atlanta trip, which would be going with The *Sunset Limited*. My first choice was Cliff. He had become my top waiter and I believed he was the best in the business. He was one of the waiters for the upcoming Reno trip, but it turned out he had to work Monday through Wednesday for Amtrak. The *Sunset Limited* left LA at 10:30 in the evening, so I arranged for Cliff to fly to LA after work on Wednesday to join me for the trip.

It's my modus operandi to find a way to make things work (too bad I'm not a politician) so, this is how it happened. I completed the Reno charter and on Sunday evening, after cleaning the car, I went home. Henry says he can still picture me Sunday night, sitting up in bed surrounded by cookbooks, working on my menus for the trip on Wednesday. On top of everything else, I had been told that the clients were vegetarians. It is one thing to cook one vegetarian meal, quite another to do breakfast, lunch, dinner, and snacks for four days. The hit of the meals was the artichoke frittata. I even gave the recipe to the mother as her youngest child was crazy about it. Monday, I washed all of the dirty car linen from the Reno trip and did some food shopping.

The *Tamalpais* was put on the end of the *Coast Starlight* on Tuesday, and Jon and I dead-headed it down to LA. On the way down I covered the dining room table and turned it into an ironing board, ironing all of the table cloths, napkins, my outfit, and the waiter's jackets, hanging them up on the dining room's hat rack. Looking in the windows as we sped by, people must have wondered at my laundry display.

The *Tam* arrived in the evening and I slept onboard. The next morning, Ron came and drove me to several stores to pick up the rest of my supplies. I had to stock everything for the entire trip, so my list was pretty extensive. Cliff arrived that evening before our guests, so he quickly made up the beds. Luckily, the flowers from the Reno trip were fresh enough for this second trip.

The clients were a family of five from Malibu who were taking their sixteen-year-old daughter, Samantha, to a ballet school in Atlanta. The other children were a boy of seventeen, Spencer, and little Sophie, who was eight (all of them good looking kids). Their next-door neighbors were Dick Van Dyke and Mel Gibson, so you knew they had money, but they were the most unpretentious, charming, interesting family you could ever meet. The father, Ozzie, was a lot of fun, and his wife was so unassuming. She was quite a bit younger than he was, but not what you might call a "trophy wife." She was pretty enough, but down to earth and a terrific mom. Spencer wanted to be an actor, but it was clear that college had to come first. Knowing kids were going to be onboard, I brought some videos I thought they'd enjoy, but was I ever wrong! They all brought books (thick books) and spent their time either reading or playing games with each other (not video games). They were well behaved and respectful. Those parents had done a fabulous job.

The car had to be taken off the train in New Orleans and attached to a train going to Washington, D.C. We had a ten-hour window for this transfer, but unfortunately, found that our train was going to be twelve hours late. Samantha's orientation was due to begin the following day. I explained the family's options: Samantha and her mother could fly to Atlanta and the rest of the family could leave the next day by train to join them; The whole family could terminate their train trip in New Orleans and fly to Atlanta; The family could take the train the next day and be a day late to Atlanta. Or, it might be possible, although terribly expensive, to charter an engine to take the *Tamalpais* alone to Atlanta. They decided to stay together and go by rail the following day.

Our late arrival gave all of us time to visit New Orleans. The family wanted to go out for dinner that evening and I recommended they dine at Commander's Palace. Dating from 1893, this historical, first class restaurant captures the essence and charm of New Orleans. They got all dressed up and took a cab to the restaurant. Cliff and I had a great time. We got some Popeye's chicken that we consumed while sitting on a bench watching the big ships come up the Mississippi River. When New Orleans was devastated by Hurricane Katrina in 2005 I thought about that day, and was saddened to see that disaster happen in such a wonderful place. The Commander's Palace endured extensive damage and has since been fully restored.

The rest of the trip was uneventful, and the family got off in Atlanta. I had let Sophie take Tammy Boy, the *Tamalpais* car's mascot, to bed with her during the trip and she loved him so much that I gave him to her for a souvenir. I am a huge believer that good kids should be rewarded. I figured I could find another leprechaun like Tammy Boy, but I never did find another like him.

After Atlanta, Cliff and I had the car to ourselves. For a change, we got to sit out on the rear platform and play railroad baron. Cliff was so much fun to be with and such wonderful company, I had come to think of him as my best friend. After so much work in one week, it was wonderful to be able to relax and enjoy the car and the scenery.

Everything was great, until we got to D.C. to reach the station the train had to go through a tunnel. Cliff and I were sitting in the dining room when there was a loud explosion at the end of the car. Sparks Cascaded down its sides and we thought we had been bombed. This trip was after 9/11 and I thought maybe someone targeted us, thinking there was a political VIP on board. It was very frightening. When we got to the station, we found out the top of our car had snagged an electric cable on the roof of the tunnel. Here it was, commute time, and the whole local system was shut down. Our own communication system had been wiped out and we were being blamed for the accident. We had to contact Jon and have him fax schematics of the car before Amtrak finally admitted it was their wire that was hanging too low.

We were moved to the private rail car track, which was right inside the station where all the commuters walked by on both sides of the car. Cliff had planned to fly home in the afternoon to go back to work, but I was able to stay overnight. Before he left, Cliff set a beautiful table in the dining room. My sister, Letty, was working in Washington and I'd invited her and her friend, and four other friends of mine who lived in the area, to dinner on the car. I put out the red carpet, and, with the flowers and candlelight on the car, it was quite an impressive sight and wowed the commuters going by. I had to fly home myself the day after, and one of the owners flew out to accompany the car back to Oakland.

Sake and Cheese

One trip on the *Tamalpais* was for some international biotech scientists, going from Oakland to Los Angeles for a convention. They were mostly European and Japanese. I cooked American style food, but wanted a couple of culinary touches to make them feel at home. I decided to serve Sake and an afternoon offering of wine, cheese and fresh fruit. I wasn't very familiar with Sake, so I inquired at my local BevMo and was advised to serve it both cold and hot. I bought a good brand, but when I asked how hot it should be the clerk couldn't tell me. I then bought two Sake carafes and several little cups. I also bought about eight kinds of cheese and some nice California wines.

When it came time to serve the Sake, I poured some of it in a saucepan and put it on the stove. The waiters and I all stood over it, watching the pan. "How hot should it be?" "I haven't the slightest idea." I finally stuck my finger into the liquid and said, "Feels right to me." We all laughed and I poured the Sake into one of the carafes and served it, along with the cold carafe. A little while later, one of the Japanese men came back to the kitchen, bowed, and said (with a heavy Japanese accent), "Ooooh, do you know your Sake!" If he only knew! My waiters heard him and it was all they could do to keep straight faces.

I cut up the fruit and put it on a platter with all of the un-wrapped cheeses. The selection of wines and wine glasses and small serving plates and napkins completed the table. The group were all standing around the table and I got called from the kitchen. The guests wanted to know what kind the various cheeses were. Whoops! I had simply opened the packages and put the cheese on the platter, throwing away the wrappings. I had selected an assortment of cheeses for them that looked and sounded interesting and didn't have a clue as to their identities. Without missing a beat, I explained to them an old American tradition of guessing what kind of cheese was being served. They really got into the "game" and I think a German won. Was he right? Beats me! If you ever hear of this "old American tradition", you now know its origin.

On my regular buffets, I used to serve five cheeses: sharp cheddar; Monterey jack, Swiss, harvarti with dill, and blue cheese. This was a combination I found most everyone enjoyed. I'd cut each cheese into a different, bite-size shape and serve them all on a tray with a mound of grapes.

Although I provided the food and drinks, guests were welcome to bring what ever they wanted on the train. One time, a 'yuppie" group from Marin County, north of San Francisco brought their own designer breads and "fancy" cheeses onboard. I quickly removed my cheeses, as I knew that my "low brow" selection might offend their refined palates! I had one group who brought their own selection of wines and they asked my waiter to ring the dinner chime each time I placed a new item on the buffet table so they could pair a wine with the new food item (even the deviled eggs). With all of that wine drinking, it was amazing that this group stayed sober. I think it was because of so much food.

The Arthur Murray Dancers

I had a charter to Reno, taking a group of Arthur Murray dance instructors to a dance competition. The cars used were the *Plaza Santa Fe* and the *Royal Gorge*. My waiter and I were invited to see the competition, and now, when I watch "Dancing with the Stars" I'm reminded of that trip. These dancers were really good, and it was fun watching them. On the way home I asked if they taught the bop. They were all pretty young and none of them knew how to do it. Well, I was a teenager in the 50s and loved to dance. There were two different bop styles—east coast and west coast. They asked for a demonstration, so I took off my shoes (they didn't call the fifties dance parties sock-hops for nothing) and proceeded to show them both styles.

From seventh grade all the way through high school, almost every kid in my class could bop. None of these professional dancers could get it. When dancing from the 50s is portrayed, it goes right from the jitterbug and swing straight to the twist, monkey, swim, and all the other novelty dances popular in the 60s, but the bop is most often ignored—probably because dance teachers can't figure out how to do it!

The Karaoke Bar

Sometimes Cliff and I would sing together for the groups on the train, usually *Chattanooga Choo Choo*. How we first came to sing together is a funny story. Our mutual friend, Chuck, my yearly dance partner, had more friends than anyone I knew. His birthday was celebrated at a San Francisco restaurant one year and probably a hundred or so people were there. After dinner, about a dozen of us wanted to keep the party going, so it was decided that we would go to a karaoke bar. This was quite a while ago, and I didn't even know what a karaoke bar was.

We went to this dive on Market Street. There was a long bar down the middle of the room, open on both sides. General seating was to the right of the bar, and the karaoke setup and small dance floor were on the left side with some tables at the rear of the space where our group sat. I told Henry that I needed to visit the restroom, in the rear of the right side. While waiting for the restroom to be unoccupied, I heard laughing from the other side of its door. Out tumbled two girls, and when I looked in I saw it was a tiny restroom. "Well, that's odd", I thought. Then, when walking around the bar to rejoin my friends, I saw men dancing with men and women sitting with women. "Henry, Henry," I whispered, "I think this is a gay bar!" "You think?" he said.

Well, we ordered drinks and had a great time. We had a pretty mixed group of people ourselves. All the guys in our party got up and sang "San Antonio Rose." It was pretty awful, but that didn't matter. We were all laughing and having a lot of fun. Undetected by my friends, I signed up to sing. The stool and screen were in the front of the room and my gang, especially Henry, was surprised to hear my name called. I sat on the stool and sang "Sentimental Journey." (A train song of course!) I had a very deep singing voice and Henry said later I sounded like Marlene Dietrich. Chuck said, "I didn't know Connie could sing like that." Then Henry said, "I didn't know she could sing like that, either." Well, I finished to thunderous applause. When I returned to our table, Cliff said, "Connie, Connie, I want to sing with you." So we sang *Chattanooga Choo Choo* together.

When I told my kids about my hit at the karaoke bar, they both said, "Mom, don't you realize what they thought? No wonder you were such a hit! With your low voice, they probably thought you were in drag!" So, I got this crazy idea, and it's one of my greatest regrets that I never acted upon it. I was going to rent a white, stretch limousine once a month and dress up as a famous personality. From my drama class experience in college, I knew that with greasepaint, costume, and padding (especially padding in my case!), you can transform yourself into almost anyone. I could go as Judy Garland, Marlene Dietrich, Mae West—so many! The limo would drive up to the dive on Market Street and I would make a grand entrance, dragging my boa behind me. I would sit down, sing one song, and leave without saying a word. Herb Caen was still writing his column in the San Francisco Examiner, and I knew I'd be in it. In case people started following the limo, I'd change enroute, back to just me, and when no one was looking I'd slip out of the car with my costume in a bag. When the limo stopped again, the door would be opened and the vehicle mysteriously empty!

I was really going to do it, but didn't because I was worried when people found out I really was a woman (which would eventually happen), I'd offend someone who thought I was making fun of them. I've talked with a lot of people since then, who assured me that no offense would have been taken.

Harold and Maude

The Western Railway Museum in Rio Vista, California, is mainly a trolley museum, although they do have some non-electric-powered rail equipment. One of their old railway cars has been converted into a diner and the organization has an amazing collection of original railway china and silver, which is used for meals service. The diner's small galley has a wood burning stove that uses presto logs for fuel (not easy to find nowadays). I had always wanted to cook on one (just to be able to say I had) and I got my chance when I was asked to cater a lunch on the car. I've since catered several meals there, but I remember that first one. I served Beef Wellington. Instead of the traditional leaf-shaped pastry decoration on top, I created tiny pastry trolley cars stamped from a flat Christmas ornament. The car was stationary, so it was easier to work in its kitchen than if it had been on a moving train. For that lunch and future catering jobs at the Junction, Cliff was my waiter.

Another car in the museum's collection is *Western Pacific Lounge #653*, built in 1931—a very famous and well-known car, as it was used for Maude's "home" in the classic film *Harold and Maude*, a 1960s movie that has a "cult" following.

I wanted to hold a complimentary invitation-only party for twenty guests, ten of my choosing and ten chosen by the Western Rail Museum. I would provide the wine and the meal served in the diner, followed by a showing of *Harold and Maude*—in Maude's car. I was even going to rent a hearse to transport guests from the upper parking lot to the dining car (and have it pass by a Harold look-alike, lying alongside the road with a knife sticking out of him). If you've never seen the movie, this will make no sense to you, but it's such a classic, you should go and rent it! Also, the guests would be encouraged to come in costume, either as a character from the movie or in 60s attire. I was even going to try to get Bud Cort, the actor who played Harold, to attend. To my great disappointment, Rio Vista nixed my idea. I thought after my first "Harold and Maude Party" the museum could continue to do it themselves, and sell it to the public. Limited to twenty guests, it would be quite exclusive, and they would be able to charge a high price. I couldn't persuade them, but I still think it's a great idea and maybe one day they'll reconsider and give it a try, with or without me.

My Mini-Me

One of my other trips also had a movie connection. Sometimes our office staff at Key Holidays would have a movie night. We had all recently seen the *Austin Powers* film and "one million dollars" became a catchword in the office.

I had a trip to LA using the *Royal Gorge* (used as the piano/lounge car on the *Fun Train*), so I hired Jeff, the piano player from the *Fun Train* to entertain. I had also started looking for an assistant, whom I could train to replace me on some of my trips.

I asked Michael's friend Michele if she would consider it, and she agreed to come with me on this trip. I had known Michele since she was in high school and at one point she almost came to live with us. She had worked for me on several New Year's Eve trips and I knew her to be a hard worker and a really good person.

I had her wear an outfit identical to mine, and I started to refer to her as "Mini-Me". We had so much fun on that trip. With Jeff playing the piano, Cliff and I sang our "*Chattanooga Choo Choo*" (talk about a captive audience). When we arrived in LA, Michele and I posed for a picture standing by the car. Well, I was standing. She got down on her knees and put her shoes in front of her apron. Our picture was taken as we were saying, "one million dollars!"

The crew and I stayed at a hotel in Chinatown, fairly close to the station. I used to double up my waiters in the hotel rooms, and on this trip I paired Jeff with my waiter, Richard. Well, it seemed Jeff had a terrible snoring problem. Richard couldn't sleep at all and was screaming at Jeff to wake up and stop snoring. After this trip, my waiters always got a single room.

Richard, who was from Wales, could have easily played

Pierce Brosnan's little brother, and he loved to sing. We often used to sing together in the kitchen. My grandmother was Welsh, and Richard always said it was my Welsh blood that made me want to sing.

Michele didn't end up being a chef. She is a fantastic artist and that became her life's passion and work. She was too much of an original to be anyone's "mini-me!".

The Thanksgiving Turkey Sandwich

One season, I had the *Silver Solarium* dome car on the end of the *Fun Train*. The *Silver* Solarium was built by the Budd Co. in 1948 and was one of six observation lounge-sleepers used on Western Pacific's famed *California Zephyr*. Ownership was transferred to Amtrak in 1971 and the *Silver Solarium* (the name was retained by Amtrak) was used in service throughout the country until it was retired in 1978. In 1985 it was sold to a private party who restored it for private charter service and in 2002 the *Silver Solarium* was purchased by Rail Journeys West. Today, it is the only one of the six original cars running in private charter service.

The problem with the *Solarium* is the location of the kitchen which was installed when the car was restored. The kitchen is across the forward end of the car. The stove and sink are on one side of the aisle and the counter and cupboards are on the other side and there is a work/serving counter that can be raised that completely blocks the aisle. The vestibule used for loading is adjacent to the kitchen and is the only access as The *Silver Solarium* has a round-end observation lounge on the rear of the car. This was not a problem when the car was attached to high-level Amtrak trains, as no through passage was possible. Now that it sometimes ran with other private cars, or, in this case, with the *Fun Train*, access was possible from car to car and visiting guests had to pass through the kitchen to get to both the dome and the round-end observation lounge.

I had decided to try something new, offering a sit-down lunch in the dome of the *Silver Solarium* to *Fun Train* passengers. I had two sittings and three entree selections and reservations were taken before the trip.

There was a large bedroom suite next to the kitchen, and I set that up to be a staging area for the food. My private dining car for the public turned out to be a whole lot more trouble than it was worth, even though the guests who experienced it loved it. It's hard enough to cook on a moving train in a tiny kitchen without a steady stream of passengers walking through. The food staging area was a good idea, however, and I used it on other trips.

On one *Fun Train* trip I had a group on the car using the *Silver Solarium*. On the menu was my special turkey sandwiches (prepared on a table in the staging room). Earlier, would roast a whole turkey and make stuffing and gravy. Setting up an assembly line, I would lay down the bread (both white and wheat), add butter and mayonnaise, gravy, stuffing, thick slices of turkey, and cranberry sauce. Hence, my Thanksgiving Turkey Sandwich.

I was so busy that day, I asked one of my waiters to assemble the sandwiches. I went to check on him, and he had completed just three sandwiches. He was being so careful, wanting to do it just right for me. They needed to get done a lot quicker, so I sent him back out to wait on the guests and grabbed Richard. "Come on, help me get these done." With our two-man assembly line, we were batting the sandwiches out. Instead of singing, for some reason Richard started clucking like a chicken. I don't know why it struck us so funny, but we were laughing the whole time.

I think part of the reason we all laughed so much on our trips was from being so tired and going with little sleep. If people had seen us being so silly behind the scenes they might have tried to have us "committed", but it is how we kept stress from getting to us. In many stressful jobs humor is an important safety valve, releasing pressure to maintain sanity.

The Las Vegas *Fun Train*

We had been running the *Reno Fun Train* for several years, when Henry decided to run a *Las Vegas Fun Train*. A week after the last run to Reno, the entire *Fun Train* consist was deadheaded to Los Angeles. Our onboard entertainers, crew, and most of our office staff went to Los Angeles too where we had reserved rooms right across from the Union Station, at the Metro Plaza Hotel. On the Las Vegas trip there was no private car on the end of the train, so I just played the part of owner's wife. (To tell the truth, I would rather have been working in a kitchen on the train.) The Lieutenant Governor of Nevada and her husband were on-board, so our train made excellent time.

You've heard the saying "The operation was a success, but the patient died!" Well, the *Las Vegas Fun Train* was a great success, and the people who went thought it was wonderful. Unfortunately, we didn't sell enough seats to make it worth doing again. (It had no mountain snow, spectacular scenery, or decades old history to attract riders like the Reno train did.)

After returning to LA, Henry treated the whole gang to dinner at a Mexican Restaurant on Olivera Street near our hotel. There were probably about twenty of us sitting at two long tables. One of our co-workers, Jean, was unable to make the trip, so before we were served dinner, we decided to call her and all say hello. Henry called her on his cell phone and when she answered, he held it up and we all shouted "Hi, Jean". We've often wondered what the kitchen staff must have thought. Imagine, owning a restaurant, and having that many people out front shouting out what sounded exactly like "hygiene"!

Olivera Street is one of Los Angeles' original Spanish settlements, where the oldest adobe building in LA is located. Today the street is a great attraction featuring entertainment, shops, and great Mexican food.

Another landmark close to the Union Station is Filipe's, featuring the best French-dipped sandwich in the world (they claim to have invented it). They also feature a delicious hot sauce to put on the sandwich. I always swear I'm going to put on just a little, but it's so good, it always get liberally added. Luckily, there's a good supply of napkins to keep the perspiration out of your eyes! Filipe's is a large place with long tables and sawdust on the floor. Orders are taken at a long deli counter from multiple lines, and the place is usually packed with customers from all parts of society. The walls are covered with a variety of memorabilia, and there is a train room in the back with display cases of old model trains. For me, it's inconceivable to go to LA by train and not eat at Filipe's. My mouth waters just thinking about it!

The *Tamalpais* Ghost

A lot of groups went year after year on the private cars, and became good friends. One couple, Bill and Judy, used to go every year with their family and friends. They would always remain on the car to Sparks and stay at John Ascuaga's Nugget Hotel. They had two sons, Will and Todd. Will worked for a time in the office at Key Holidays, and Todd started working for me as a waiter when he was just eighteen and in college.

Of all my waiters, Todd was by far the funniest. After working quite a few trips for me (and after graduating college), he got a job as a waiter in a big hotel. (As he was a college graduate, there was a method to his madness!). He then started applying for jobs on cruise lines. He was hired by Holland America Line, and eventually became the youngest assistant cruise director in their history. When offered the position of cruise director, he didn't want to commit to that much more time, so he moved on.

He went to Las Vegas where he put together shows and wrote for comics. Todd is bright and funny, and easily could have been a stand-up comic himself, if he had so chosen. When he worked for me, he kept everyone in stitches.

His parents had chartered the *Tamalpais* for their yearly trip and Todd was my waiter. Also on-board, as mechanic, was Lou, one of the owners of the car. On Saturday, Lou, Todd, and I were all on the Tamalpais as it sat in Sparks. It had been taken off the *California Zephyr* and put on the private car track located in the middle of the yard. I was doing some cooking on Saturday for the return trip on Sunday, and Todd was cleaning the car. Lou said he was going into Reno and would be back later.

The car had a telephone and we received a call for Lou. It seemed his Dad had been in an accident. This was before anyone had a cell phone, so we said we would have Lou call home as soon as he returned.

Todd's family was having a get-together at the hotel, within walking distance of the car, and I insisted he join them. There was still some polishing to do, but I was done in the kitchen, and didn't mind finishing up the cleaning. I was there anyway, waiting for Lou to relay the message, so off Todd went. It was actually one of my favorite things to work alone on private cars while they sat in the yards. It was so quiet and peaceful. No one ever bothered you, but once in a while, we would get a "foamer" poking around the car. There are railfans and then there are "foamers" — a term for over-the-top (rabid) railfans. Their whole lives seem to revolve around trains, and the term is used to describe the foam around their mouths! (a tongue in cheek description).

Anything old, whether it is a rail car, house, automobile, or just about anything (including people), needs to be kept up (and given a lot of TLC), or it will look shabby. The oak paneling and brass on the *Tam* required constant polishing, and the mirrors, sinks and windows needed cleaning all the time. So, there I was, happy as a clam (I've always wondered why clams are so darn happy!), polishing up a storm, waiting for Lou.

I was in the kitchen at the front end of the car. It was a warm day, so I had the top of the Dutch door at that end and the door to the rear platform open, to get a breeze through the car. I heard Lou get on the rear platform, so I ran through the car to tell him about his Dad. He wasn't on the car, so I looked outside, down both sides of the car—no Lou. That's strange, I thought, but went back to my polishing. I was now in the rear lounge, when I heard someone at the other end of the car. There's no way Lou would climb through the open top half of the door, so I figured I had an intruder. "Who's there?" I called, but again, no one. Mustering all the courage I possessed, I gingerly made my way through the car. Finding no one onboard. I was sufficiently spooked to lock both of the doors, but I figured it must be kids, messing with me and staying out of sight under the car.

Lou finally came back and got his message. It wasn't serious enough for him to fly home, so he stayed with the car. The "intruder" incident was out of my mind and I never mentioned it.

On the way home on Sunday, a freight train ahead of us had derailed in the mountains. It had been carrying some chemicals, and some hazmat experts had to be brought in to see if it was dangerous. We were on the end of the *California Zephyr*, and were stopped in Truckee, right across the street from a row of quaint shops and restaurants. As we had no idea when we would get the OK to proceed, the passengers weren't allowed off the train. It became obvious that we would have to serve something for dinner, so I got the attention of a local kid and paid him to run to the store and pick up some chicken.

We ended up sitting there for four hours. I was in the kitchen, and Lou was standing in the doorway talking with me. He casually said something about the ghost on the *Tamalpais*. I thought I was hearing things. Lou was a down to earth guy, and an engineer for the Union Pacific, not someone you would expect to be talking about the supernatural. "Oh, yeah, right Lou" "No really. There really is a ghost on the car, but he's a friendly ghost, who just likes to play tricks. I'll lay out all the tools I need to work on something, and one will go missing. I'll find it later in some strange place". I wasn't buying it! Then he said "He manifests himself the most when you're polishing the car". I looked down to see all the hairs on my arms standing straight up.

After that trip, I heard a lot of stories about our ghost. One concerned the car when it was being worked on at a facility in Redwood City. Whenever the car was stationary between trips, a long, gray runner was unrolled to cover the carpet. It had been raining, and the ground outside was quite muddy. One morning, it was discovered that the rear platform door to the lounge had been forced open. (This was before the security system had been installed.) There were a couple of sets of muddy footprints on the gray runner, leading down the hall past the bedrooms. At the entrance to the dining room, the footprints stopped abruptly, and long "running" footprints, leading back toward the rear lounge could be seen on the runner. The shoe size was not large, so it was probably adolescents. The break-in wasn't discovered until the morning, so it wasn't like they'd been caught. It just didn't make sense that after they'd gone to all of the trouble and risk of breaking in, the whole car wasn't explored. Something scared those kids off the car! Another time, there was a fire (perhaps electrical) inside a wall. A blaze that should have spread and destroyed the car was mysteriously put out. Even my waiter, Tom, had an experience. He was alone, accompanying the car on a deadhead move, and the rear platform kept falling for no reason, hitting him on the leg. He told me he felt silly, but had a little talk with the ghost and said he wasn't going to hurt the car. After that, there was no more problem with the platform.

The best story was about a family traveling cross-country. It was at night, and the parents and friends were sitting in the dining room. They had a little daughter who had gone to the rear lounge. The girl came into the dining room and asked who the man was in the rear lounge. Thinking someone may have gotten on during a stop, they all ran back and looked—no one was there. The little girl stuck to her story, describing her traveling companion "He was really, really dark and was wearing a funny jacket and an ice cream hat." What she had accurately described was what a Santa Fe porter would have looked like in the 20s.

But, all of this is hearsay, kind of like hearing of other people's experiences with UFOs, interesting, but hardly proof.

I had a trip to Reno on the *Tamalpais* and my waiters were Greg (who had married Michele), and Darrel. We were going to spend the night on the car rather than in a hotel. Michele's college-age brother and a friend lived near Reno and we all had dinner in town on Saturday night. The boys wanted to see the car, and we got back to it pretty late. They certainly weren't drunk, but they had had a few beers, and we told them to stay on the car until morning. We were all wide awake, and Darrel and Greg said they would get the car ready for the morning, I decided to pre-cook my breakfast meats, and we all got to work. Darrel and Greg vacuumed the car and set the table. The boys were in the rear lounge, playing cards and listening to music. (I use that term loosely). They had put on a tape they brought in from their truck. To me, heavy metal is not music; just irritating noise, but it was keeping them entertained.

Greg came into the kitchen, and asked if I had put the light on in the crew room. I said I hadn't but went to look. There is a toggle switch on the wall right inside the room. It was off. The light that was on was a reading light by the window. I used the crew room for storage, and it was so crowded it would have been hard to get to that light to turn it on. Greg said all of the bedroom lights and fans kept coming on and he kept turning them off. I said there was probably a short somewhere in the wiring.

I had finished cooking the bacon and sausage (using a baking pan in the oven), and had the pan on top of the sink, half filled with water to soak it. Darrel had been setting the table, and had taken a break to come in to talk with me. I was leaning back against the stove and Darrel was facing me, standing in front of the freezer. Suddenly, I felt a sharp rap on my back from the stove, and the water in the pan on the sink began to slosh back and forth. The car was sitting all by itself in the yard, with no other cars or engines around it, and even if the boys wanted to play a prank on me and run full force against the car (a heavy-weight), we would not feel a thing. "Darrel, I think we just had an earthquake!" We went to the lounge, where Greg and the boys were, "Hey, did you just feel that earthquake?" "No." "Wait a minute, you can't have an earthquake at one end of a railroad car and not at the other end. That's impossible!""

Darrel, Greg and I were in the dining room trying to figure out what could have caused the bump, when the boys came running down the hall, genuinely terrified. The one who'd been sitting on the couch got bumped from the back, and the tape they had been playing came out and shot across the room. They were visibly shaken, and said they were going to get off the car for a smoke. Greg said he'd join them, but first he'd make sure all of the bedroom lights were off. When he stepped off the train, he looked up to see the light on in bedroom A. Darrel and I were the only ones on the car (so we thought!), and we were together in the dining room. I can't swear the lights, tape and couch bump happened. What I can swear to is what happened to me in the kitchen, and Darrel was my witness. Over the years, I've tried to find a logical explanation for these events, but no one has ever given me a satisfactory answer. When I told Henry, he asked if Darrel and I were finished with our work. When I said no, he said it was almost like I was rapped in the back to "stop talking and get back to work"!

The oddest thing was that we all stayed on the car that night, and didn't feel afraid. I stayed in Bedroom A, and I remember saying out loud "OK, you know I love this car and take good care of it, but I'm a rather modest person, so if you could please stay out of the room when I'm getting undressed and keep out of the bathroom, we'll get along just fine!"

In this story, I've called him a ghost. I actually think of him as "The Guardian" of the *Tamalpais*. I've told this story many times, and have had people tell me they've also felt a presence on the car. I think, if I have an angel residing on my shoulder, then why not?

Cliff and the Wheelchair

One time, Cliff and I went up to Reno with a group on the back of a *Snow Train*. Our rooms were at Harrah's Hotel. We had just been up five days earlier on the *Fun Train*, and Cliff had left something in his room at Harrah's on that previous trip. He called housekeeping to see if it had been turned in, and they said they would check, and to call back later.

A mezzanine, accessible by two escalators, separates the East tower and the West tower at Harrah's. Located on the mezzanine are restaurants and slot machines. We had just ridden the escalator up from the West tower, when Cliff spotted a house telephone on a large pillar. "Just a minute, I want to call housekeeping," Cliff said as he sat down to make the call. Now, for most people, this would be a short call, but for Cliff (who could be a bit dramatic) it was a long, drawn- out inquiry.

A very nicely dressed man around sixty years of age came up and stood waiting. Cliff put up his finger, indicating "just one minute", and continued talking. The man stood there, patiently waiting and Cliff put up his finger again, "one more minute". When he was finally finished, the man, who we had both assumed was waiting for the phone, said, very politely "May I please have my wheelchair?" Cliff had just sat down in it, figuring it belonged to the hotel. Well, with his best "Little Richard" scream, he jumped up, mortified! The man wheeled the chair over to a slot machine, where a man who looked to be in his nineties very shakily got into it (I imagine that he was the man's father.) We made a hasty departure, taking the escalator down and went outside to Virginia Street. We laughed all night long, and it's one of my favorite "Cliff" stories. I only wish I had a picture of his face when it happened.

Shopping in Reno

Most all of my trips to Reno were for two nights, and I would go shopping for supplies on the middle day. Both Ron and Cliff loved to go shopping with me. Ron's favorite "game" was to slip items into my basket, things I would never, ever buy. As hard as I tried, I could never catch him doing it. I'd get up to the check-out with pork rinds, spam, cheese whiz, and the like. I think he topped himself, when there was a package of Depends in my basket. Ron always wanted to have a private rail car chef cook-off, where the challenge would be to make the worst hors d'oeuvres ever. I might have had a shot at winning with cheese whiz on pork rinds, garnished with bacon bits, but it never happened. Perhaps we were just easily amused, but we always had fun on those shopping trips.

One time, Cliff and I had some bigwigs from Harrah's on one of our trips. They asked us what we were planning to do when we got to Reno. We told them we had planned on shopping that evening, as the train was returning the next day. They said when we were ready to go, they would arrange for one of their limousines to take us. After we checked in, we went to the valet parking and there, waiting for us, was a long, white, stretch Limo. I can still see Cliff, hopping all over the seating area in the car, checking everything out. When we got to the grocery store, we emerged from the limo (both wearing jeans and sweatshirts) to the amazement of the other shoppers. The driver waited for us and when we returned to the limo with our cart he insisted on loading all of the groceries. He then drove us to the rail yard in Sparks and helped us load everything onto the car. Boy, were we ever spoiled!

I usually rented an automobile up in Reno, and on one trip Cliff wanted to look for curtains. He had just moved to a new flat in San Francisco, and couldn't find anything he liked for his bathroom. We drove all over Reno and Sparks, looking for those darn curtains. Finally I said, "Why don't we go to a fabric store and you can pick out just what you want." "Well, I don't sew and I don't know anybody that sews," he protested. "Oh for heaven's sake, I'll sew them for you!"

We went to a fabric store and found the most unique material. It's hard to describe, but it was very sheer, with African animals embossed on it. When I got home, I tried to sew the curtains on my sewing machine (I'm such a dinosaur that I sew on an old Singer treadle sewing machine.) The needle kept catching the sheer material, and I ended up doing the whole thing by hand. I went back East by train to visit my sister, Letty, and my brother, Bill. I took the material on the train with me and finished the curtains before I got home. People kept asking me if I was working on a bridal veil. I would hold the material up, so they could see the animals. It was so pretty, they would ask where I had purchased it, and were amazed when I said Sparks, Nevada. Later, Cliff moved again, and needed another panel. I went back to the fabric store and they no longer carried it. I looked for it at several fabric shops, but never could find it again.

Cliff was so much fun to be with. Up in Reno, we would shop together, eat together and gamble together. We were there together so often that people thought we were married. So, when I would go to Reno with Henry I'd get these terrible looks from everyone who assumed I was cheating on Cliff! Henry was my husband and Cliff was my best friend.

Bob and Cleo

Bob and Cleo were a couple who had been together forever. They decided to go to Reno with a group of their friends to get married, and they booked the *Tamalpais* for the trip. For this trip Mike Biehn was my waiter. Bob and Cleo had a suite at the Eldorado Hotel. The maid of honor slipped me a key to their room and while they were off getting married, Mike and I brought in champagne, wine, and a wedding cake and decorated the room. What a surprise for them when they returned. Mike even wore his waiter's outfit to serve them.

On the way home, we were on the end of the train, so I put a "just married" sign on the back platform. I joked that I was going to drag old shoes and cans behind the train. Of course, this could never be done. There were sensors in the tracks to detect anything dragging under a train. If the sensors went off, an automated voice (urgently and loudly) would say, "Stop the train! Stop the train!" Then, when the train was stopped, the length of the it would have to be walked, and inspected visually. I wasn't about to drag anything!

For several years, the same group of friends went to Reno on the *Tam* to celebrate Bob and Cleo's anniversary, and Mike always came as my waiter for the reunion.

The Liberty Belle Saloon

In 1898, Charles Fey invented the first 3-reel slot machine in San Francisco. It was called "The Liberty Bell". His son carried on the business and registered twenty-one patents on coin-operated amusement machines. As children, Henry and I would have seen many of these in San Francisco at the Cliff House and at the early amusement park, Playland at the Beach. Playland was built at Ocean Beach in 1863, near the Cliff House. In 1884, its gravity railroad roller coaster attracted visitors, and there was also the popular Ocean Beach Pavilion for concerts and dancing. The area was serviced first by a trolley line in 1890, and that was followed by the *Ferries and Cliff House Railroad*, the *Park and Ocean Railroad*, and the *Sutro Railroad*. Sadly, Playland at the Beach met its fate in 1972 when it was razed to make way for condominiums.

In 1958 Fey's grandsons, Frank and Marshall, took the original Liberty Bell slot machine to Reno, where they opened up the Liberty Belle Saloon on Virginia Street.

It became a tradition that I would take my guys to dinner at the Liberty Belle when initiating a new waiter. The establishment was so much more than a saloon. Besides great food (my mouth still drools when recalling their lobster!), the brothers amassed a huge collection of antiques and memorabilia. On the roof were several antique wagons and the front door was saved from the original Palace Hotel in San Francisco. The fabulous Palace Hotel was built in 1875 and completely destroyed by the massive fire which ravaged The City after the 1906 earthquake. A new Palace Hotel was constructed in1909 and today is one of San Francisco's most beautiful and historic hotels.

Marshall Fey wrote a beautiful book in 1994 called (what else) *Slot Machines*, and the Liberty Belle had hundreds of unique and rare machines on display including a 1900 cast iron Roovers Donkey—a mechanical, fortune-telling, donkey smartly clad in a red velvet dress. For a nickel she would activate, bringing a monocle up to her eye, turning her head, and striking a "wheel of fortune" with the little baton in her hoof. I'd give each of my waiters a nickel and we would all give it a turn. Oddly enough, the wheel would almost always land on "food" or "work" for me. One time, Darrel received the fortune of "twins". His wife was pregnant at the time, and I thought he was going to faint.

Another thing we always did was to visit a picture hung above one of the dining tables. It was a color broadside issued about 1895 by the Centlivres Brewing Company. It depicted a

1800s dining rail car, with a railway waiter serving a bottle of Centlivres Nickel Plated bottled beer to a very fashionable couple. The car interior was exquisite with its' dark wood and leaded glass windows. I always referred to it as "my picture"' and tried (unsuccessfully) to get the bartender, Jeff (Fay's great grandson), to make a copy for me.

The Reno Sparks Convention and Visitors Authority (RSCVA) had built a huge complex, whose parking lot completely surrounded the Liberty Belle, and they wanted it torn down for more parking. This was not only a travesty in my mind, but the locals were outraged. The way the building was constructed made it impossible to physically move it, and a two-year battle to save the landmark ensued. The Feys were finally defeated by a regulation regarding the sprinkler system, and the Liberty Belle closed in 2006. I saw Jeff right before they closed, and said I would like to purchase "my picture". I was too late; everything was going to be auctioned off. Not deterred, I attended the auction. I took the train by myself to Reno, where I stayed with Rose-Marie and Dan, who now lived in Reno.

I had never participated in an auction before (ironically held at the RSCVA), and it was sad to see so many of the Fey family treasures, all 597 of them, being dispersed to strangers. I told Jeff I didn't know how he could take being there, and he said he almost didn't come.

When the auction began, it was so fast paced and as I looked around and saw the other bidders I could tell I was definitely out of my league. The little fortune-telling donkey was number 15. "Oh," I thought, "Wouldn't it be fun to get that." My whimsical notion was shattered when the bid went to $35,000.00! My picture was number 33, and I was getting sweaty palms, thinking, "What am I doing here?" When #33 was presented, a man working the auction held it up over his head and walked across the front of the room with it. "No, no, don't show my picture to everyone," I thought. The bidding started, and the other bidders had suddenly become my mortal enemies. There were two men standing in the front, wearing cowboy hats, acknowledging the bids as auction cards were raised. When they spotted a new bid, they would take off their hats and yell a kind of whoop, making the proceedings both exciting and entertaining. I had set a limit beforehand, an amount I quickly disregarded, when the bidding left my limit in the dust. But I knew I was the rightful owner, and was not to be defeated. Finally, thank goodness, the bidding stopped, and I was now the legitimate and proud owner of "my picture". I ran up to Jeff and he congratulated me, knowing his picture would be lovingly held in my trust.

The picture was too big to bring back with me on the train, so I left it with Rose-Marie until we could drive up and get it. Today, it's one of my most treasured possessions. I never told Henry what I paid for it until a friend who was quite knowledgable about the value of railroadiana said it was worth about four times what I paid. Luckily, I have never been tempted to attend another auction.

Prepping for a Trip

Whenever I got a request for a private car charter, the first thing I did was to reserve a car. The car owners would always handle the arrangement with Amtrak for me to put the private car on the end of the train. The next thing was to line up my waiters. As these trips were not consistent, all my waiters had other jobs and were not always available, although there was usually ample time for them to make arrangements.

During the twenty-five years I was doing the trips, a lot happened to everyone—marriage, kids, divorce, and even some deaths. I think it's called *life*. It was not uncommon in the business for both waiters and chefs to get burned out. I loved what I did so much I never even came close to burning out, but I could certainly understand it. I used to say, if I didn't love it so much I would hate it.

Cooking on a train is really, really difficult and it can also be stressful. People would ask me what it was like cooking on a train, and I would tell them it was like cooking in a 7.5 earthquake! Just balancing on a train uses muscles you don't normally use. I used to joke that if you ever saw someone walking straight on a train, they were drunk! Yet, I think the hardest part was all the shopping involved and loading the car.

After going over the menu with the client, I would start two lists. One was for food and supplies to purchase and the other was what I needed to take to the railcar. I usually had to go to several stores to get everything I needed for just one trip. Loading the car was a challenge. The best way, was to lower the trap on the vestibule and lift everything up. It was a lot easier for the guys, but I'm not all that tall or strong. I usually had help, but sometimes I'd go to the yards the night before a trip and stay overnight on the car, to avoid getting struck in traffic on the way to the train in the morning. On these occasions I usually did the loading myself. I think the actual cooking on the train was the easiest part.

Chef for a Day

There was a large and popular restaurant in San Francisco that offered a program called "Chef for a Day". For $100.00, you could go and spend a day working there as a "chef". Henry bought it for me, thinking it would be good for me to see how things were handled in a restaurant. I think most people who did this were probably housewives and retired people, not professional chefs. I took BART (Bay Area Rapid Transit) to the City and arrived for duty. I have to say the first egregious thing they did was to put me to work and *not* tell me to wash my hands. After taking public transit, I can't imagine what nasty germs I carried into the restaurant. Of course, I knew to wash my hands, but that did shock me.

The first thing they did was to introduce me to the head pastry chef who showed me around. He told me they featured three different kinds of freshly baked bread. There were three baking racks, each holding a different type of bread. He walked up to the first rack, took a whole loaf, broke it half, gouged some bread from the center to taste, and offered the loaf to me to do likewise. "It's OK," he said with no enthusiasm describing the first bread. We then stopped by the second rack and he did the same thing, "This one's not bad". At the third rack, after tasting the bread he proudly said, "This one is really good". I never reacted or said anything, but I remember thinking if he worked for me, I'd fire him so fast it would make his head spin! Besides wasting three loaves of bread, he was only proud of one. Why in the world would a professional chef worth his or her salt ever make mediocre food and then have the audacity to sell it?

The first thing they had me do was to cut up old croissants for bread pudding. The cheap knife they gave me to work with was so dull, and the handle so uncomfortable, that I got a blister. If I had known, I would have brought my own knives.

Probably the most enjoyable thing I did was to drip melted sugar around a wooden dowel, and slip it off when it hardened (to make a dessert garnish). There was a long sink nearby where all the lettuce was washed, but I noticed the pastry cooks didn't even speak to the lettuce washers. (No one spoke to or even smiled at the busboys and dishwashers either. Granted, it's probable some of these workers spoke no English, but a smile is a smile in any language.) After the lettuce was washed, the sink was empty. One of the pastry cooks was making tiramisu and beat the eggs in a big Hobart mixer. She then took the beaters and laid them on the sink counter. I started to spray them off with water from the hose that was hanging right above the sink. "No," she said, "Leave them. *They* have to clean them," and she

nodded dismissively toward the dishwashers at the other end
of the room. She didn't even place the beaters down in the sink
where they could drain off but let them make a new mess on the
counter. After a while, I went upstairs to work on the salad line,
and passed through the kitchen where the chef and *sous* chefs
were working. What drama! Everybody was yelling and carrying on.

Henry met me there for dinner, and when he arrived, dinner
was on the house. They said they had never before had anyone
work so fast and for so long . When we got our food, Henry
whispered to me "I'm glad we're not paying for this (their prices
were not cheap). Your food is so much better!"

On the way home, I said I could never work in a restaurant.
I couldn't stand the pecking order and all the drama. On the private car, at least on my private cars, there were no prima donnas.
No one looked down their nose at the dish washer since that is
the same job shared by the chef! We worked as a team, and I
never asked my guys to do anything I wouldn't do myself. (I
even helped wash the outside windows.) I didn't have to tell
anyone what to do, or how to do it. They knew their job and just
did it. In fact, whenever I left the kitchen, one of them would
sneak in and wash dishes! One of my waiters told me that working on other cars was work, but working for me was fun!

Finding a Chef

I really needed to find an assistant chef whom I could trust
to go out in my place, and eventually take over when I finally
retired. One chef I tried out was a woman who was a teacher at
a culinary school. Our relationship ended, when she rearranged
my kitchen on our first trip.

Another chef was a young guy who had just graduated from
culinary school. He criticized almost everything I did. and was
very condescending. My waiters couldn't believe the way he

acted toward me. We were on the back of a *Fun Train*, and half way through the trip, on the way home, his demeanor changed and he started to act more respectfully. After we got back his ride didn't show up, so I offered to give him a lift home. When we reached his place, he turned to me and said, "Why didn't you tell me?" "Why didn't I tell you what?" "That you owned the train." "I don't own the train. What are you talking about?" I guess someone on the train heard the way he had been talking to me, and told him that Henry and I owned Key Holidays and that the *Fun Train* was ours. I think he had thought I was just some (uneducated) cook, hired to do the trip. He said he really wanted to work for me, but the damage had been done. If I had to be the owner's wife to get respect, I didn't want it.

I bought my meat through a wholesaler in Oakland, and was telling the butcher with whom I worked about trying to find a chef. He recommended a young guy (22 years old) who had worked in local restaurants. I gave this young chef a call and hired him to help me with a trip. His name was Keon, a black kid from Oakland who also did rap music. We really clicked on that first trip. He wasn't exactly skinny, and we were both working in the little *Tamalpais* kitchen, but we worked so well together that it wasn't a problem. His style of cooking matched mine and he managed to do well in that small space. Most chefs coming from restaurants don't adapt to kitchens on private cars, with no one to wash the dishes (or the pots and pans) and the small amount of counter space — not to mention the movement of the train. Most importantly, Keon got along with my waiters and appreciated the car.

On the next trip out, I had two cars on the back of the *Fun Train* and five waiters. Keon agreed to come again, and I just wanted to make him laugh and feel like part of the group. I have a really off-the-wall sense of humor, and decided to write and perform a rap about cooking on private rail cars. Before we left the yards, we called Keon into the *Tam* dining room. My waiters stood behind me (they were my back-up group) and I told Keon I had a surprise for him—a rap. His eyes rolled and his jaw dropped. I said I couldn't do any hand gestures because, after all, I was an old, white woman. In fact, I said this was an Ogden Nash Rap. (He was probably too young to have a clue who Ogden Nash was and never did ask.) My "group" started making back up percussion sounds, and I proceeded to perform my rap. Pretty soon, the word spread throughout the train, and I was doing my silly rap for everybody.

On my last trip on the *Plaza Santa Fe* in 2008, there was a fellow videotaping the *Fun Train*. He was walking through with Rick, the *Fun Train* Manager. Rick said, "You should film Connie's rap." He took one look at me and then looked at Rick, like he had made a funny joke of some kind. "No, really," Rick said, "She does a rap". So he filmed my rap, and then said, "Do you mind if I put this on YouTube?" Now, I've mentioned what a dinosaur I am. I didn't even know what YouTube was, so I said, "OK". He asked my full name, and when I said my last name was Luna, I said, "You know, like in Lunatic." Well, he also put that on YouTube (the voice from above saying, "Gotcha again!") If you're curious enough to look it up, it's under Connie Luna, *Grandma Rap*. People have asked me for a sequel, but I tell them, "I'm a one rap wonder!"

T. Bone Towser Lives On

I escorted a group to Sparks on the *California Zephyr*. The *Virginia City* was on the end of the train with a group that was getting off in Reno. I told my group they could ride the *Virginia City* from Reno to Sparks (this was a great way to drum up future private car charters). So we got off in Reno and started walking toward the end of the train. One couple in my group were both blind and had their seeing-eye dog with them. I didn't want to separate them from their group and it was my responsibility to get them off the train in Sparks, so they, along with their dog, came with us. We had to walk on the outside of the train and half way down, the conductor said we couldn't change cars and told us to go back to our car on Amtrak. Somehow, my blind couple didn't understand what was happening and continued on down the tracks. They were put aboard the *Virginia City*, so the only people who got to see the car, couldn't! When we all got off the train in Sparks, the couple said their dog could tell another dog had been on the *Virginia City*. He went straight to Bedroom C and sniffed all around. It had probably been over thirty years since T. Bone Towser had ridden the car with Beebe and Clegg, but somehow he's still there!

Dining by Rail

When private cars are in the rail yards the crews often visit each other's cars, which are all historic and unique. When Cliff and I were in New Orleans, we introduced ourselves to another crew and they said to me, "Oh, we know who you are." I heard this from other crews too, and hadn't the slightest idea why — still don't!

Every March in Stockton, there was a big rail fair drawing people from all over the country — Winterail. One year, Henry and I attended. He usually went with much more avid (or is that rabid!) railfans than I, but this year he took me. One of the booths featured railroad books and I spotted a book I wanted to read: *Dining by Rail*, by James D. Porterfield. I rarely ask for anything, so when I do Henry is more than happy to comply, and he bought me that book. (I'm a cheap date!) We were going to Hawaii on vacation and I took the book along with me to read. I read it during our vacation and for most of the long flight home, finishing it right before we landed.

When I went into work the next day there was a pile of pink "call back" slips on my desk. Working with so many groups, I regularly communicated with a lot of people. One of the slips said to call a Jim Porterfield. The name sounded familiar, but I just thought he was from one of the groups. When I called, he told me he was an author and was writing a new book about railroad cooking. He said he wanted me to be in it. I don't know if he ever believed my story about reading his other book on the plane from Hawaii the night before, but it's absolutely true.

I couldn't imagine how Jim had heard of me (he was in Pennsylvania). I was so afraid it was a mistake that I didn't ask! He wanted a short autobiography and recipes from my private car menus. I did send my contribution to him and it was published in his book, the title of which is *From the Dining Car*.

I never met Jim in person, but talked with him several times. What a nice guy, and so knowledgeable. He has an ongoing feature, called *On the Menu*, in the magazine *Railfan and Railroad*, and he related my tale of the "spaghetti train" in the April 2005 issue.

My Zany Waiters

My waiters were just as silly as I was, which made for some fun times. They could turn almost any negative into a positive.

I used to send information about the trip out with the travel documents. It was always suggested that two small suitcases were desirable rather than one large one, as they had to be lifted on and off the train. (I always thought giving a reason why, helped people understand better the request.) Most of our guests complied, but some packed as if they were going on a three week trip, not two nights in Reno (I suspect they never read the information sent). Some bags were so heavy I was convinced that gold bullion smuggling was going on!

On one trip, I was still in the kitchen when the guys started taking off the luggage in Reno. I heard all this laughing and the "Death March" being hummed. I ran to the rear lounge to see

my four waiters somberly carrying a suitcase as large as a
steamer trunk, on their shoulders like a coffin. Not only was it
funny, but I'm sure the owner of the suitcase also got the message. When a train stops at a station and blocks a street, it can
only stop for ten minutes or is liable for a fine.
So many of my groups were seniors and were slow getting on
and off the train. In order not to exceed the ten minute limit, the
luggage had to be expedited quickly It was a group effort (often
including me) with all of us transferring luggage like a bucket
brigade at a fire. The worst part was when a guest wanted to
help. It was quite a trick to say "sit" without it sounding like a
command to a German shepherd!

Blocking the traffic (including emergency vehicles) in Reno
was not the only problem with the tracks running right through
the town. Although the daily *California* Zephyr and the seasonal
Fun and Snow Trains are the only passenger trains that stop in
Reno, the Union Pacific tracks are heavily used by freight trains.
The blocks in Reno are small, and every train (by law) has to
blow it's horn at every crossing. Most of the freight engineers
just "sat" on the horn all the way through Reno. The noise was
bad enough during the day, but at night it was terrible, especially as major hotels were built right next to the tracks.

In 1938, engineers recommended a railroad trench be built
through Reno. The idea was not acted upon but was the source
of bitter contention for sixty four years. Finally approved, construction on the 2.25 mile project known as ReTrac started in
2002 and was completed in 2006. The SP depot (now owned by
the City of Reno) was built in 1926 and is on the National Regis-
ter of Historical Places. A bottom floor was added to accommodate passengers getting on and off trains in the trench and there
is no more ten minute rule to contend with. The naysayers pre-
dicting disasters such as earthquakes and flooding are pretty
quiet now and the trench is lauded as a tremendous improve-
ment in Reno.

Most of my groups went year after year, and knew what to expect, even with the food. I'd sometimes think they must be tired of the same menu, but then had to remind myself that even though I fixed a lot of the same food so often, the groups were eating it just once a year. One time I didn't make the Grand Mariner French toast, and I thought the group was going to throw me off the train. They said they had been looking forward to it for a whole year!

Over the years I've cooked on so many private cars and had so many dinner parties at my home that I can't begin to remember my menus for each and every occasion. But I often talk to people who remember every detail of a meal I've served them. Memories are certainly not a one-way street. I've learned that all of my experiences on the private cars are now shared memories with so many people.

Two of my waiters, George and Jim, were from Southern California (the same Jim who crimped the wire on the Native Son!). Jim is also a railroad chef, but when he worked for me it was as a waiter. He is one of the nicest guys you'd ever want to meet—good natured, always smiling, quick-witted and fun (he is a minister, too). George and Jim are great friends and when together, are like a comedy team. George called Jim "Himie", and their back and forth banter was hilarious. George is something else! He was quite young when he first worked for me, but he knew everything about working on the private cars. Although he is white, we all said he must be a reincarnation of a Pullman porter (who were all called "George" after George Mortimer Pullman). Our George had an appropriate outfit for every occasion. If he helped to wash dishes, he would change out of his waiter's outfit into a dishwasher's attire. He worked for me on the *Native Son*. Our groups were usually thirty-two passengers, which meant a lot of glasses. There were racks in the kitchen to accommodate all the different sized glasses. I used to wash them, and put them in the racks to air dry. George insisted on drying each one, so there

would be no water spots. He also polished all of the flatware—
very precise and particular.

Probably the most energetic waiter I had was Ollie. I used to
call him a whirling dervish. He was a bit of a loner, and when we
got to Reno, he would sometimes join us for dinner and sometimes he wouldn't. It was nothing for him to walk from Reno to
Sparks, and I don't think I ever saw him tired, even on the
"spaghetti train".

On one of my trips on the *Native Son* for our regular group
from St. Kevin's, my waiters were Michael, Tom, and Darrel. They
decided to serve the food in character as "The Blues Brothers".
After choreographing their moves in the kitchen, they put on dark
glasses and delivered the food to the great enjoyment of all. That
was one group we could be really silly around.

Each of my waiters had his own unique personality, yet when
working together on the train they were like a well-oiled machine.
The one thing we all had in common, was a great sense of humor
and a deep appreciation of the cars we worked on. There was a
genuine feeling of family, and a mutual love and respect for each
other.

These feelings also applied to the car owners. A lot of people
thought all the private cars were just expensive whims of the
wealthy. That couldn't be farther from the truth. First of all, I think
most owners are rail fans. Some of them are quite wealthy, but
most of the car owners I dealt with were not. Two of the owners
were CPAs, another was an electrician, another worked for the
County in mosquito abatement, and another, an Amtrak engineer.
What they all had in common was a love of trains. All of the cars
I worked on would have been scrapped if it were not for these
owners, and pretty much any money they made from the cars
(and then some) went right back into their maintenance. I would
sometimes get queries from an interested party regarding buying
a private car. I would tell them, "Owning a private rail car makes
owning a yacht seem like a sound financial investment!"

Some of the owners don suits and go on the trips as "owners", but most of the ones I worked with were more likely to be wearing jeans or overalls. They loved their cars and came on the trips in the role of mechanic and maintenance man (acting like the father of a very needy child)!

I never had to sign a contract, and was never cheated or overcharged. The car owners were honest and honorable, and it was a pleasure doing business with them.

Rocking The Train

One of the most common and difficult repairs on the cars was replacing a broken window. The trains ran through some bad neighborhoods where they could be subjected to rock throwing. This was done by kids who were not taught respect for anything, including themselves. On a freight train, they aimed for the engine. On a passenger train any window was the target, with the grand prize being the private cars on the end of the train. The windows had mandatory safety glass, so, although they shattered, no glass went flying. But a rock hitting a train sounded like a gunshot and was very frightening when it happened (I always worried about my seniors having heart attacks!), and the windows had to be replaced. The *Tamalpais* always carried a spare window pane, which was kept under the double bed in bedroom A, so the repair could be made before the trip home. One time I helped Jon Kirchanski replace a broken window in Sparks. What a laborious endeavor. There was so much maintenance from normal wear and tear on these old cars that having to repair such unnecessary damage was really maddening.

There was a danger of people on the rear platform being hit, so we would often move passengers inside when we knew we'd be going through the bad neighborhoods. The biggest danger to people was on the freight trains. If a rock came through the open window, it could injure or even kill one of the engine crew.

I had a freight engineer tell me about this one section they went through, where they were "rocked" consistently and how the crew dealt with it. On one trip the engine crew carried a box of ballast and, when the rocks started flying, they threw them too, but not back at the kids. The houses these kids lived in were on the other side of the train, so the engine crew's rocks went toward the houses. After the train had passed by, there stood the kids, rocks in hand, facing some pretty angry neighbors. Even the kids thought they had overthrown the rocks and hit their own houses. The engineer told me they felt bad throwing rocks at the houses, but they never had problems in that neighborhood again!

When I was a kid, most parents taught their children to respect other people and their property, and when you didn't there were consequences. There was very little litter, no graffiti, and people didn't have to lock their cars and houses.

The speed of all of our technological advances seems to have left our morals and manners in the dust. I think one of the reasons I liked private cars so much, was, as I said before, that it was like being in a time-machine, transporting one to a far more kind and gentle time.

Me, probably telling a story, onboard the Virginia City.

John Fiore and me, entertaining onboard the Virginia City.

The Native Son with a new paint job.

George Heflin, me, and "My Boy" Henry.

PLA member Dave Burla and me cooking on the All Day Lunch Car in Niles Canyon.

AT & SF #33 Tamalpais

Me, right after I "blew up" the Tamalpais kitchen.

Todd Utikal, Tom Nelson, and Darrel Saunders on the "Tam."

More views of the Tamalpais.

The elegant Chapel Hill.

Bubba Paris and me on the Reno Fun Train.

Michele Stevens, my "mini me," working on the Royal Gorge.

Round-end observation car—the Silver Solarium.

Henry and me onboard the Las Vegas Fun Train.

Keon Stewart and me in the Virginia City kitchen.

Me and my back-up rap group—Front, Todd and Grant. Back, Todd's friend, Keon, me, Cliff, and Ollie.

Chapter 111 Train Tours

Hearst Castle

Henry started the Hearst Castle tour when he worked for Great Western Tours. For the tour, he started a bus company, San Simeon Stages, to provide ground transportation from the train depot in San Luis Obispo. When Key Tours was started, the two main tours offered were Reno via the *California Zephyr* (the *Fun-Train* came later) and Hearst Castle. Key Tours was a tour wholesaler, so we not only sold directly to the public, but the bulk of our sales went through travel agents. These popular tours were unescorted and departed daily.

The Hearst Castle tour included Amtrak from both northern and southern California, narrated motor coach transportation, hotel accommodations and the Hearst Castle tour.

I used to handle all of the groups on Key Holiday's package tours as well as the private car groups. With groups on our package tours, I could deviate from the standard tour and often included meals and side trips and went along as an escort. The best way to persuade travel agents to sell our tours was to have them go on the tour themselves. I used to escort travel agents on familiarization (fam) trips, to show them Key Holiday's Hearst Castle package tour. It was a joint fam trip with Amtrak, who would have a sales rep go along to promote train travel. Often, half of the travel agents would travel by train from Los Angeles to San Luis Obispo and the other half would come down from Oakland with me. Many agents had never traveled on a train before and the fam trip was a great introduction to Amtrak.

I always used to bring a large cooler full of hors d'oeuvres for the evening's sales presentation and would wrap the cooler with bungee cords to prevent it from accidentally opening. As it was both heavy and bulky, I would check it rather than carry it on the car with me. On one trip there was a very officious agent at the station who said he couldn't put my cooler in the baggage car. I was already carrying a lot and didn't want to have to load it on the coach. The Amtrak rep who was with me on the fam said, "Oh for heaven's sake! Just load it." "No, we can't carry food in the baggage car." "What food?" I said, looking him straight in face. "Those are books!" "What?" "Those are books," I said, staring him down with my best "Mother" look. Well, after he put it in the baggage car, we were on our way.

San Simeon Stages picked up passengers from both the south and north bound trains. If the trains were on time, the passengers from both trains were combined. If one of the trains was late, the driver would take the first group downtown to the Mission San Luis Obispo to occupy their time while waiting for the second train before the transfer to the hotel. Were lucky to have our manager, Anne, as the primary driver/narrator. Her knowledge of the area and of Hearst Castle was outstanding, but even more enduring was her personality. Everyone just loved Anne and our tour could not have been in better hands.

Because of the unreliability of the train schedule, the actual Hearst Castle tour was on the next morning. After the tour, we stopped for lunch in the charming little village of Cambria (where the movie *Arachnophobia* was filmed) and then proceeded to Morro Bay for lunch and then to San Luis Obispo to catch the afternoon train (for both north and southbound). These trains were often late, especially the southbound coming from Seattle, so Anne would call ahead to check the train status. If there was time, we'd make an extra stop at the Madonna Inn in San "Louie". Alex Madonna, who made his money in construction, built the Madonna Inn in 1958. It started out with just twelve rooms and today is one of the most unique hotels you'll ever see.

It now has a hundred and ten rooms, each one decorated in a different theme, including the "Caveman Room". There is an excellent restaurant, a coffee shop, a gift shop and a bakery. (Anne used to say of the bakery, "You can hear your arteries slamming shut!") Alex's wife Phyllis' favorite color was pink, so almost everything was pink, even at one time the coke machine and stop signs. It was a fun place to stop. Much of the building, inside and out, was constructed with rocks quarried by Alex Madonna. The big fireplace in the main lobby is made of these rocks, and one of them has embedded in it the vertebrae of a prehistoric animal.

On one of the fam trips both trains were late for the trip home and we stopped at the Madonna Inn. I told the group on the bus about the fireplace before we got there, admittedly exaggerating by calling the vertebrae dinosaur bones. I was the last one off the bus, and I spied a couple of the travel agents standing by the fireplace. I walked over, pointed to the stone and said, "See, here are the dinosaur bones". Two elderly ladies were sitting in chairs in front of the fireplace waiting for their tour bus to leave. "What did you say?" one asked with a very strong New York accent. I pointed to the stone and said, "These are dinosaur bones". I think she may have been a little hard of hearing. With an absolutely incredulous look on her face, she said, "Those are Dinah Shore's bones?" What did she think? That somehow, Alex Madonna got a hold of Dinah Shores body and stuck her bones up in his fireplace! "No, no! Those are dinosaur bones!" Real life is so much more funny than made up jokes!

On another fam trip, we arrived at Hearst Castle for the tour and found the visitors center dark—not a good sign. Apparently, a transformer had exploded, leaving San Simeon (the Castle's location) and Cambria without power. The Hearst Castle visitors center had a skylight ceiling, so we could see. We waited quite a while, hoping the lights would come back on, but they never did, and we had to leave. It was getting close to lunchtime. Most everything in the area was closed, but we saw cars in front of a local coffee shop and we stopped. They had a gas stove and had stayed open, putting candles on all of the tables. They only offered one meal: scrambled eggs, pancakes, and bacon. A lot of the customers pitched in (I can still picture our bus driver walking around with a pitcher of syrup), and the food was delicious. Key Holidays paid for our group's meal and we left. It was a Hearst Castle fam—with no Hearst Castle tour! Later, I heard from several travel agents, saying it was the best fam they had ever been on.

On another fam trip, the entire group of travel agents came up from Southern California. At the end of the tour the group boarded the southbound train for the trip home and I took the northbound *Coast Starlight* back to Oakland by myself.
I sat in the observation car, watching the scenery. All of the seats face the windows with an aisle down the center. The train stopped in the middle of nowhere and sat there for a long time. Two Amtrak car attendants passed by each other in the center aisle right behind me. "Any idea why we're stopped?" asked one. "The crew died." said the other as they continued walking and left the car.

The news soon spread throughout the car. "The crew's dead!" "What do you think killed them?" "Do you think it was gas?" Panic was setting in. I finally stood up, "Excuse me, may I please have your attention?" I explained that the crew wasn't actually dead. They had run out of legal operating hours and we were waiting for a new crew to arrive, The passengers were greatly relieved!

I thought about how easily a miscommunication can cause trouble. In the old days there was a signal stand alongside the tracks with a ball on it. When the ball was in the topmost position, it meant the train was leaving the station—hence the term "highball". Once on a private car, when the train started to move I said, "Highball!" One of my passengers looked up and said,

"Oh, I'll have a vodka tonic." On another trip, there was a freight car carrying mail on Amtrak. We were on the rear of the train next to it and could see the back end of the car through the rear window of the *Tamalpais*. I called my waiters to look. Stenciled on the back of the car, in big letters, was "Do not hump". I couldn't resist. "Why?" I asked with a serious face, "Why would anyone do that?" We are still laughing about it. A "hump yard" is a rail yard that uses gravity from a man-made hill or "hump", together with powered switches, to sort incoming trains onto the correct tracks. "Do not hump" signs are placed on cars that must not use a hump yard because of cargo restrictions or car age, not some misguided advice on kinky behavior!

The most memorable Hearst Castle tour turned out to be the start of a great love story. A travel agency in Portland, Oregon used to bring a group on the *Coast Starlight* every year on a grand tour. I would join them in Oakland, and we'd get off the train in Salinas. There, we'd be met by our Hearst Castle bus, San Simeon Stages. Our driver, Bob, was like family. He wasn't a "typical" bus driver. He was college educated, loved history, wrote music, sang, played the piano, and had an ambition to own a bookstore. (he was also cute!). For these tours we had overnight accommodations in Monterey, where we would visit the fabulous Monterey Aquarium and take the famous 17 Mile Drive to Carmel. We would then bus over to Yosemite and stay at the historic Wawona Hotel, located at the southern end of Yosemite.

Built in 1879, The Wawona Hotel was maintained beautifully as a historic treasure. A host of dignitaries have stayed there, including Ulysses S. Grant and President Theodore Roosevelt. Its main building had a wide veranda with white wicker furniture, a beautiful dining room and a Victorian lounge off the main lobby. There was an antique piano in the lounge that had been used to accompany the singer of *The Indian Love Call*, performed during the famous fire falls in the Yosemite Valley. The fire falls were created in 1872 by dropping burning embers off the top of

Glacier Point. This ritual was begun to attract people to Yosemite and was discontinued in 1968, when an overwhelming number of visitors was endangering the natural environment. The piano was placed in a shed at Camp Curry and was deteriorating. There was always a natural competitiveness between the different accommodation sites in Yosemite, so in the middle of the night, workers from the Wawona Hotel raided the shed at Camp Curry and relocated the piano (via a garbage truck) to the Wawona, where it was restored. The piano was played by Tom Bopp (almost nightly) since 1983. He was just wonderful. Much more than a singer and piano player, he was a consummate performer (he was also the Wawona historian).

From Yosemite, our tour would go to Morro Bay and then tour Hearst Castle, with a side trip to Solvang (a historic Danish community). The group would go back north by train, leaving from San Luis Obispo. The Portland group went on this grand tour for several years, and I would go along to assist their escort.

One year, the Portland agency's regular escort couldn't come, and in her place they sent another agent, Sue. Both Bob and Sue had been through rough divorces, and had been on their own for some time. I could see there was a mutual, but very cautious attraction. When we got to Morro Bay, our group (being seniors) went to bed early. Morro Bay is really quiet at night, but there was a karaoke bar a couple of miles away. Bob drove Sue and me there, and we were all going to sing. Unfortunately, it closed before we got a chance, and we said we would do it the next year. The trip concluded and we went on home.

The next year, Sue escorted the trip again. I was busy with a private railcar trip when the group came, so I asked one of my waiters, Richard, if he could escort the group as far a Monterey. After my trip I was able to relieve Richard and join the group in Yosemite.

Well, when I saw Bob and Sue, I could tell the sparks were flying. We were sitting in the lounge listening to Tom Bopp, when he took a break. Tom knew me from escorting several groups there, and I asked him if Bob could play the piano while he was on break. He said normally, he would say no, but for me he'd say yes. Bob played and sang one of his own (romantic) songs. I could see he was playing it for Sue, and he was really good. When we got to Morro Bay, we went back to the karaoke bar and Sue sang a country and western song. She was terrific. (turned out she had been practicing a whole year to impress Bob). That night, we were walking down a street in Morro Bay and I turned to them and said, "Here's the deal. Here's the deal. You have to promise me that neither one of you will ever hurt the other". I felt rather responsible for the situation.

The next morning, when I got on the bus I looked at Bob's face and he looked like a beaten puppy with puffy eyes. Sue got on, and she was a mess too. After they left me the night before they had decided it just couldn't work, with Sue and her kids up in Portland and Bob and his kids in Morro Bay. They looked so sad and heartbroken. When I escorted groups to Hearst Castle, I'd always take the driver to breakfast while the group was touring the Castle. Bob and I were having breakfast at the San Simeon Lodge, when he said he wanted to buy some roses to give to Sue. I said that wasn't a good idea, because not only would the flowers die, but Sue might get in trouble with the agency for fraternizing with the bus driver while escorting a tour. The group wasn't stupid, and her getting the roses would get back to the agency. I suggested they write to each other and take some time to see if things could work out, so Bob bought some pretty writing paper. There was a gift shop with some cute, stuffed animals for sale. I told Bob to trust me—if he wanted to give her a gift, make it a cuddly dog. He was pretty dubious, but picked out an adorable St. Bernard puppy. I told him I would give it to her on the train, in her compartment, so the group wouldn't know. After breakfast, Bob and I sat on the bus waiting for the group. He took some of the writing paper, and wrote a note to Sue. When she got on, he handed the stationary and the note to her. I watched her read it, a big smile spreading on her face. She took a sheet and furiously wrote an answer to him. When we got to the station, they couldn't even hug goodbye with the group watching. On the train, I gave the dog to Sue. She cried and cried, and hugged it so hard, I thought the stuffing was going to pop out.

A few weeks later, I talked to Bob and he said they were getting married. WHAT? It seems Bob had been hired for a charter, driving a bus to Oregon, and while it was there, Sue followed the bus to be with Bob at the charter stops. They told me they were getting married in Las Vegas on Nov. 4, and Sue said if I could make it, she would like me to be her Matron of Honor. Those two were so much in love, being pen pals was simply not going to suffice! I booked a flight to Las Vegas and bought a pretty little music box for a wedding present. A funny thing happened at the airport. I left on Nov. 3, right after 9/11. The security was tight, and I only had carry-on luggage. I think it was random (I never thought of myself as looking suspiciously sinister), but another fellow and I were picked to stand out of the line while they went through our luggage, We started talking and I said I had a wrapped gift of a music box, and I hoped the mechanism wouldn't look like a bomb in the X- ray. (I could just see them blowing it up!). He then told me his bag was even more suspicious. "What's in it?" I asked. "Dead ants," he said. I couldn't believe my ears. "Dead ants? Did you say dead ants?" It seemed he was a scientist who studied ants and was taking some specimens to another scientist in Las Vegas. It's a wonder the two of us got on that plane.

It was a beautiful wedding. Bob and Sue now live in St. Louis. He went on to get his Masters degree and works as a historian at National Parks. At this writing, they've been married for twelve years, and are as much in love as ever. They still have the music box and the stuffed St. Bernard puppy. (They named him Willy, after William Randolph Hearst).

I used to be invited to a special annual dinner and performance of Tom Bopp, held at the Women's Faculty Club at UC,
Berkeley. It was in a very intimate setting, with banter between
Tom and the audience. I went up to Tom and told him about Bob
and Sue getting married. Of course he remembered them, and I
asked him if he could play and sing for them. Tom was a romantic and readily agreed. I phoned Bob and Sue and held up the
phone so they could hear Tom serenading them. I just love
"Happily ever after"!

There was a funny side story to that last tour with Sue. One
of her group was an Episcopalian Bishop on a little R & R. He
was so funny, and liked to give me a hard time. In Cambria, we
were in a shop that had been an old home. The sales counter was
in the middle of the room, and as I was paying for something,
he snuck up to the counter, pointed at me and whispered to the
clerk "I'd keep my eyes on that one if I were you". He did look
rather official, and I did get an odd look from her.

On the bus, I'd often take the mike and tell humorous stories (my
captive audience). I was telling about the time I was hosing
down the cement around our pool, and thousands of ants
poured out of the wooden dividers. It became a war. I would
hose them down the drain, and they would keep coming. It was-
n't thousands. I think it was millions. I used so much water it
could have filled the pool. I had never seen so many ants in my
life! As soon as I hosed them all down the drain, they were replaced with twice as many. I became obsessed with defeating
them. Suddenly, I was struck with the strangest thought. What
if God was an ant, and he just said we were made in his image
to trick us? When we died, we would have to face him, and try
to explain all of the drownings, the poison, the squishing. The
only people in heaven would be Albert Schweitzer and a bunch
of Buddhists! Everyone else was laughing, but the Bishop was
taking notes. I suspected he was going to try and work my story

into a sermon. I had the horrible thought that I would hear on the news that an Episcopalian Bishop was being excommunicated for claiming God was an ant, and his only defense was that it was only a joke!

Beautiful Yosemite

Another popular Amtrak tour offered by Key Holidays is Yosemite. It is an unescorted tour for individuals that can be done in a day or overnight. The train used for this tour is the *San Joaquin* that runs between Oakland and Bakersfield down the center of California, and the stop for the Yosemite tour is Merced. There is a bus connection between Bakersfield and Los Angeles, but, as it is almost a hundred miles and takes three hours, almost all of the people on the tour come from the North. A tour bus transfers passengers from Merced to Yosemite. Included is a Valley Floor Tour—a two hour, narrated, open-air tram tour. For Yosemite-In-A-Day tours, after the Valley Floor Tour, passengers return by bus to Merced where they take the train back home. Yosemite Overnight includes hotel accommodations.

For my groups, I put together quite a comprehensive trip and would escort it myself. We would start by taking Amtrak's *San Joaquin* to Merced where we would be met by our chartered tour bus. Our first stop was the Castle Air Museum located close by in Atwater. When I first started taking groups there it was still an active Air Force Base, now it's just the museum. There were over fifty restored planes from World War ll, the Korean War and the Cold War, and there was an indoor museum. There was also a lunchroom. I usually don't pre-select meals for my groups, but Castle had the best hamburgers and soft ice cream, so that's what we had for lunch. My groups for this tour were always seniors and they really identified with those WWll planes. One day there was an argument (good natured) on the bus regarding who had won the war, the Army or the Navy. Finally, one little old lady ended it by loudly proclaiming, "We all won the war!" I used to look at my group, enjoying their hamburgers and ice cream while sitting next to tables of young Air Force guys, and think, "The men in my group were these fresh faced kids fifty years ago."

After lunch, we would visit the Merced County Courthouse Museum. The old courthouse was built in 1875 and had wonderful exhibits. I think one of the oddest things about the building was the wood. The doors and walls were made of redwood, hand painted to look like oak. Redwood is so beautiful, I can't imagine anyone wanting to paint it, but I guess it was the style at the time. The drive into Yosemite followed the Merced River, and we would stay the first night at the Yosemite Lodge, located in Yosemite Valley. In the morning, after an open-air tram ride through the valley, we would head south in our bus and, after a stop at the Mariposa Big Trees (site of the Giant Sequoias—the largest trees in the world).

We'd spend the second night at the Wawona, and the next morning we would go to the tiny settlement of Fishcamp and ride the *Yosemite Mountain Sugar Pine Lumber Railroad*. This railroad runs on four miles of the original line of the Madera Sugar Pine Lumber Co. Started in 1899, it featured a fifty-four-mile flume, where the logs would cascade down the water to Madera. The logging train operation closed in 1931, and reopened as a tourist railroad in 1961, Today, two Shay engines wind their way through the forest: #15 built in 1913 and #10 built in 1928. I'd always arrange for two of my group to ride up front in the engine (one in each direction). After the train ride, we would bus through Mariposa (California is full of Spanish names; Mariposa means butterfly) to Fresno, and have lunch at a wonderful Basque restaurant across the street from the depot, before taking The *San Joaquin* back home.

It always amazed me how many Californians have never

been to Yosemite, a place that attracts people from all over the world, but I think that's true of a lot of people everywhere. We tend to ignore what's in our own back yard. Yosemite is one of the most beautiful and spectacular places on earth and should be on everyone's "must see" list. I believe that a person might enter Yosemite not believing in God, but it would be hard to leave that place thinking a supreme being didn't have a hand in its creation!

(Another Love story!) Yosemite was also the site of my son's wedding to Michelle. Michelle's mother Cheryl and I were good friends in high school. In fact, Tod and I double-dated with Cheryl and her date, Bob, for our high school grad night. After school, Cheryl moved to Florida where she met her husband, Mike, in college, Her daughter Michelle was born about three weeks after Jade, and they came for a visit when the girls were four and I was pregnant with Michael. When Michael was going to Sacramento State, he, Tom and Darrel roomed together in Sacramento. Cheryl called to say Michelle was moving from LA to the Bay Area, and asked if she could stay with me until she found a job and a place to live. As Michael's bedroom was available, I said of course. I hadn't seen Michelle since she was four. I still remember when Michael came home from college (with a bag of laundry, of course) and met Michelle. I don't know what she expected but I don't think it was a tall, handsome boy! As the song goes "Zing went the strings of my heart".

The night before the wedding, we all stayed at the Wawona and enjoyed a barbecue (rehearsal) dinner outside. Michelle's little sister, Cherie, played the piano and Jade's oldest daughter, Katie, sang (both beautifully), and, they performed a duet at the wedding. Cherie lived in Michigan and Katie in California, so they hadn't ever performed together until Tom Bopp let them rehearse, using the piano at the Wawona. Those two girls amazed everyone with their outstanding performance at the wedding which was performed by Don McGinnis—the same minister who had married Henry and me. The site of the wedding was the little, historic Yosemite Chapel and the reception was held at the famous Ahwahnee Hotel in the Yosemite Valley. The Yosemite Chapel was built in 1878, and sustained damage in the great Yosemite flood in 1997 (the water reached halfway up the pews). It was restored just in time for the wedding.

Romance of the Rails

Henry's long history of putting together and running train tours started with the PLA in 1961. His tours had such a good reputation that he had a following who would go with him anywhere, and over the years he put together hundreds of train tours all over the world.

The groups I handled were based on our package tours but I had an idea for a cross-country tour and my boss (Henry!) allowed me to put together my own tour, I named it the "Romance of the Rails". It was exactly three weeks long, and, because we used all first class sleeping accommodations, it was pretty expensive. Nine people signed up for it, and it turned out to be a wonderful tour.

We took the *California Zephyr* from Oakland to Chicago. There, we took a tour of the Pullman District. In the 1880s George Pullman (Pullman's Palace Car Co.) built an entire community for his workers on a 4000 acre tract. One thousand homes and public buildings were erected in this planned, model industrial town, including a church, hotel, post office, bank and library. Today it's protected as a National Historic Landmark. We also went to the Museum of Science and Industry to see the *Pioneer Zephyr* (nicknamed *Silver Streak*). Built by Budd in 1934 for Burlington, it broke a world record on a run between Chicago and Denver traveling 1,015 miles in 13 hours and 5 minutes and attaining a top speed of 112.5 miles an hour. After an overnight stay in Chicago we traveled to Jackson, where our tour bus met us.

Our first stop was at the Casey Jones Home and Train Museum and it struck me the way someone in history was often immortalized because someone wrote a song. My group comprised well-traveled, highly educated seniors, and their enthusiasm at all of our stops made the trip not only enjoyable, but also educational. From Jackson we drove to Nashville. On entering the city, our driver asked if we wanted to stop at the Parthenon. I knew Nashville was the home of the Grand Ole Opry, but the Parthenon? It turns out that Nashville's full-size replica was built in 1897 for the Tennessee Centennial Exposition. It featured a forty-two-foot-high statue of Athena Parthenos and around the perimeter were plaster casts of the Elgin Marbles—fragments of larger-than-life-size figures. The figures seemed familiar and I remembered that I had seen the originals at the British Museum during our travels to England. The lower floor of the replica in Nashville housed an art exhibit.

The original Parthenon in Greece was partially destroyed in 1656 when explosives stored there by the Ottoman Turks was blown up and half of that building is missing. To see the whole Parthenon, you have to go to Tennessee!

We stayed at the fabulous Union Station Hotel. This railroad terminal was built in 1900, and opened as a hotel in 1986. As so many classic buildings have been demolished, it was wonderful to see such a beautiful, historic building preserved for future generations. I think we have to turn to the past to find true elegance. Another example is air travel. When airplanes first offered passenger service, the interior of a plane emulated a rail car, and I have a picture of my Aunt Ellis serving coffee from a silver pitcher.

After Nashville, we went to Chattanooga where we took the *Incline Railway* up Lookout Mountain. At the top, there was a Civil War memorial battleground. I am always struck by the beauty and peacefulness of Civil War sites. It's as if time and nature are the great healers, erasing the horror and ugliness of war.

Of course, we had to stay at the Chattanooga Choo Choo Hotel. There was so much to see, it was a shame we were only there for one night. When I think back on it, the model train layout stands out the most in my memory.

Our next leg of the tour was by riverboat back to Memphis. Al Harvey and his wife Marian were on the tour. Al was not only the PLA historian and the "Voice of the *Snow Train*", but he also did little theater and loved to sing. We were walking in the hallway on the boat, and he started to sing. I told him he should be in the passenger talent show. He said he would only do it if I did it also, so we two "hams" signed up. Al was fantastic and stole the show. I did stand-up comedy and finished with my rendition of *Chattanooga Choo Choo*.

I had done stand-up once before on a cruise Henry and I had taken to Mexico. There were about five hundred people in the audience of the passenger's talent show and I must say, it was the most frightening thing I have ever done. Henry asked me where I got my material and I said, "Don't you notice that I say funny things all the time?" People came up to me afterward to ask where they could catch my act, which horrified Henry. He made me promise to only do it on ships (figuring we would never see the people from the ship again). I think it often happens that husbands like their wives to have a good sense of humor, but only want them to be funny around a handful of people. With my daughter, I could only be funny around her. Around other people she was mortified and I would hear a drawn out "Mother" or if people didn't know who I was, she would pretend I was a complete stranger. I think she could say Mom, Mother or Mommy in eight different tones. With Michael it was a different story. He liked having a funny mother, the sillier the better! Michael was definitely my best audience.

One time, after we were married, Henry said to me "You are so strange!" "Look" I said "You knew I was strange before we got married". "Yes, I know, but I didn't know how strange!" He never knows what I'm going to do next, but after more than thirty six years, I can't even get him to raise an eyebrow.

In Memphis, we went to the Peabody Hotel. This grand old southern hotel was built in 1923. In 1930 the general manager and a friend went duck hunting, and returned to the hotel with some live decoys. Having imbibed quite a bit of Tennessee whiskey, they thought it would be humorous to put the ducks in the beautiful Italian fountain in the lobby of the hotel. The ducks were an overnight sensation, and are still the highlight attraction of the hotel. The ducks reside on an upper floor, and arrive at the lobby by elevator. A red carpet is rolled down between the elevator and the fountain, and at 11:00 am the elevator doors open, the ducks march down the carpet to a John Phillip Souza march, and hop into the fountain. They are served their midday meal in a silver container by a uniformed duck-master, and they march back down the carpet and into the elevator at 5:00 pm. When we were there the hotel lobby and balcony were packed with spectators for every performance.

We traveled by train on the *City of New Orleans* from Memphis to New Orleans where we stayed in the French Quarter for three nights. One night, Al wanted to go to Bourbon Street, but Marian didn't. I talked her into letting Al go with me, promising to keep him out of trouble. We squeezed into Preservation Hall to listen to Jazz. Then we walked down the middle of Bourbon Street where we saw a crowd below a balcony. Guys on the balcony were throwing bead necklaces into the crowd, apparently to reward girls for showing their attributes. Al (who was in his mid seventies) suddenly turned to me and said, "I'm going in!" Before I could say anything, he disappeared into the crowd. After much bead-throwing and cheering from the throng, Al emerged, eyes twinkling, wearing the biggest grin. My lips remained sealed until after Marian's death as she definitely would not have been amused. Al has now joined her, and hopefully, the event has been forgiven.

Our group went to the New Orleans Cooking School, where we learned how to make gumbo, jambalaya and bread pudding. One of the husbands in the group groused about attending a cooking school, but at the end of the trip, when I asked everyone what their favorite memory was, he said his was the cooking school. I came away with what (with a little tweaking of the recipe) came to be one of my signature dishes, mango bread pudding.

The trip from New Orleans to Los Angeles was relaxing and uneventful. There is no better way to see our country than from a window of a train and one gets a sense of the magnitude of it. While traveling through the thousands of acres of farmland, I'd have loved it if the farmers had put up signs facing the train to identify their crops!

When we arrived in Los Angeles, we transferred to Long Beach and stayed on the *Queen Mary*. Al said he had returned from serving in WWII on the *Queen Mary*, and he pointed out the place where he had slept on the deck. We enjoyed our farewell dinner in Sir Winston's restaurant on the ship.

We took the *Coast Starlight* back to Oakland the next day which was on October 31st (Halloween). I had asked everyone to buy a feathered mask in New Orleans, and we all wore them in the first class lounge on the train. We had the Amtrak attendant judge them, and the winner got some souvenirs I had picked up in New Orleans, a fitting end to our wonderful tour. To me, New Orleans is not just a geographical location, but also a frame of mind—a place where cares are replaced with a light-hearted celebration of life, and fun rules.

The *Coast Starlight* runs between Los Angeles and Seattle. It is 464 miles from LA to Oakland and 113 miles of that is right next to the Pacific Ocean. No matter how many times I've taken the train on this route, it never ceases to enthrall me.

Throughout our tour we traveled thousands of miles and experienced a patch-work quilt of American life. The sights we saw, the food we ate, and the people we met all verified our appreciation to live in and be part of such a magnificent country. The best souvenirs we all brought home with us were our memories, but as nice as it is to travel, it's oh so good to get home.

The Balloon and Air Races

Every September, Reno featured the Balloon Races the weekend after Labor Day and the Air Races a week later. I put together a tour to the Balloon Race using the *Native Son*.

It was fun finding balloon-themed decorations for the car and we stayed at the Circus-Circus. On Saturday morning, we took a bus to the Rancho San Rafael Park, where the hot air balloons were preparing for the first feature of the event, the "Dawn Patrol". Just a few of the balloons participate—balloons qualified to fly at night. These balloons ascend and shine lights, making the balloons look like glowing giant Christmas ornaments in the darkened sky, all accompanied by choreographed music. The Dawn Patrol started at 5:30 am and we had to leave the hotel at 5:00. It was rather cold, so we all sat on the bus to await the ascension—and we waited, and waited. We could see balloons being inflated, but then they started to deflate. It seemed the winds were too strong for a safe flight, and the Dawn Patrol was canceled. Needless to say, my group was disappointed However we made up for it the next morning. I arranged to have hot coffee and doughnuts on the bus, and this time it was safe enough to let the balloons fly. The mass ascension occurred at 6:45 a.m. and our bus chased the balloons, which were a myriad of sizes, shapes, and colors. They were so graceful and beautiful and we could only imagine the fantastic views the occupants of the balloons were seeing. The winds determine the path of the balloons, so chasing them in a bus was rather challenging. One thing I learned was that the balloons will come down pretty much wherever they want. Each balloon had a chase vehicle and the speed at which they collected up the deflated balloons was amazing.

In the afternoon, we went to Virginia City where they had the Camel Races. Camels actually have a history in Nevada where they were used in the desert during the gold mining days. But the Camel Races started as a joke in 1959 when the editor of the *Territorial Enterprise* in Virginia City announced a fictitious race featuring camels. All the other newspaper editors knew it was a joke, but the San Francisco Chronicle editor called his bluff and sent a borrowed camel from the SF Zoo to compete, along with a rider, (the Hollywood director, John Huston). So, the Camel Race was created, and is still going strong. The jockeys are local celebrities and ride untrained camels that do whatever they want.

At the race we attended, one camel ran straight towards the finish line leaving all of the other camels in the dust. It came to an abrupt stop just short of the line and no prodding by its rider could make it move one more inch. The announcer laughed so hard he couldn't talk and his laughing was contagious to the whole crowd. All of this was accompanied by music from banjos and harmonicas, and it was one of the funniest things I had ever seen. There was ostrich racing too. Ostriches are huge, strong birds and it took about ten minutes and four men to attach a cart to one of them. The rider jumped in the cart and when the starting gun went off the ostriches ran so fast that if you blinked you missed the race. There was also a Brahma bull rider, and I've heard that some years there were even zebra races. I can just imagine what Mark Twain would have written had this event occurred during his lifetime. He would have loved it!

One year, I took a group on the *Native* Son to the Reno Air Races. The Reno Air Races were started in 1964 by a WWll flying ace named Bill Stead. They took place at the Reno Stead Airport (formerly Stead Air Force Base),which was named after Bill's brother, Crosten. Some of the guests on the train were pilots themselves and their shared knowledge made the tour educational as well as enjoyable. The most impressive feature I remember was a plane piloted by Bob Hoover (a former USAF test pilot and fighter pilot). It was quite large, and both engines were turned off, as he silently coasted in for a landing. In reading information about him, I wonder if such an American hero can be produced today. It was an honor and a privilege to have witnessed him flying.

When I was watching all of the vintage airplanes, I thought about how the people who appreciate vintage rail cars also appreciate most everything else of worth that is vintage. The quality of workmanship in the past was extraordinary, and I fear it may be lost to the ages.

As consumers, we have been inundated with a barrage of mass-produced products, a great many of them plastic. However, one can still find the creations of artisans and craftsmen (usually at street fairs) and hopefully, the knowledge and skills required to hone their crafts will be passed down to future generations. There is a level of joy and satisfaction that is reached when creating something unique and we all profit by the inclusion of such artists in our midst.

Chapter IV   A Busman's Holiday

Traveling with Friends

In 1984, Holland America offered a repositioning cruise on the *Rotterdam* between Vancouver and San Francisco. A repositioning cruise occurs when a ship needs to be moved to another location to commence it's cruise schedule. Rather than dead-heading an empty ship, space is sold to the public at a very reasonable fare.

Henry and I decided to go with a group of our friends. All together, there were fifteen of us. This was not a tour and we were not going as tour escorts. We took Amtrak's *Coast Starlight* to Seattle and the *Princess Marguerite* ferry to Vancouver where we boarded the *Rotterdam.*

On the *Coast Starlight,* we had a double bedroom that opened up to the next bedroom to make a suite. Dan and Rose-Marie were in the next room, so we sat together during the day. The small toilet doubled as a shower and as I was going in to use the facilities, Henry said "Whatever you do, what ever you do, don't push the wrong button!" (If he hadn't said anything, I would have been alright.) Sure enough, I pushed the wrong button and activated the shower. I thought if I pushed it again it would turn off the water—wrong! It just doubled the shower time. So there I was—fully clothed, looking like a drowned rat, not even having a towel to dry off. I had to emerge from my humiliating circumstance eventually and have never heard the end of it. I think I was not the only victim of this button arrangement because later model cars have the flush and shower buttons spaced farther apart.

Private railcars and ships often change their names and, with ships, the same name may be used for several different vessels. The *Princess Marguerite III* was a former BC Ferry constructed in 1965, originally named *Queen of Burnaby* and later MV *Royal Victorian*. In 1999 she was returned to BC Ferries and is running today with the *Princess Marguerite* moniker. The original Princess *Marguerite I* was built in 1926 for the Canadian Pacific Railroad which was replaced by *Princess Marguerite II*, built in 1949 and retired in 1979. There have been six ships named *Rotterdam* since 1872. The one on which we sailed was #5, built in 1958 for trans-Atlantic service. She became a full time cruise ship in 1969—spending summers in Alaska and winters in the Caribbean, with an occasional round-the-world cruise. One of the last steam-powered ocean liners, *Rotterdam* #5 was classically beautiful and I think she was probably the cleanest ship afloat. The Dutch run a tight ship and passengers were not even allowed to throw serpentine off her decks. She is retired now and is permanently moored in the city of Rotterdam, in the Netherlands, as a museum/hotel.

Our cruise on the *Rotterdam* left from Vancouver, with a stop in Victoria before sailing to San Francisco. Victoria was terrific. Of course, we had to have high tea at the Empress Hotel, built in 1904 by the Canadian Pacific Railway as a terminus hotel for the Canadian Pacific Steamship Line It's a beautiful, chateau-style hotel made of stone, which was almost torn down in 1965. Luckily, the building was restored and designated a National Historical Site in Canada. In all of our travels in England, I don't think we experienced anything quite so British as high tea at the Empress in Canada. We also toured Butchart Gardens. This was originally the site of a 1904 cement quarry. The wife of the owner, Jennie Butchart, started creating a sunken garden in 1909, completing it in 1921. Today, the botanical gardens cover fifty-five acres and feature the Sunken Garden, Rose Garden, Italian Garden and Mediterranean Garden. There is statuary throughout as well as a koi pond. Flowers abound profusely and it is truly magical and magnificent—well worth a trip to Victoria. Henry always gets a little nervous when I am exposed to beautiful gardens and koi ponds. The look in my eye reveals the state of my mind, whirling madly around, planning future embellishments for our garden at home.

Over the years, Henry and I have escorted many tours, sometimes together and sometimes on our own. When you're the escort, you never completely relax, because you are responsible for making sure everything goes smoothly as planned and the group is happy. On this trip with our friends we were able to sit back and enjoy everything, making it one of our fondest travel experiences.

Rail-Fanning in the USA

Even though I love trains, cook on private railcars, and am a member of PLA, I am not a true rail fan. That distinction in our family belongs to Henry. When one is married to a rail fan, pretty much every personal vacation is going to have a train in it somewhere.

PLA has an active steam train department, which restore and run the trains in Niles Canyon. Two of the members of that department, Alan and Jeff, decided to fly back to South Dakota to ride the *Black Hills Central* steam train in 2007. Henry and I planned a rail-fanning, cross-country road trip, driving to meet them in South Dakota. The first train on our itinerary was Nevada Northern Railway's *Ghost Train* in Ely, Nevada. The Nevada Northern has the best preserved, least altered and most complete main yard that remains from the steam railroad era. Started in 1906, its trains were used to transport ore, mostly copper, from the Kennecott Mining Company. The *Ghost Train* is pulled by engine #40, built by Baldwin in 1910. The many trains on the line were once a common sight, but the one train running today is like a ghost from another era—hence, the name. The Ely depot is featured in one of my favorite movies, *Rat Race.*

Our next stop was in Heber City, Utah to ride the *Heber Creeper.* The Denver and Rio Grande started a branch line in 1899 to run between Heber and Provo. The line shut down in 1967. Opened up again as a tourist railroad in 1970, it again shut down in the late eighties. The Heber Valley Historic Railroad Authority was created in the 1990s, and runs the train today. We rode the train to Vivian for a thirty-one mile round trip, and Henry got to ride in the engine on the way back (making him a very happy puppy, indeed)!

From Heber we drove to Rapid City, South Dakota, where we picked up Alan and Jeff at the airport. On the way to Hill City, we drove through a wild game park, where we kept the windows up. There were bears, wolves and big horn sheep right outside our car! The next morning we rode the Black Hills Central's *1880 Train*—a tourist passenger excursion train The ride was two hours long and we traveled twenty miles round-trip. Afterwards I did laundry at the hotel while the guys chased the afternoon train that left at 1:15. Women who complain about their rail-fan husbands or boyfriends should think again! I'd rather have Henry chasing trains than chasing women!

Originally a Keystone branch of the Burlington Northern Railroad built by the Chicago, Burlington and Quincy Railroad as a mining railroad for gold in the Black Hills. The train was later used to haul equipment used to carve the nearby Mt. Rushmore. In 1957, the Black Hills Central Railroad began running the *1880 Train* over the line.

The next day after chasing the *1880 Train* to Keystone, we played tourists, visiting Mt. Rushmore and driving through Custer National Park, where we saw elk, buffalo, wild burros, and wild turkeys. After a stop at the South Dakota Air and Space Museum at Ellsworth Air Force Base near Rapid City, Henry and I dropped Alan and Jeff off at the airport and continued our rail-fanning road trip.

Alan and Jeff are old friends, and before they both got married and had children of their own, they often came to our house for dinner and to watch rail videos. They also traveled with Henry on some of his train tours. I mentioned in an earlier story how Henry took a group to Cuba. As I was dropping him off at the San Francisco Airport, we met Alan and Jeff who also went on the tour. The last thing I said to them was "Take good care of my boy." When I picked Henry up at the end of the tour, he had this huge gash on his forehead. Apparently, he had fallen down a flight of stairs at the hotel in Havana and Alan and Jeff, afraid to face me when they got home, worried that I would hold them responsible. Of course it wasn't their fault, but I love to tease them about it.

After South Dakota, our first stop was Georgetown, Colorado where we rode the narrow gauge *Georgetown Loop*. This railroad was first built in the 1880s to service the gold and silver mining activity in the area and it traversed some very challenging topography for a railroad. The *Georgetown Loop* features three hairpin turns, four bridges and a 30-degree horseshoe curve. The old train was pulled by #9, a shay logging engine, originally from the *Westside Lumber Company* of Tuolumne, California. The spectacular scenery on the line soon became a favorite early tourist attraction.

The railroad was dismantled in 1938, but became a subject of interest for the Colorado Historical Society, when they were planning the 1959 celebration of the discovery of gold. Reconstruction was started in 1973 and was completed in 1984, on the 100-year anniversary of the original construction of the Devil's Gate High Bridge.

When we went on the *Georgetown* Loop, we rode behind #12, a Baldwin 2-6-2, built in 1929 for use by the *Kahului Railroad* in Hawaii, which transported sugar cane and pineapples until 1966. On our train the consist was a combination of open and closed vintage coaches (of course we rode in an open car), and we were impressed by both the scenery and the engineering marvels along the line.

On our way back home we stopped in Golden, Colorado for a visit with Richard Luckin. I had worked with him on the *Niles Canyon Railway* china, and it was such a pleasure to see him again. He had sold a lot of his vintage railroad china collection, but still had an impressive collection of all the china he had produced.

While in Golden, we also visited the Colorado Railroad Museum. Started in 1959, it highlights the area's history with narrow gauge railroads. The museum is in a replica of an 1880s style depot and houses and extensive collection of train photographs, paintings, and model trains. There is a library and model train layout and outside a round house and turntable. On display outside is over one hundred historic narrow and standard gauge locomotive and cars.

On our wedding anniversary we were in Denver. I had told Henry when we were planning the trip, that I wanted to have dinner at Morton's, where Cliff and I had his birthday dinner two years earlier. So Henry and I had reservations. When we walked in, we were greeted by the same gracious maitre d, and he greeted me like an old friend. I certainly wasn't wearing jeans and a sweatshirt this time, and I couldn't believe he recognized me. He started to seat us in the smoking section, but then remembered I had sat there before out of necessity. After taking us to our table, he took Henry's drink order and then said to me "You're not a drinker, right?" He had remembered. We were handed a special printed menu that started with "Happy Anniversary, Mr. and Mrs. Henry Luna". I spotted the waitress across the room who had served Cliff and me. When she was free, she hurried up to us and gave me a big hug. Wow! I could only surmise that they really, really loved that bread pudding. (Henry was very impressed.) It was another fabulous dinner and

I've recommended Morton's in Denver to a lot of people.

Next on our list of "must ride" trains was the *Manitou and Pikes Peak Railroad*. Pikes Peak is located in the Front Range of the Rocky Mountains, ten miles west of Colorado Springs. Prior to 1891, the only way to get to the summit (14,110 feet) was to hike or go by mule. A conventional railway uses wheel friction on the rail (called "adhesion") to provide locomotive power But the maximum grade that can use this system is nine percent. Pikes Peak has grades up to twenty-five percent, and the only rail system that works is a cog or "rack" railroad. The cog wheel on the engine meshes into the rack rail, which is mounted in the middle between the outer rails. The train was originally pulled by steam powered Baldwin engines. A gasoline engine was used in 1938. Since 1939 it's been pulled by diesel engines. Switzerland has the most cog rail lines in the world, and much of the equipment used on Pikes Peak came from Switzerland. But the distinction of being the cog railway with the highest elevation in the world goes to Pikes Peak.

From the bottom to the top, the train goes through four life zones, so the flora and fauna is quite unique and varied. There is an abundance of wild life, including large herds of bighorn sheep, and growing on the mountain are bristlecone pines as old as 2000 years. The scenery is spectacular. At the top is the Summit House, built in 1963—primarily a cafe (famous for their fresh doughnuts) and a gift shop. There is also a side room where passengers affected by altitude sickness can be treated. When we were there, we all had to wait inside the cafe as there was a lightning storm occurring. Although Pikes Peak is not the highest mountain in Colorado, you still feel like you're on top of the world. After she traveled to the top via prairie wagon and mule in 1893, the view inspired Katharine Lee Bates, an English professor from Wellesley College, to write *"America the Beautiful"*.

From Pikes Peak, we drove to Chama, New Mexico. In 1880, the San Juan Extension of the Denver and Rio Grande ran tracks

through the ore-rich Rocky Mountains from Denver to Silverton
in Colorado and then on to Santa Fe, New Mexico, to accommodate the silver mining operations. Traversing the steep passes
and deep gorges, it was an engineering marvel of its time. When
the line was abandoned in 1969, the most scenic part of the route,
equipment and buildings were saved, and now runs as the Cumbres and Toltec Scenic Railroad, a 64 mile ride between Antonito,
Colorado, and Chama, New Mexico and the Cumbres and Toltec
is jointly owned by the two states. We took the coal-fired, narrow
gauge train one way from Chama to Antonito, with a stop for
lunch in a bona fide ghost town deep in the Rocky Mountains—
Osier, Colorado. It was once a thriving railroad town with several hundred residents, a post office, and a saloon, besides the
many railroad facilities. Today, most of the railroad buildings
are still standing. The *Cumbres and Toltec Scenic Railroad* built a
kitchen and dining facility in Osier, and a home-style, all-you-
can-eat buffet is included in the cost of the trip. A bus took us
back to Chama.

On to Durango, Colorado to ride the last train in our cross-
country odyssey. Durango was founded in 1879 by the Denver
and Rio Grande Railroad. The line from Durango to Silverton
was built in 1881 to transport supplies and people into the San
Juan Mountains, and bring gold and silver out. This forty-five
mile, narrow gauge rail line has been running steam locomotives
continuously since it opened. The Denver and Rio Grande sold
the rail line in 1981 to the Denver and Silverton Narrow Gauge
Railroad where it operates as a tourist railroad. The depot in Durango, built in 1882, has been preserved in its original state. The
train follows the Animas River, a tributary of the San Juan River,
and as we wound our way around the cliffs overlooking the
river below, we could see kayakers traversing the white-water
rapids. It appeared grueling for the kayakers, who went for
miles, paddling furiously with no chance to rest at all, and it demanded their complete physical and mental commitment. I re-

marked to the conductor that it seemed terribly dangerous, and he said two kayakers had drowned just the week before. One thing I surely appreciate about riding trains—they are really, really safe!

Rail-Fanning in England

For our honeymoon Henry and I had flown to England from San Francisco. In London, we went sight-seeing during the day and went to theaters in the evening. After attending a performance of *The Mousetrap* (I am a huge Agatha Christie fan) we were going to enjoy an after-theater dinner. I was all dressed up and thought we would be going to an elegant restaurant. We started walking, and Henry said he was looking for a special place. We walked and walked and I was wearing high-heeled shoes! Finally, he spotted what he had been searching for. It was called Wimpies. Wimpie was a character in the Popeye comic strip and cartoon. He was always eating an enormous hamburger, stacked high with all the trimmings. (At home growing up, we always had hamburgers on Saturday night, and always called them "Wimpies") We were the only people there who were dressed up, and everyone was giving us strange looks. Henry went up to the counter and returned with what was supposed to be hamburgers. To this day, I'm not sure what it was. There were no condiments and I remember putting some malt vinegar on it to give it some moisture and flavor. Henry had been to England before and said you hadn't lived until you experienced a "Wimpie". He has a strange way of seeing the uniqueness in bad things (he also loves lightning and earthquakes!) I must admit, it is one of my favorite stories and much more memorable than if we had gone to a fancy restaurant.

We took the boat-train from London to Southhampton where we sailed on the QEll ocean liner to New York. In 1980, there was very little concern for extra security. In fact, on the flight over on

British Air, somehow the crew knew we were on our honeymoon and we were invited up to the cockpit. I remember being
surprised that it was so small of a space on such a big plane (a
747). We were introduced to the pilot and he was so handsome
and charming with his clipped English accent, that I had a dis-
concerting thought that he was really an actor in the role of a
pilot! When boarding the QE II, we had to go through some tight
security because of the concerns in England regarding the IRA.
After being frisked, we had to walk single file across the covered
ramp to the ship. Henry was in front of me, so I was conversing
with the couple behind me. As we stepped onto the deck, the
ship's photographer was taking the first of the many souvenir
pictures taken on the ship. After settling in our cabin, we found
the ship's daily newsletter informing us of all the onboard news
and activities. It was noted that joining us on the cruise was the
American actor, Jack Gilford. We looked in vain for three days
trying to spot him. Our embarkation photos had been posted
and when we found ours, I couldn't believe my eyes. Standing
right behind me in the picture was Jack Gilford and his wife–the
couple I had been chatting with. I hadn't recognized him as he
had grown a beard.

We only had time to do a small amount of sightseeing in London, and had promised ourselves a trip back to England for a
more extensive tour and to ride some trains.

Being in the travel business, we put together many tours
around the world, booking and paying for accommodations and
activities in advance. Oddly, for our own personal travel, we
hardly ever make reservations. There's a wonderful word in the
English language—serendipity It's described in Webster's dic-
tionary as "an apparent aptitude for making fortunate discov-
eries accidentally". Because we travel like this, we have had the
most amazing experiences and met the most amazing people
imaginable. Many people need the feeling of security that planning in advance can give, but we've never had a problem trav-

eling serendipitously. For our return trip to England, we made a list of what we wanted to see. As the rail fan, Henry got to choose all of the railroad sites. I chose the tourist sightseeing. I love history, so places like Stonehenge, castles and the city of Bath were high on my list. We rented a car, and drove all over England and Wales.

Our first train ride was on the Bluebell Railroad. Originally the Lewes and East Grinstead Railway, it was built in 1882 along the border of East and West Sussex between Sheffield Park and East Grinstead. It's run as the Bluebell Railroad, since 1960, and it is the first preserved standard gauge steam-operated passenger railway in the world to operate a public service. They have the largest collection of steam locomotives (over 30) after the National Railway Museum in York, and over 150 carriages and coaches. I wondered why it was called the Bluebell Railroad, until the train passed through acres and acres of wild bluebells—quite lovely. I like to joke that if the words "lovely" and "brilliant" were stricken from the language, the English would be rendered mute—but the bluebells were truly lovely.

Our next stop was one of the most impressive for me, Stonehenge. The building of Stonehenge was accomplished in three distinct phases, Originally, it was a large circular earthwork, probably used as a burial site and a ceremonial meeting place, about 5,000 years ago. This was followed by timber settings between 4,900 and 4,600 years ago. The final phase came with the building of the standing stone circles. First, 'bluestones' were brought from the Preseli Mountains in Wales, two hundred and forty miles away to form the inner circle. Then came the sarsen stones of the outer circle, some weighing up to 50 tons, from the Marlborough Downs, twenty miles away. In a sequence of settings between 4,500 and 4,000 years ago, Stonehenge finally took the form of the prehistoric temple, the ruins of which we see today.

There was a fierce storm on the day we saw Stonehenge. At

the gift shop, we purchased a huge, heavy-duty umbrella. The wind and rain were howling and blowing horizontally, and we both huddled behind the umbrella as we made our way around the monument. (I think today you can no longer walk all the way around it.) It seemed fitting to view such an ancient, mysterious temple in such wild, dramatic weather. The question as to how it was built has been fairly determined. Why it was built, by a people with primitive tools of stones, flint and antlers, over a span of a thousand years, will probably never be known.

As we drove to our next train in Wales, the scenery reminded me of the movie *Mary Poppins*, the scene where Mary and Bert ride their carousel horses through the English countryside. The rolling green hills were segmented by miles of low stone fences, interspersed with trees. I remember thinking it was no wonder fortresses had to be constructed for defense, the openness offered so little protection.

The ancestors of my father's mother immigrated to America from Wales in the 1700s, and I have always felt a Welsh connection. (It also was the source for my curly hair and dark complexion).

I always wondered how the Welsh had been able to maintain their own identity and language. It became apparent as soon as we entered Wales. With its steep cliffs and wild nature, it was so different from the rolling hills of England. Although part of The United Kingdom since 1801, it definitely is its own country and culture. The signs there are written in both Welsh and English. To the uninitiated, Welsh seems a crazy, ancient, Gaelic language that underuses and overuses vowels and double consonants. It's as if extra letters are thrown in a word willy-nilly or vowels omitted where you'd think there should be one, with no rhyme or reason. When I told my Welsh waiter, Richard, that I couldn't possibly pronounce the words, he said that he was from Wales and he couldn't pronounce them either! Lest you think I'm exaggerating, there is a railway located on the island of Anglesey in Wales called *Llanfairpwllgwyngyllgogerychwyrndrobwll-lantysiliogogogoch*! (*Llanfairpwll* for short.) The name was conceived in the 1860s as a publicity stunt in an attempt to develop a tourist attraction. I have no proof, but I suspect that, like the ducks at the Peabody Hotel in Memphis, the idea came to fruition after a few too many pints of ale at the local pub!

The Welsh can trace their roots back long before the Roman conquest in AD 43. It is believed there was a Celtic migration from the Iberian Peninsula to the British Isles after the last ice age around 10,000 years ago, resulting in a link between peoples of Ireland,Scotland and Wales and the Basque people in Spain and France.

Our destination was the Ffestiniog and Welsh Highlands Railway, located in Gwynedd, Wales. It is the oldest surviving railway company in the world. This narrow gauge railroad was built in 1836, running 13 1/2 miles between the harbor at Porthmadog and the slate mining town of Blanau Ffestiniog. Originally, the slate- loaded cars were powered by gravity going downhill, and pulled by horses on the return uphill. In 1863, a steam engine replaced the horses, although the gravity aspect of the operation wasn't replaced until 1939. By 1951 the railway was abandoned and in derelict condition. Probably the most famous railfan in England, Alan Pegler, paid off the debt and obtained control of the railway. With his leadership as chairman and his infectious enthusiasm, the Ffestiniog and Welsh Highlands Railway was restored and became the second largest Welsh tourist attraction (the first being Caernarvon Castle). The train runs through forested and mountainous scenery, past piles of slate, and was well worth our trip to Wales. Alan Pegler remained fully involved with the railroad until his death in 2012 at the age of ninety-one.

Before heading to our next train in Pickering, North Yorkshire, we stayed at a hotel in Bath, Somerset, because the Roman Baths there were on my list. Predating the Roman Baths was a shrine to the local deity of the thermal spring that feeds the spa, the Celtic goddess Sulis. At the hot springs (the only hot springs found in England), the Celts believed it was possible to communicate with the underworld through the religious caste of Druids, but the Goddess would first have to be placated with offerings. The Romans actually respected native deities, and instead of replacing Sulis after their conquest, they decided she was the same as their goddess, Minerva, and the name at the baths became Sulis Minerva. The Roman baths are a masterpiece of civil engineering, constructed over a period of three hundred years, and the Roman plumbing is still working today. Bathing was extremely important in Roman society, and the spa provided a place for business, philosophical, and social activities. The present day tradition of throwing coins in a fountain for good luck or to make a wish is not new. Many Roman coins were thrown into the Sacred Spring, and over 12,000 have been recovered. The complex is extensive and is located today below the modern day street level.

Bath is located at the southernmost edge of the Cotswold region, a range of hills twenty-five miles across and ninety miles long, and we crossed the Cotswolds on our way to North Yorkshire. The highest hill (Cleve Hill) is 1,083 feet high. The area is very picturesque, and is designated an Area of Outstanding Natural Beauty. The region boasts castles, abbeys, halls, palaces, mansions, museums, parks, and Shakespeare's home at Stratford-upon Avon (where he was born in 1594).

The hotel where we stayed at Bath was the site of the elevated modern bathtub that I mentioned in connection with the English and traditions. There was a group of seniors from Scotland on a tour of the Cotswolds staying at our hotel. I met one of the ladies from the group and she was was telling us about her tour. I asked her how she managed to get in and out of the high tub. "Oh, my dear" she said, with a charming Scottish accent, "I just wash up. I'd probably be killed getting in that tub"! When we were leaving the hotel, we saw her group on their tour bus. She got off the bus and ran up to us with brochures about the Cotswolds. Henry gave her a hug, and she not only hugged him back, but also gave him a big kiss, to the cheers of the group on the bus. "Oh" she gushed "I haven't been kissed by a Yank since the war"! She was still quite attractive, and would have been a real beauty in the '40s. I bet she did get kissed by a Yank, probably more than one!

When we arrived in Pickering to ride on the North Yorkshire Moors Railway, we looked for accommodations. The Black Swan looked interesting, and we went in to book a room for the night. The Inn dates back to the 17th century, and the computer sitting on the counter behind the check-in desk seemed a little incongruous in its surroundings. The elderly gentleman who waited on us looked a bit muddled as he went on the computer to check availability. We stood waiting while he laboriously searched for a room, I looked behind the desk to see wooden cubbyholes, and there was an old-fashioned key in one of them. After about fifteen minutes, he looked up from his keyboard and said there was just one room left. "We'll take it," we said, and he went back to his computer to complete the transaction. Finally, after another ten minutes, he turned around and removed the key from the cubbyhole. "How many rooms do you have?" I asked, as we took the key. "Nine." he answered. Sure enough, there were only nine cubbyholes. Not wanting to start an international incident and be the "ugly Americans", we didn't laugh until we were in our room.

The Black Swan is quite historic. It used to be a stagecoach stop that featured a lively pub on the lower floor. I seem to remember a sign stating that Charles Dickens had lodged there. I bet he got his room in under a minute! Ah, progress!!!

There's an interesting fact about the swans in England. Some people think the Queen owns all of the swans in England, but only the "mute" swans are owned by the Queen. The origin of

this specie of swan is eurasia although fossils as old as six-thou-
sand years have been found in the post-glacial peat beds in Great
Britain. This large swan is always white, and has an orange bill
bordered with black. They aren't really mute, just less noisy than
other species of swans. The black swans aren't native to England—they were imported from Australia. Swans were also the
symbol for alchemy—the chemistry of the middle ages, the chief
aims of which were to change the baser metals into gold, and to
discover the elixir of perpetual youth. Swans make me think of
Hans Christian Anderson's story of *The Ugly Duckling*, written
in 1844. The theme of the "ugly duckling" changing into a beautiful, graceful swan seems to correlate to the choice of the swan
as the symbol of alchemy.

In the morning, we walked from the Black Swan to the railway station to ride the train. First established in 1836 as Whitby
and Pickering Railway, it transported goods to the inland from
Whitby, then an important seaport. The railway shut down in
1965, and was reopened in 1973 as the North Yorkshire Moors
Railway. Running 18 miles across wind-swept moors and spectacular scenery, it's one of England's most popular heritage railways. The coach in which we rode had a high partition between
the seats, so we could not see our traveling companions. We
could hear them, however, and the couple in the seats next to us
were bickering non-stop for the entire trip. They were completely oblivious to the other passengers in the car, and I imagine
they probably bickered all of the time. It was so unbelievable
that it was funny (We're so easily amused!). When we got back
to the station, we followed them off the train just to see what
they looked like. They appeared to be just an average, ordinary
couple (until they opened their mouths). They kept up their
bickering until we lost sight of them. It's funny how certain
memories like that just stick in your mind.

Back at the station, we saw a sign advertising a Pullman dinner train. We asked the ticket agent if there was any room on the

evening's train. It was not only sold out, but she said they never had no-shows or cancellations, since it was pre-paid. She was very surprised that we stuck around anyway, and kept on checking as the departure time neared. About ten minutes before the train left, she called us over and told us she was astonished to have just received a call with a cancellation for two seats. So we not only got the last room at the Black Swan, but the last two seats on the dinner train — a bit of serendipity at work. The dinner and service were outstanding.

Next, we were off to the city of York to visit the National Railway Museum, where we found there was almost too much to see. The locomotives were in pristine condition and beautifully displayed. The engine that impressed me the most had been cut in half, so you could see the entire inside of the unit. The most famous steam locomotive in the world, #4472 — *The Flying Scotsman*, also resides at the museum. Built in 1923 for the London and North Eastern Railway, it was called upon to pull the first non-stop train, 393 miles between the capitals of England (London) and Scotland (Edinburgh) in 1928. The *Flying Scotsman* also has the distinction of being the first steam locomotive to officially be clocked at 100 miles per hour (in 1934) and making the longest non-stop run by steam — 422 miles (in Australia, 1989). Alan Pegler rescued the *Flying Scotsman* from oblivion in 1961 and took it on a worldwide tour for a "Buy British" exhibition between 1969 and 1972. It wasn't at the museum when we were there, but Henry and I had ridden it when it was in San Francisco at Fisherman's Wharf in 1972. Henry had reserved the entire train for a two-hour PLA railfan special, running alongside the San Francisco Bay between Aquatic Park and Pier 38. The consist of that train was Engine #4472, a First and Second Class compartment coach, the Pullman *Lydia,* and an Observation-Pub car. What I remember most about that trip was Alan Pegler pointing out the compartment in which Winston Churchill had ridden. What Henry remembers the most was that Alan Pegler could drink everyone else under the table. That skill didn't seem to hurt him, however, as he did live to be ninety-one! I remember him as warm and engaging, and unabashedly in love with his train! Unfortunately, although the tour was popular and had many visitors, it was a financial disaster for him, resulting in bankruptcy. Alan Pegler worked his way home on a P&O cruise ship, lecturing about trains and travel. He later became an actor, portraying Henry Vlll in over 700 performances at the Tower of London. He also continued lecturing, and was honored with the Order of the British Empire in 2006.

When we got back to London, we visited the London Transport Museum in Covent Garden. The museum featured buses, trams, trolley buses and rail vehicles from the 19th and 20th centuries. There was a simulator for driving a train through the London Underground. Henry, who is a qualified steam train engineer, was pretty good, but I was terrible. Thank goodness it wasn't a real train. I was determined to master it, playing it over and over, and Henry had to drag me away. It would have been a crime against humanity had I ever become an engineer!

South of London we visited Leeds Castle — touted as "The loveliest castle in the world". Located in Maidstone, Kent, the castle was built in 1119 on two small islands in the middle of a lake. It was the residence of several kings and queens, most notably, Henry Vlll. The castle has passed through many hands and has been restored numerous times. The five-hundred acre grounds include a duckery, a wood garden, a mill, a flower garden, an aviary, a maze, a grotto, a greenhouse and a vineyard. The last private owner, Lady Baillie, established a charity specifically for the purpose of preserving Leeds Castle in perpetuity, for the benefit and enjoyment of the public. Leeds Castle plays host to a number of events, including concerts, hot air balloon races and fireworks displays. It is also used for national and international medical seminars, as well as artistic and cultural events and conferences.

After Leeds Castle, we drove to Portsmouth, where two historic ships were on display. One was the *HMS Victory*, built between 1759 and 1765. It was used to fight in the Battle of Trafalgar where Vice-Admiral Horatio Nelson was killed. The other was the *HMS Warrior*, England's first iron-hulled warship, built in 1860.

As I stood in Portsmouth gazing out at the sea, I tried to envision the scene from the 1600s. The dock would have been the last sight of England for immigrants going to the new world aboard the tall sailing ships, not even sure they would reach their destination alive. Did my own ancestors leave from this very spot? What kind of people were they? My maiden name is Collins. My ancestor, John Collins, was a shoemaker and tanner, son of John Collins of Suffolk, England. He was born in 1616 and came to America before 1638.

The United States is so aptly named. Not only were states united to make one country, but every nationality of the world united to make one people, the American. When asked my nationality, I always say, American Mutt, and proud of it. After visiting Bath and Stonehenge, I realized that the age of our country is like a blink of an eye in the annals of time, but there has never been another country like it—a patch-work quilt made up of all people from everywhere, living together in peace. I have always believed that DNA is so much more than physical transference. I think the bravery and character of our ancestors, who risked their lives for a better one, is in us all.

Before we left Portsmouth, Henry was feeling so British that he yearned for a gin and tonic, so we popped into a local pub. They were astounded when he asked for ice and a wedge of lime in his drink, identifying him as an obvious Yank!

The last train trip of our holiday was also the most decadent thing we have ever done. We took the morning *Eurostar*, the high-speed channel tunnel train from London to Paris. We had lunch in the Eiffel Tower and then rode the train back to London in the afternoon. We went over in coach class, and splurged by returning in first class. Being a private railcar chef myself, I was eager to experience dining in first class on the train. What a disappointment! Our seats were the same as the ones in coach class. I expected to be called to a dining car to eat, but we were served right at our seats. Before we got our meal, we were given plastic glasses and told not to dispose of them, as they were running short. We then each got a little split of French wine with a screw top and an airline-style packaged meal with plastic utensils. There was no choice of food. It was chicken. I guess what made it "first class" was the daub of *foie gras* on top. Unbelievable!

The Chunnel train reaches a depth of 250 feet under the English Channel and travels up to 186 MPH. It also travels the farthest underwater than any other train in the world, 23.5 miles.

We were sorry we didn't have time to include Scotland and Ireland in our itinerary, and couldn't believe how fast the time had flown. We left with a realization of the immense participation of rail enthusiast in England. Restoration and maintenance are top drawer, and even the gardens around the depots are lovingly maintained. Railfans everywhere owe a debt of gratitude to the multitude of volunteers who make visits like ours so fulfilling and enjoyable.

Life's Drama on Amtrak

Our friends, Rose-Marie and Dan had moved from Redwood City to Virginia, and we decided to pay them a visit. We traveled by plane when time or logistics demanded it, but given a choice, we always preferred the train, so we booked a deluxe bedroom on the *California Zephyr*. We met the most memorable couple on the train, on their way to Denver. The husband was a radio disc jockey, and pretty soon it seemed like the entire train knew who he was. The thing that made him unusual, was that he couldn't talk! In his job, he had a machine where he could type in the words, and the machine talked for him. On the train, he had a tablet, and communicated by writing on it. His personality far outshone his disability, and after a while, you forgot he couldn't talk. He spent most of his day in the observation lounge car, where he would spot wildlife before anyone else, jot down where to look, and hold up the tablet. He kept the other passengers really seeing what they were looking at.

His wife was so friendly. She was going to Denver to meet the son she had given up for adoption when she was a teenager. He was married with children of his own, and had been searching for his biological mother for some time. We were sitting together, talking before the train reached Denver. She was nervous and said she didn't know what would happen when they met. I said first they would hug, and then they would cry. When the train arrived, there was an extended station stop, and when the couple left the train, about thirty passengers got off with them to watch the reunion. At the top of the ramp, a young man stood waiting with his wife and two small children. When his mother realized who it was, she ran up the ramp, hugged him and they both cried. They weren't the only ones. When we got back onboard the train, I don't think there was a dry eye among all of us who had witnessed the reunion.

The Train to Machu Picchu

I had always been fascinated with Machu Picchu, especially since my trip around South America so many years before with my daughter. When Jade and I visited Peru, we toured a two thousand-year-old temple site near Lima, but didn't have time for further excursions outside of the city. I was ecstatic when Henry suggested we take Peru Rail from Cusco to Machu Picchu for our own holiday.

We flew to Lima and then to Cusco, which had been the capital of the Inca Empire. When Jade and I were in Lima we visited a museum. In one room, there was a large glass jar holding the remains of an ancient Peruvian. It was small so I thought it was a child, but was told it was an adult. In another room there was a glass-encased mannequin which was used to display a royal Incan outfit that had been excavated from a tomb. It almost never rains in Lima, so the material was perfectly preserved. The Incan garment was displayed on a mannequin that appeared to be about six and a half feet tall. The Incas, a pastoral tribe in the twelfth century, originated in the Cusco area. They soon expanded, eventually subduing the other Peruvian tribes. I remember thinking, no wonder the Incas were able to dominate the other tribes so easily considering the disparity in size. This was only my observation, and I have never read or heard of it from any other source, but to me it seemed obvious. The native indigenous people of Peru today tend to be quite short.

After previous attempts to conquer the native population, the Spanish conquistador, Francisco Pizarro, overthrew the Incan empire in 1535. Although he was outnumbered, the Spanish had horses and superior armaments, and the Incas were further decimated by smallpox, introduced by the Spanish. Although Machu Picchu is less than forty-five miles from Cusco, it remained unknown to the Spanish. Although the locals knew of it, it wasn't "discovered" until 1911, by an American historian, Hiram Bingham.

It is believed that Machu Picchu was built as a family home or summer retreat for the Incan Emperor Pachacuti. It was also thought to be an agricultural station and, like Stonehenge in England, it was a sacred religious site constructed with astrological alignments. The stonework is unbelievable. We saw one ancient stone wall where, even though no mortar was used, a piece of paper could not be inserted between the rocks. The rocks were perfectly hewn to fit each other, and one stone was as large as a bus. Knowing this was accomplished with no modern power or machinery just boggles the mind.

get the altitude at all.

We had a little time before the train to Machu Picchu departed, and Henry opted to go on a local tour around the town. I wanted to poke around on my own, and went into the shops around the public square. One shop was a grocery store and they were selling boxes of coca tea bags. I bought a box and was told by someone at our hotel that I couldn't take it home, as it was a product made from the coca plant. It was just a box of tea, and I said I would put it in full view in my suitcase, and if they took it, they took it. Well, nobody even looked, and I still have some. It obviously didn't make me an addict (I've never used drugs of any kind), but it surely seemed to help with the altitude.

As high as Machu Picchu is, it is 3230 feet lower than Cusco. No wonder people get altitude sickness on Pikes Peak at 14,110 feet. The funny thing is, if you didn't know the altitude of these three locations, you would think Machu Picchu was the highest.

One of the most important features of the Inca empire was it's system of roads. Part of the construction of the roads was accomplished by cultures that preceded the conquest of the Incas in 1438, who then claimed exclusive rights over the numerous traditional routes. The fact that, after four-hundred years, many of the roads today are in good condition is indicative of the quality of construction. The most important route, (named Camino Real by the Spanish), was 3,200 miles long extending from Quito in Ecuador to Argentina.

The two main uses of the network of roads was communication via messages carried by runners and of the transportation of goods using llamas and alpacas as pack animals. Also of importance was the military and religious purposes. The Inca Empire was vast and the roads enabled soldiers to be dispatched expediently. Also, to the Incas, the mountains were objects of worship and rituals were conducted on top of mountains, which included the sacrifice of children, goods and llamas. Many shrines and religious sites were located along the trails and ordinary people were not allowed to travel along the roads without official permission.

The Inca hierarchy maintained absolute power over the populous. The Inca trail was called Camino Inca and today Machu Picchu can still be reached by hiking the Inca Trail (a four or five day trek). The trail is the sight of the world's most difficult marathon (twenty-six miles). The record for this marathon is about six and a half hours.

Rail Peru was founded in 1999 for tourist, freight, and charter services in Southern Peru which provided a new route to Machu Picchu. They used refurbished 1965 German Ferrostaal railcars, and ran on a three-foot gauge. We took the Vista Dome train for the hour-and-a-half ride, and were fascinated by the passing scenery. It seemed like every bit of ground was used for agriculture, even on terraces on the hills. We also passed by sites where adobe bricks were being made (most all of the homes in Cusco are constructed of adobe). We sat in the first two seats on our car where we had the best view. After a while I needed to visit the restroom located at the other end of the car. Occupying the rest of the Vista Dome was a large group of tourists from a European country that shall remain nameless. Let's just say this group had not availed themselves of the modern day marvel called deodorant. I really don't know if the car had air conditioning, but I do remember it was a hot day. I got halfway down the aisle and had to turn back, as I was about to lose my breakfast. My need for the facilities was just going to have to wait.

Our destination was the tiny town of Aguas Calientes—the closest point on the rail line to Machu Picchu. There are no roads leading to Aquas Calientes and the only access is by rail. After we detrained, buses took us up a switch-back road to the summit. We traveled through a jungle carpeted with flowers, and I remember thinking "Oh, they've planted impatiens", but then realized these impatiens were growing wild. How pretty they were. Machu Picchu is extraordinary. If you can't see it in person, I would recommend at least watching travel documentaries. It exceeded everything I ever imagined. Three things I vividly recall: One was a star constellation etched in a rock, not only was it etched accurately, but it was also a constellation that can only be seen from the Northern Hemisphere! The second was another constellation of stars, again accurately etched, and depicted not as viewed from the earth, but as if it were being viewed from its other side, as if looking through it toward earth. It's hard enough on the human mind to try to explain how so many single socks can get lost in a clothes drier, without also expecting it to contemplate such unexplained mysteries of the universe as these! My third vivid memory from Macchu Picchu is of the docile alpacas, grazing peacefully on the ancient terraces of the Incas.

On the train trip back, some of the train crew walked through the train using the aisle as a fashion runway, modeling alpaca quality wear. It was entertaining and fun, and, of course, they finished by offering the merchandise for sale.

When we got back to the hotel, we had a little time before venturing out for dinner. All around the open lobby were up-scale stores, one being a jewelry store. There was a beautiful gold necklace in its display case in the lobby. Henry was always trying to buy me jewelry, but I never wanted it. I liked jewelry, just not on me. (He really didn't realize just how lucky he was!) We went inside this store and Henry asked the clerk the cost of the necklace. "6,000. American" said the clerk. As Henry blanched, I gave him a wistful look, batted my eyelashes, and purred "Oh Honey, I want it". The clerk looked expectantly at Henry and I put on my best "pout face" (remember, I'm an actress), and said,

"Oh, it's so pretty, pleeease." The look on Henry's face was priceless! Henry told the clerk we'd think it over, and we got out of there. Outside, I laughed and took a picture of the necklace. I told Henry I was going to take that to parties.

The meals and service we experienced in Cusco were outstanding and we ate many delicious varieties of food that have a long history in South America. Corn has been cultivated in Peru since 1200 BC and today they have a fifty-five varieties in a myriad of shapes and colors. I've always associated potatoes with Ireland, but potatoes weren't introduced to Europe until they were discovered in Peru by the Spanish conquistadors in 1536. Potatoes in Peru have been around for 8,000 years and today Peruvians enjoy about 4,000 varieties of that vegetable. Tomatoes originated in the Andes mountains in South America where they grew wild but were first cultivated by the Aztecs in Mexico. Avocados, on the other hand, originated in Mexico before "migrating' south to Peru. Like the potato, these foods were brought back to Europe by the early Spanish explorers. Fresh fish in the region is obtained from the Urubamba, Villcanota and Lares Rivers. The Urubamba starts at the headwaters of the Amazon high in the Andes and flows through the Sacred Valley below Machu Picchu (our train to Machu Picchu from Cusco traveled alongside it during much of its route).

One dish I especially enjoyed was the fish soup—so fresh. The tuxedoed waiters (unexpected in a town with adobe houses) provided service to rival the best waiters in San Francisco or any other place,

We took a side tour by bus which stopped at an establishment that seemed to be in the middle of nowhere, but was noted for a local alcoholic drink. The group went in, but, as I didn't drink alcohol, I walked around the building. I found a barn. The door was open, and there was a two-foot barrier across the bottom of the opening. When I looked in, I saw hundreds of guinea pigs scurrying around. They were every size and color, and were so cute. I knew that they were being raised for food, and was tempted to place a little ramp inside so they could escape to freedom. It struck me that perhaps Hindus are similarly tempted to knock down fences at cattle ranches in the US. Of course, when traveling you have to respect the host culture, and I didn't install the ramp—but I wish I would have. At a later stop in a local village, we saw a community oven from which roasted guinea pigs were being withdrawn with a long-handled paddle. The little crispy critters looked like they went in whole (you could still see their little teeth). I suppose if I were starving, I could bring myself to eat one, but I think I would have to be pretty darned hungry!

Chapter V   Henry's PLA Tours

Over the more than fifty years that Henry has been the PLA excursion director, he has put together hundreds of rail tours. Many of them were joint tours with the Central Coast Railway Club—a chapter of the National Railway Historical Society (NRHS). His counterpart with that organization was Art Lloyd—an icon in the rail community and a good friend of ours.

I accompanied Henry on a number of these rail tours and I'll share some of my personal recollections of them here.

McCloud River Railway

Located near Mt. Shasta, 296 miles north of San Francisco, the town of McCloud has fewer than 1,500 residents. In the heart of timber country, it was the site of the McCloud River Lumber Company sawmill, and the McCloud River Railroad Company was built to transport lumber and passengers. Completed in 1897, it featured a large switching yard, a roundhouse, and a complete shop facility. The train ran 17.8 miles between Mt. Shasta and McCloud with a switchback (rare for a mainline railway) at Signal Butte (switchback is a method of climbing steep gradients by reversing direction on a second track). It offered both freight and regular passenger service until 1952 when the passenger service was discontinued. In 1992 the operation became the McCloud Railway, running freight service and the *Shasta Dinner Sunset Train*. The passenger coaches were kept and used for group charters. The PLA started chartering the train in the winter of 1964 and went almost every year. The highlight of this excursion was the vintage steam engine and snowplow.

When Key Holidays was running the *Reno Fun Train*, it didn't operate over the President's Day holiday in February, so Henry scheduled a the PLA trip to McCloud every year during this time.

Our favorite place to stay was the elegant, historic McCloud Hotel Bed and Breakfast, located right across the road from the railroad. It was built in 1915 by the McCloud River Lumber Co. to house single men working at the lumber mill, but by the late 1980s it was a condemned derelict. In the early 1990s, new owners, after an extensive restoration, opened it as a hotel and restaurant achieving a a four and a half star rating.

In the middle of February, there was usually deep snow in McCloud, and the train needed a snow plow to clear the tracks. This made the photo run-bys of the steam train quite spectacular, with the steam and smoke billowing in the frosty air. In 1951, a Jordon Spreader replaced the bucker plows used to clear the snow. The bucker plow (originally made of wood) was a heavy wedge that simply pushed the snow off the tracks which required a tremendous amount of locomotive power. The Jordon Spreader was developed to dig and clean ditches, regulate ballast as well as remove snow. It had a large blade on the front as well as 'wings', which pushed the snow back away from the tracks.

On one of the trips, we had just left town and the train was running through the forest. I had my eyes trained on the beautiful Currier and Ives scene passing by outside the window, when I spotted an animal running into the woods through the snow. There was no doubt in my mind that it was a wolf (it definitely wasn't a dog, fox, or coyote). It happened so fast, apparently, I was the only one who saw it. Today, the train no longer runs, but there are still wolves, wild and beautiful, running through that snowy forest in the winter.

Our friends, Al and Marian used to go on the McCloud trip every year. One thing about Marian—she hated fish, I mean she really, really hated fish. We ate out many times with them, and I think she didn't even like other people eating fish around her. On this one trip, the McCloud Railway had put a big pot of soup on board to be served to the passengers. It was fish soup (I thought an odd choice to serve to a group) and had been placed in a little side room next to the vestibule. People were walking through the train, and Marian, along with another woman, backed into the room to let them pass. I don't know if the train lurched, but that pot tipped over and hot soup sloshed on both of them. The one woman was burned pretty badly, and we had to stop the train at a crossing where she could be taken off for medical attention. Marian was burned too (not as badly), but she insisted on staying on the train. She was wearing jeans that had been saturated with the soup, and she reeked of fish. Of all of the people on the train, it had to happen to Marian. To this day, that particular trip is always referred to as the time the fish soup got Marian

The last time we rode the train it had a strange looking double-deck car with an open top. It was snowing and freezing, yet the upper deck was crammed with rail fans. I always liked to joke that rail fans weren't quite right in their heads, and here was my proof!

The Great Slave Lake Rail Tour

Henry and Art had put together a joint PLA/NHRS tour to Great Slave Lake in Canada. There were sixty-five of us, with Art and Ellie Lloyd and Henry and me as escorts. The tour started out of Vancouver, part of the group arriving there by train and the rest (including Henry and me) by air. We had exclusive use of some VIA rail cars — three sleepers, a diner (featuring VIA's "Blue and Silver" service) and a Park Observation car which had been added to the *Canadian* in Vancouver.

When we got to Edmonton, our cars were taken off the train

and two locomotives took us north over the *Great Slave Lake Railway*, normally used only for freight.

Our rail journey from Vancouver to Hay River in the Northwest Territories was 1,225 miles. When our train arrived in Hay River, there was a big sign stretched across the street welcoming us. Everybody in town knew who we were, and they were so excited to have a passenger train come to their town. At our hotel, the gift shop was selling homemade preserves made from a local berry. When Henry and I went to buy it, they were sold out. The clerk called a relative, who she knew had made some, and when it was brought to the hotel, she insisted on giving the preserves to Henry and me as a gift. The people of Hay River were so friendly and gracious. The town is located on Great Slave Lake (a lake that is wider than California), and while we were there we witnessed the Northern Lights (Aurora Borealis)—just breathtaking.

I can't say enough about the Canadian train service. (I wish Amtrak could emulate their level of professionalism.)

Steam Trains in China

The last country to use steam locomotives on a mainline was China. The *Jitong Railway* ran 587 miles in Inner Mongolia between Jining and Tongliao, for both freight and passenger service. It was opened in 1995, and the steam engines were built as late as the 1980s. Many of the locomotives were the large 2-10-2 type engines, and some trains ran with two engines on their head end. The use of steam was made possible by low labor costs and the abundance of coal for fuel in the region. China's last steam train ran on December 8, 2005. Railfans from all over the world made their way to Inner Mongolia to witness the last throes of steam in China.

We flew to Hong Kong from San Francisco, and traveled by train to Beijing and thence to the autonomous region of Inner

Mongolia. We had sleeping accommodations on the trains, and ironically the class was called "Soft Sleeper". Each room had two upper and lower berths, and the beds were like sleeping on a piece of plywood. In fact, all of the beds encountered during our tour, even in the hotels, were all really hard. The bed linen consisted of comforters, and we found ourselves putting them under us for padding. I could have made a fortune if I had brought a supply of cheap air mattresses with me and sold them.

Henry had paid for all four accommodations in each of the bedrooms on the train, even though only two of our group were booked in each room. The trains in China are all owned and run by the government, and if they had wanted to, they could have put strangers in the extra beds, even though we'd paid for them. We were lucky that didn't happen. The official description of the "Soft Sleeper" class noted: "Passengers share with other passengers, but this is no problem, and a good way to meet people". Sitting with strangers at a dining table or in a coach seat is one thing, but sharing a bedroom with total strangers (especially when we did not share a common language) is not my idea of a good way to meet people! Henry instructed our group to put items on the extra bunks, so that the conductor would think the "empty" (paid for) beds were occupied. Apparently the ruse worked.

On the train to Inner Mongolia, the dining car had menus in both Chinese and English. Almost no one who worked in the car spoke English, so you just had to point to what you wanted. I managed to convey to the waiter, through the help of another passenger who spoke a little English, that I was a cook on a train in the USA and wondered if I could see the kitchen. After a while, he returned from the kitchen and said I couldn't see it. I certainly would have been satisfied with any number of reasons for that decision, but the excuse given was rather unsettling. The cooks, it seems, were embarrassed because their kitchen was so dirty. Since I was about to be served food coming out of that kitchen, I wished they had just said it was against regulations!

The best way to see any countryside is from the window of a train. We were astonished to see the thousands of acres of corn and sunflowers growing. We had not remotely associated corn with China, even though it was added to most of their cuisine. The only corn I recalled eating in Chinese restaurants at home was baby corn. In China, corn kernels were used.

It is always my practice when riding trains to look for wildlife in the passing scenery. In China I saw absolutely nothing. Even when I later walked on the grasslands of Inner Mongolia, I never even saw an ant. I got our entire group to start looking, and outside of a handful of birds, as far as we could tell, the countryside was completely devoid of any fauna at all. The portion of the Great Wall we visited was in a remote forested area. I asked the guide if there were any wild animals there, and she almost laughed at my question. In fact, the only animals we saw in China were those at the Beijing Zoo and the pedigree dogs being walked in Beijing by what appeared to be a Chinese version of yuppies. Several Chinese whom I consulted have verified my summation of this phenomenon. Everything has either been eaten, or the fragile chain of co-existence in nature has been broken. It's a wonder their crops get pollinated (with so many people, maybe it's done by hand)! Perhaps environmentalists would be of better use if they left the tiny fish in the California Delta alone and looked into this possibly irreversible problem in China.

Beijing is an ultra modern city, where we went to a nine-story department store that made Neiman Marcus look like a Penney's by comparison. Unfortunately, the modern and upscale style of the store was not reflected in the restrooms. There are western style toilets in hotels and new apartment complexes, but the facilities at public places such as department stores, train stations, restaurants, and at the Great Wall and Forbidden City comprise a hole in the floor. Western muscles are simply not adapted to perch in such a precarious position.

As we traveled from Beijing to Inner Mongolia it was like being in a time machine, going back centuries. It was common to see people working in the fields with no modern machinery, and donkeys pulling hand-hewn carts piled high with corn or sunflower stalks.

We stayed in the railroad town of Daban and took bus trips to various sites in the area. Our travel guide in Mongolia was a woman employed by the Jitong Railway. Her name was Loren, and not only was she knowledgeable and helpful, but also charming and personable. Our bus driver did not have an English name, but after riding in his bus, from which the right-of-way was determined by the honking of a horn (without the bus slowing down), we dubbed him Louie (after Louie Armstrong– the man with a horn!). On one of our bus rides, we started some sing-along songs, and were rewarded by Loren and Louie singing some Chinese songs. We chased the train, an iron behemoth traveling along the grasslands that were once the domain of Mongolian ponies ridden by the warriors of Genghis Khan. At one of our stops, Loren prepared our lunch by the side of the bus. We were served what looked like hot dogs. Visions of Wimpies danced in my head as I attempted to associate what I was eating with an all-American hot dog. Trust me. If it walks like a duck, looks like a duck and quacks like a duck, it is not necessarily a duck!

We stopped at some yurts. Yurts were the portable dwellings used by nomads as far back as three thousand years in the steppes of central Asia. They were round tents made of skins or felt stretched over a wooden frame and are still in use today. The basic design has been copied throughout the world with adaptations for climate and use. The yurts at which we stopped appeared to be a "dude ranch" for Chinese tourists. There were four or five small units and a large one for group dining and activities. A saddled Mongolian pony was brought out from behind the yurts and Loren mounted it, posing for pictures for our group. That is my favorite memory of her, and after we returned home, we sent her a red Stetson cowboy hat made in the USA! (red being a lucky color in Chinese culture).

One day, our group was getting a tour of the railroad maintenance facility, and rather than take the tour, I, along with two other wives from the group, Jessie and Wendy, opted to explore the town of Daban. No one spoke English there and for some, we were the first Westerners they had ever seen. My curly hair received a lot of attention, with children wanting to pat my head. Even with the language barrier, everyone we met graciously received us. We came across a walled compound, which turned out to be a historic Buddhist complex including a temple. It was so interesting, I talked Henry into stopping at there later with the whole group. There was an entrance fee, and since we were the only tourists there I imagine our contribution was quite welcome. Our "host" was a diminutive, elderly Buddhist Monk. He was so cute, laughing and smiling, running from exhibit to exhibit. He insisted we ring the bells, and inside the temple he lowered the silk ropes so we could walk right up to the altar. There were three younger Monks, standing quietly to the side, watching us with somber faces. After we left, I said something to Loren about the head Monk being so joyful. Turned out, he was a neophyte, and one of the younger Monks was in charge.

We had two or three birthdays in our group, and Henry decided to buy a birthday cake. We had seen a bakery in the town, and went in to order one. The proprietor spoke no English, and when we pointed to a birthday cake, he thought we wanted that particular one, and, as it was made for someone else, he just kept shaking his head "no". Finally, after much gesticulation, we managed to order the cake. We watched them decorate it. They spun it around on a lazy Susan and embellished it with unbelievable speed, creating an artistic marvel. The oddest thing was that all of the birthday cakes said "Happy Birthday" in English—this in a town where no English was spoken. Included with the cake was a bag of birthday paraphernalia (candles, serpentine, balloons, and a musical card playing Happy Birthday). I do believe the most used word in the world is "OK", and the most popular song is "Happy Birthday"!

When we returned to Beijing we toured the Forbidden City and the Great Wall. The bus transporting us to these sites had to contend with the congested traffic in Beijing. Driving there is not for the feint of heart! Hundreds of bicycles were darting in and out everywhere and the only traffic regulation seemed to be that the largest vehicle with the loudest horn had the right-of-way. I was reminded how thousands of blind bats are able to fly together in unison avoiding mass destruction.

The Forbidden City was built (by over a million workers) between 1406 and 1420. The 178 acre walled "city" was surrounded by a moat and contained ninety palaces and courtyards, 980 buildings and 8,704 rooms. It served as the Chinese Imperial Palace for the Emperors of the Ming Dynasty (1368 to 1644) and the Qing Dynasty (1644 to 1911) Throughout it's history there were twenty-four Emperors and uninvited guests were dealt with by instant execution. Today it is the largest ancient palatial structure in the world and is visited by millions of tourists. (Luckily for us, the execution order had been rescinded!). We had been drinking nothing but tea since our arrival in China, and at the Forbidden City, one of our group located a Starbucks. That just didn't seem right (almost sacrilegious), but I must admit that the coffee tasted as good as manna from heaven!

The Great Wall (the longest wall in the world) is 13,170 miles long. Construction of the wall started 2,300 years ago to prevent invasion from the north and to protect the "silk road" trade. Over the centuries, the level of interest and activity in the building of the wall varied according to the Emperor in power. It was built by soldiers, commoners and convicts (a "works project" on a massive scale). Although it deterred invasion, it did not entirely prevent it and the wall came to be more of a psychological barrier between Chinese civilization and the rest of the world. Even today, the Great Wall is a powerful symbol of enduring strength. When I think of all the amazing things I've experienced during my life, walking on the Great Wall of China is on the zenith of my list.

We went to a large railroad museum full of huge steam engines, and on the front of each one was a large round picture of Mao Tse-tung. Touring the museum at the same time was another railfan group from the USA. Our group got talking with them, and we mentioned that the next day we were scheduled to visit a little mining operation, where they were going to steam up and run (a short distance) a little engine. Some of the rail fans in the other group were furious that their tour was including a visit to the Great Wall. Even though this was their first visit to China, they were such "foamers" that they were only interested in the trains of that country, and they asked if they could join us. I think I pointed out to Henry that "foaming" just might be grounds for divorce!

Chapter VI   The Derailment

When choosing a title for this phase of my life, *The Derailment* seemed like such an appropriate metaphor for what happened. The engineer on a train is in control only if the train is on the track. In a derailment, there is no control at all; just hope that the damage will be minimal, and no lives will be lost. Your fate is completely out of your hands and the only power you have is faith.

The Hostile Takeover

Henry retired from Key Holidays in 2004, after twenty-one years. We were happy to turn the business over to Jade and Michael, but when asked what happened, we told people (with a straight face) that it was a hostile takeover. After the expected reaction of shock and dismay, we laughed and said that Henry and I had gotten hostile, and made the kids take it over! Although technically I retired too, I still continued doing the private railcar trips.

Jade had worked at Key Holidays since it opened in 1983, and not only was she good at it, but she loved the business. It wasn't Michael's cup of tea, and Jade bought him out.

Michael mentioned to me his idea to become "The Ladle King", explaining to me his quest to be a soup chef like the "Soup Nazi" on TV's Jerry Seinfeld show. Michael made terrific soups, and I talked him into partnering with me to open a restaurant. It had always been my dream to have my own little restaurant , and here was the first time I was able to achieve that goal, now that Henry was retired.

We looked for over a year for a location, finally finding a potential spot in Martinez. Although there had been a full-sized
restaurant at the location, all that was left of the kitchen was the
range hood that hadn't been cleaned for years. The owners of
the building wanted the space to be used for something other
than a restaurant. The building was owned by the United Steel
Workers Union and, in trying to convince them to lease the
space to us, Michael and I offered to provide a complimentary
dinner for one of their union meetings (an offer they couldn't refuse), cooking the type of food we planned to serve if they rented
us the space. Well, I guess they liked the food, because they said,
"Yes." and we got the space on a handshake in January, 2008. So
our little restaurant, Connie's Kitchen, became a reality and
Michael and I were filled with euphoric enthusiasm for our new
venture.

The Symptoms

In March of that year I was working on private railcars on
the *Fun* Train and the *Snow Train*, doing four back-to-back trips.
The last trip was on the St. Patrick's Day weekend returning
March 17. My energy and endurance were legendary, leading
my waiters to call me the Energizer Bunny. I never got sick, not
even headaches, and took no pills at all. I didn't drink alcohol—
I had stopped in 2000 (I was gaining too much weight and decided it was easier to stop completely, than go to a party and try
to remember whether I had had one or three glasses of wine).
Besides adding weight, drinking simply isn't very good for you.
I never did smoke or do any drugs (I was practically a Saint!),
but on this St. Patrick's Day trip, I wasn't feeling well. I had a
swollen gland on the right side of my neck, and thought I must
have an infection somewhere in my body. I didn't look sick, and
the video of me performing my rap, filmed on this particular
trip, shows no signs of anything wrong. When I got home, how-

ever, I went to bed for four days and remember telling Henry, "I think there's something very, very wrong with me".

The Diagnosis

In May I went to a doctor and was tested for all sorts of things—with no definite results. Years before I'd had a full-screen x-ray done that showed spots on my thyroid. I went to a thyroid specialist who advised surgery to remove my thyroid. I didn't particularly like that prognosis and got a second opinion. The second doctor said it wasn't serious and to just have my thyroid monitored occasionally. Of course I preferred this diagnosis (considering the coming events, this was probably the biggest error of judgement in my life!). When I mentioned this to the doctor, he immediately had tests done on my thyroid, taking a biopsy.

While awaiting the results, I drove with Cliff to Southern California to participate in the Fullerton Train Days, where Key Holidays had a booth. After the train event Cliff stayed in Los Angeles. He owned and rented out his old family home, and it had a "mother-in law" cottage he maintained for his own visits there. After the train event I drove on to Las Vegas to visit the father of my high school boyfriend, Tod. We had dated steadily for four years in high school and I thought of his family as my own. We were inseparable (our friends even referred to us as Cod and Tonnie!) but, as happens in many teen-age romances, we went our separate ways during college. We had been not only sweethearts, but friends, and true friendship remains and goes on. We reconnected by mail thirty years later. He was happily married too, had two grown sons, lived in Washington, D.C., and we were still friends. He told me his sister, Nikki, lived in Hayward, California and his other sister, Laine, lived in Santa Rosa. In high school, they had been like my little sisters, and today we are still "sisters in heart." Their parents were living in

Las Vegas and I visited them both there. After his mother passed away, Laine went to live with their father to care for him.

When I arrived, I found that both Tod and Nikki were there on a visit. I hadn't seen Tod for thirty-three years and we were catching up with our lives when I told him I had never done drugs. I said "Can you imagine me on drugs?" He replied, "How could you tell!" I must admit, that was pretty funny! (I think perhaps I might be the proverbial bullet that he had dodged).

Before leaving, I told the girls when the sad day came when they lost their Dad (whom I just loved), I wouldn't send flowers. Instead, I would come to Las Vegas and cater the funeral.

I picked up Cliff in LA on the way home. By this time, I knew the results of the biopsy would be available. The doctors had my cell phone number and I hadn't received a call, so I convinced myself that no news was good news. Boy, was I wrong! I got my diagnosis on May 8 and the biopsy came back positive for cancer. I was going to have to have surgery to remove my thyroid. My surgeon, Dr. Deborah Kerlin, said she did all of her thyroid surgeries on Mondays and her first open date was in July. My thyroid doctor had advised me to have the surgery as soon as possible, so I had him call her. I don't know what was said, but my surgery got scheduled for a Friday in June. It was actually on Friday, the 13th! I joked with Dr. Kerlin that the only patients having surgery on that day would be all of the accident victims and me!

Dr Kerlin is a "star" at John Muir Hospital in Walnut Creek. When she took out my thyroid, she could see the cancer and aggressively removed as much as she could see. If she hadn't done that, and only removed my thyroid, I wouldn't be here today, but a nerve in my vocal chords had to be sacrificed and I was left with a "helium gas" voice. I remember waking up after surgery to hear Dr, Kerlin say "Your singing career is over!". Oh, how would I break the news to Cliff! I told Henry I could now get work as a voice-over for cartoons. Before the surgery, I spread the rumor that Henry was paying extra to have a "mute" button inserted in my neck that would be hooked up to the TV remote. I imagined God saying, "Connie, Connie, Connie. I gave you lots of chances to stop talking so much, but did you listen to me? Noooo!"

The type of cancer I had was identified by a biopsy from the surgery and it didn't look good, so further tests were done at both UCSF (University of California San Francisco) and Stanford in hopes of a different conclusion. But all of the results were the same. I had anaplastic cancer. It doesn't even sound like cancer, more like something you'd buy at Home Depot in a can. "I'd like a gallon of anaplastic, please".   My thyroid doctor was the first one to tell me what I had. When I asked him what I could do, he said "Pray". Good advice, but not especially comforting coming from a doctor. The survival rate was 2 to 5% to live past six months! It's quite a rare cancer, accounting for just 1% of thyroid cancers. Lucky me! Essentially, I had been handed a death sentence. It was surreal. I remember waking up at night thinking it was just a bad dream. Of all my doctors, only my oncologist, Dr. Matthew Sirott, had had one other patient survive this. He had to fight for me to get any treatments at all and thankfully he succeeded. It's not that the other doctors didn't care, they just thought I'd be going through a tough time for nothing, and they wanted me to be able to enjoy what little life I had left.

I really had no unfinished business, but I was concerned about the effect my illness was going to have on my seven grandchildren. By nature, I was a chicken and a coward, afraid of all sorts of things—heights, speed, the dark, dogs, horses, scary movies, a lot. Now, I needed to be a good example, handle myself with dignity, and not frighten my grandchildren, so I prayed for strength and courage. The only way I can describe what happened was as if I had rubbed a magic lantern and a genie popped out to grant my wish. It was like "poof"! Suddenly I was strong and courageous. This wasn't my nature, so I knew it was a gift. I think the Angel on my shoulder had a little extra help with this one. The chicken had morphed into an eagle.

Michael told the landlord of the restaurant what was going on, and he said until we told him otherwise, he would hold the space for us.

After my surgery, but before my treatments started, my waiters and car owners surprised me with a party at my house. They brought beer and pizza. They also snuck into my commissary storeroom so they could wear white jackets and black bow ties (with their shorts and jeans) to the affair. Cliff had canceled a trip to LA to come, Tom came from Sacramento and Wayne came from Salinas. I was so touched, and it meant the world to me. When I look at the pictures taken at the party, I am reminded that there is no evidence of a scar from the thyroid surgery. I have seen other recipients of this procedure who look like they were victims of Jack the ripper. I have always thought that Dr. Kerlin showed an extra level of sensitivity to women who did not have to spend the rest of their lives wearing turtlenecks and neck scarves.

After the party, a train picture I had hanging in my bathroom had disappeared. In August I received an envelope in the mail from "TTT" addressed to Kaunie Luna. In it was a photograph of the missing picture, with a note reading "If U ever want to see this picture again — Get better soon" it was signed The Toilet Thief. It had to be Todd. He was the only one zany enough to pull such a stunt. Later in the month, I got a second letter. This time, the photograph also contained the corner of the local Penny Saver newspaper, showing the date. It read, "Your picture is fine (notice the date). Keep up your treatments and keep smiling! Or else the picture is toast". It was signed, "The Toilet Thief strikes again".

Connie's War

In the beginning, I had pretty well accepted my fate, even planning my own memorial,. (I didn't want my family to have to go through that.) I wanted the service to be held at my home, in the garden I loved so much. I wrote a three page missive, and asked Don McGinnis (the minister who had married both Henry and me and also my son Michael and his wife, Michelle) to read it at my service. I didn't show it to anyone and have not kept a copy for myself. I remember it started with "Just when you thought I had finally stopped talking, here I am". If there were to be any tears, I wanted them to be from laughing, remembering all of the funny things in my life. I was receiving hundreds of get well cards and lots of flowers and gifts (my living room looked like a florist shop). With my biggest gift of strength and courage, I was handling things pretty well. One incident really got to me though.

When I was two years old, I was given a teddy bear. Unlike kids today, we didn't have dozens of stuffed animals and tons of toys. My teddy bear, named Boo Boo (Hey, I was only two!) was my best friend. When we were children, every Christmas, our teddy bears went under our stockings, and Santa would put fresh ribbon around their necks. This tradition had been followed all my life. My kids would put their own teddy bears out and they, along with Boo Boo, would receive new Christmas ribbons. (My sisters and brother all still have their bears, too.) I used to keep my bear on my bed, and when Henry and I were dating he would always tease me about it. When we got married, Henry was moving his things into my place and in one of his boxes was a homemade, patchwork, stuffed lamb. "What the heck is that?" "That's Bambi!" "Bambi was a deer!" "That's Bambi!!!" Well, Bambi was put next to Boo Boo and they have been sitting together ever since. They both go out under the tree every Christmas, and they both get a new ribbon.

When I was planning my demise, I told Henry I wanted to be cremated and asked him if he could see if Boo Boo could be cremated with me. "No," he said. "How can you say no to me? It's my dying request!" I couldn't believe it! Henry looked at me with tears in his eyes and said, "But Bambi would be so lonely." It's the one time we both cried.

My reaction to my dire prognosis was one of fatalistic acceptance. I don't remember ever bitterly thinking, "Why Me?" or feeling resentment, but one morning I woke up around 4:30 full of anger. I usually never got angry, but this time I was livid, shaking with rage. I sat straight up in bed and said out loud "You're uninvited, you're unwelcome, you're my enemy. Get the hell out of my body! I have this great, big strong body and you're just these tiny little cells. We're fighting you and you're going to lose!" I wasn't angry that I had cancer, I was angry <u>at</u> the cancer. So, the war was on! I even made a folder when I got up titled *Connie's War*, and put articles about fighting cancer in there. I told Henry, no matter what happens, there's going to be a big party at our house, either a memorial service or a victory party. The battles to come were pretty intense. The trick was to take just one day at a time.

The Treatments

Normally, anaplastic cancer is so aggressive that radiation and chemotherapy treatments are ineffective. But in my case, I was given the chance to proceed with the treatments, and did they throw the book at me. Before starting, I had to have a device surgically inserted in my chest to serve as a portal into a vein in my neck for chemotherapy. During my surgery a two-inch-long blood clot had been discovered in the right side of my neck, so the chemotherapy device was implanted in my left side and I was put on warfarin to thin my blood. To prepare for radiation I had to have a custom, plastic mask created. A flexible piece of mesh was molded over my face and shoulders and allowed to harden. At every session the mask would be put on and then clamped to the table to prevent any movement during the radiation treatment. The mesh enabled me to breathe and to see, but it was rather claustrophobic. I remember (irrationally) thinking that if there was a big earthquake and everyone ran out of the building, there I would be, clamped to the table, unable to move or even yell for help with my new helium voice!

The forty-minute radiation treatments were given five days a week—Monday through Friday—for seven weeks. Every Friday I got chemotherapy as well. There was a waiting room for non-patients, and another for patients after they had donned their hospital gowns. There were usually four to five of us waiting our turn for radiation. I'd go in, sit down, and say "So, what are you guys in for?" which always generated a laugh (the best medicine of all). One time I found the person sitting next to me was an old friend, Dave Butts. He had worked with Henry at Great Western Tours and lived in Walnut Creek. Most of the men waiting for radiation had prostate cancer, as did Dave, and most of the women had breast cancer. The entire time I was there, I never witnessed anyone feeling sorry for themselves. The atmosphere was always upbeat and humor was welcome. I did notice that the other patient's sessions were a lot shorter than mine, usually lasting just fifteen to twenty minutes long.

During the radiation, music was played. I brought my own CD to play—*Facing Future* by IZ (Israel Kamakawiwo'ole), best known for his rendition of *Somewhere Over the Rainbow*. One of the radiation technicians, Renaldo, would always do a little hula when he put it on. I'd say "Goodbye, I'm going to Hawaii now", shut my eyes and dream of all of the beautiful things about Hawaii—one of my favorite places on earth.

Every Wednesday, I'd bring a tray of hors d'oeuvres for the staff. I think one of the worst things to do when going through an ordeal like this is to feel sorry for yourself and stop thinking of others, so this was good therapy for me as well as a way to say "Thank you" to such a caring and compassionate staff. After my last radiation, I received a "diploma". It wasn't a congratulations for being cured, it was for surviving this stage of my treatments. Jade and her two oldest daughters, Katie and Sarah, brought leis for the celebration, even one for my mask to wear.

When I had finished the thirty-five radiation and seven chemo treatments, I had to have four more, tougher chemos, three weeks apart. The radiation had burned me so badly (inside and out) that I thought I looked like those little crispy critters coming out of the oven in Peru. The scar tissue from all the radiation eventually closed off my esophagus, and I couldn't even swallow one drop of water, which resulted in more surgery to insert a feeding tube in my stomach. I had that for six months and at one point, the tube site became so painful that I had to have that one removed and a second one put in. To examine the inside of my throat, one doctor threaded a miniature camera on a thin cord through my nose and into my throat. It was extremely painful and made me gag. I told him the CIA should forget water-boarding—this procedure would elicit all the information they wanted! I had to endure it several times.

Pillars of Support

The angel on my shoulder went on some well deserved R&R, and was replaced during this whole ordeal by another angel, my daughter, Jade. Although she was running a business and had a family to take care of—five daughters (two were in college)—she kept a folder of all of my medical records (it was about four inches thick by the end), and she went with me to all of my doctor appointments. She scheduled friends and family to take me to my daily treatments and sent out e-mail updates on my condition to dozens of people. She lived about nine miles from my house, but Key Holidays was in Walnut Creek too, so every morning she would come before work and every evening she'd come after work, cleaning my house and cooking meals for Henry.

My two sisters and my brother all came (separately) for two weeks each, which really helped both Jade and Henry. Bill and his wife, Terry came from Michigan, Letty and her husband, Vince, came from Virginia and Pat came from Arizona. I needed to be isolated, as my immune system was compromised, so I moved into our guest bedroom. Henry kept tabs on me with a baby monitor, and would stay awake half the night listening to me breathe (and cough). It scared him to death whenever I was too quiet! I think what kept him sane throughout this whole ordeal was his involvement with the PLA and the Niles Canyon Railway.

My sister Pat had arrived on November 12th. On the 20th I went to the ER at the hospital. My white blood cells. which should have been at 7000, were at 500 and I was hospitalized. After that got fixed, my red blood cells were off and I was given two transfusions. I cannot say enough about the professionalism and compassion shown me at John Muir Hospital. I think it's ranked number eight in the nation, and I was so lucky to be going there.

On the 25th I came home, and that evening the NCRy was running the yearly special VIP Christmas train. Every year, Henry would ask me to provide and serve hors d'oeuvres on the train, but this time my shy sister Pat got suckered into doing it in my place. The train was a great success, and Pat had a ball. While Henry and Pat were out, I rolled my hair (all 45 strands of it that were left) in curlers, and sat real still so the curlers wouldn't fall out. (I mentioned before that I had curly hair. Big curlers are used to straighten curly hair.) When they came home, Pat saw the curlers and cracked up, but Henry didn't laugh. "Don't you think this is funny?" I asked. He said he thought I had become so eccentric that I was really trying to curl my hair.

Thanksgiving was the 27th and we went to Jade's for dinner (I sat on the couch with my feeding bag hanging from a pole, attached to a tube to my stomach). The rest of the family ate at the dining room table, but I was close enough to enjoy the festivities. Every night, when I hooked up the bags for dinner, I would describe what I was having (rack of lamb, prime rib, baked potatoes, asparagus, etc.). My taste buds were pretty well shot by this time, and even the water I used to brush my teeth tasted terrible, so I let my imagination take over.

I kept a journal and wrote in it every night. It really helped to put what I was feeling into words, and when I read it now I realize how much of what I went through, my mind has now put away on a top shelf, out of sight. I also enjoyed working *Sudoku*. I was given a one thousand game puzzle book and finished the whole thing without cheating. Another thing I did was to read the *Bible* from cover to cover. I had always intended to do that, but procrastinated, as it's a pretty difficult read (all those begats!).

When I chose to fight, I decided that I had gotten cancer for a reason, and there was a lesson I had to learn, so I started to look for the answer. My favorite verse from the Bible was Romans V, part of which says that "suffering produces endurance, and endurance produces character, and character produces hope, and hope does not disappoint us, because God's love has been poured into our hearts…". Henry said in my case it should have read "produces a character". It astounds me to this day how many people were praying for me. Even a friend of my sister Pat's was on Easter Island praying for me.

Before I got sick, Henry had put together a tour to England for the PLA, which we were both supposed to escort. He didn't want to leave me and found a substitute escort. I received in the mail a picture of the group. They were in two lines, with the front line kneeling. Each person was holding a sheet of paper with a large letter written on it, which together spelled the message, "Get well Connie We miss U!" Over their heads in the background was Stonehenge.

Entire churches of different denominations were including me in their prayers—Catholics, Baptists, Quakers, Buddhists, Mormons—more than I can name. (I'm a Presbyterian.) I never prayed myself for my life, but I'm not stupid, I prayed for my doctors! I did say the Lord's prayer every night, and the evil I was asking to be delivered from had a new face—cancer!

During this time I was given several cook books about cooking for cancer patients. The best one was called *One Bite at a Time*. In reading about fighting cancer, I came to the conclusion that the five main causes (outside of genetics) are insecticides, chemicals, smoke and smog, diet, and stress. I had been cooking most of my life and my food was certainly tasty, but I really didn't pay much attention to organic food or think about using organic ingredients. However, I came to believe that we're killing ourselves with our food and lifestyles. I think this was a lesson I had to learn, and it took a serious, life-threatening disease to make me see the light. My menu for Connie's Kitchen didn't change too much from my original plans, but the ingredients surely did.

I was so blessed to have the unconditional support of my family, and my friends were so caring. Joy, a dear friend from England who was a neighbor before Michael was born, and was my matron of honor when Henry and I married, drove with her husband, Mike, all the way from Oregon just to see me. My next-door neighbors, Leslie and David, constantly brought me flowers and gifts and moral support. My best friend from first grade, Deanie, who lived in Michigan and was going through cancer herself, made me realize the power of friendship. Al Harvey brought me flowers every week, and I received so many get-well cards, they filled an entire wall, top to bottom. My doctors told me not to be around any negative people. I told them I didn't have any negative people in my life. When I met someone like that, I wasn't rude, I just didn't have anything to do with them.

They're like vampires sucking the life out of you , bringing you down to their miserable level! Best to leave them alone.

My sense of humor had always gotten me through pretty much anything life had thrown at me, and I'd welded it like a finely-honed weapon, worn it like protective armor, and depended upon it to face my cancer. I spent so much time in bed, I lost most of my muscle. I told Henry I wasn't his trophy wife, I was his atrophy wife!

My last chemo was on December 5, but I had to wait until January 14, 2009 to take the PET scan. Before the scan, I told Dr. Sirott that the cancer was gone. He said I was probably right because people usually had a good sense about their own bodies. The results were in on January 24th, 2009. Perhaps God got tired of all the nagging, but for whatever reason, those many prayers (for which I will be eternally grateful) worked, and I was granted a miracle.

The War is Over! The War is Over!

I should have banged on a pan lid with a wooden spoon. The PET scan showed the cancer was completely gone. It's rather daunting and quite humbling to be the recipient of a miracle. Perhaps God didn't want Bambi to be lonely either.

I called Don McGinnis and asked him to burn the memorial note I had sent to him. With the evil cancer vanquished, as he looked into the fire, I told him to say "You lost and she won!" Instead of a memorial, I threw a big victory party at my home and invited all of the people who had given me so much love and support. Happily, one of my guests was Dave Butts, also cancer-free!

One morning, I was home alone and the doorbell rang. Standing there was a policeman holding my missing picture. Standing next to him was Todd, in handcuffs. "Pardon me ma'am, but I believe this is your stolen property." The next week

I received a note from our friends, Bill and Judy. It read "Connie, we were so happy to hear you beat the cancer. We've been praying for you all along. Can't wait to see you. I was also sorry to hear your bathroom was burglarized while you were ill. I've heard that the criminal was apprehended and your property returned. What sort of parents would raise such a child. All Our Love, Bill, Judy and Andy (he had Todd pegged from the beginning)". Andy is a cat, Bill and Judy are Todd's mom and dad, and the policeman (real) was a good friend of Todd's.

Jade put together a scrapbook titled "Hope" with my high school graduation picture on the front. There used to be a television show in the 50s called "This is Your Life." Well, the scrapbook was pretty much my life, with the cancer ordeal fully documented. Besides pictures, there were the update e-mails Jade had sent out and the ones she received. I just love looking through it, and still can't believe I had so many people who cared about me.

I was gradually getting stronger, but still on the feeding tube, when I received the sad news that Tod, Laine and Nikki's father had passed away in Las Vegas. He was like a father to me too, and I told Henry "I think I can do this" So, fulfilling my promise, I drove by myself to Las Vegas and catered his funeral. The feeding tube was a bit of a nuisance, but I had resigned myself to it and, like the cancer experience, I just took one day at a time (the entire picture being a little overwhelming). It wasn't any problem doing the food (I had done the same buffet dozens of times on the private rail cars) and it felt good to be cooking again. I'm an extremely independent person, and one of the hardest things was having to rely on others for everything for so long. It was wonderful to be able to use my skills to help someone else, and it was so nice to meet Tod's wife, Carol (an accomplished poet), and his two (handsome) sons.

After the second (this time successful) operation to open my throat, I could eat normally again and I had the feeding tube removed. I thought there would be a scar from the tube, but what I didn't expect was the hole that was left. It looked just like a second belly button. I tell people that, obviously, I had two mothers! As it's highly unlikely I'm going to don a bikini any time soon, it doesn't really bother me.

Michael Luna, Tom Nelson, Michele Stevens, me, Darrel Saunders at my surprise party.

Grant, Darrel, Wayne, Morris, Michele, Roy, and Todd at my surprise party.

Darrel, me, Todd, and Grant.

Wayne, Cliff (my best friend), Morris and Roy.

"If you ever want to see this picture again, get better soon!"— The Toilet Theif

Jade, me and grand daughters Sarah and Katie.

Todd (busted!)

Chapter VII   Connie's Kitchen

Building a Kitchen

Not long after I was given the green light to go on with my life (sans the feeding tube), Connie's Kitchen came off the back burner. I had lost a lot of weight (a diet I would not recommend to anyone!) and was still pretty weak, but my dream was not to be denied. Michael and I proceeded with the plans to build the kitchen at the location in Martinez and we were so excited to resume our quest. As there was nothing left in the kitchen but a hood, we had to hire an architect to design the kitchen. The six pages of blueprints had to be worked and reworked before being approved by several departments. The Union knocked down all of the existing walls and built a conference room in a third of the space. The floor and ceiling were removed and new plumbing (including a grease trap) and wiring were installed. I had a handyman (who was also a friend), Jim, who had worked for me for years, and he and Michael did most of the construction. I was getting stronger all the time and was able to work at home, wall papering and painting all of the ceiling panels (the wall paper was embossed and looked like pressed tin). I even sewed the window valance on my old treadle sewing machine. After everything was built, I did most of the painting and wall-papered the cafe area. The construction was so extensive, it took over a year to complete. For a few months during this time, I cooked food on Sunday (enough to feed around fifty people) and delivered it to a local homeless shelter. Besides keeping my cooking skills honed, it was a way of giving back. Surviving cancer gives one a different perspective regarding life's priorities.

In building the kitchen, we really didn't know what we had gotten ourselves into, and the labor and expense far exceeded our expectations. Looking back on it, we should have kept looking until we found a fully functional kitchen. But we were so happy and excited to have found a location after such a long search, we naively went into it, full steam ahead!

A Dream Come True

Our grand opening was August 14, 2010 (Michael's birthday) and he and I were elated. It was such a long, arduous road to get to this point, that we had almost come to believe this day was never going to happen. There was a pretty large crowd for the ribbon-cutting. The Mayor and some members from the Martinez Chamber of Commerce were there along with quite a few locals, and of course our family and friends. Ann, one of our friends from the PLA, was a horticulturist. The decor of Connie's Kitchen featured sunflowers and chickens and Ann had grown a large pot of sunflowers and had brought it all the way from her home in Half Moon Bay to Martinez (a distance of about sixty-five miles). The plants were in bloom and the the pot was placed next to the entrance. I had made hors' d oeuvres for the occasion and our guests all got tours of the kitchen. The cafe area was small—only seating a dozen people, but the kitchen was quite large. As kitchens go, I must say, it was just beautiful! We were ready to feed the world!

In our little office space, we had a recliner chair. By this time, I had recovered quite a bit, but I really didn't know about my stamina and thought I might need a place to rest during the day. Before the crowd came and the festivities began, I found myself alone in the kitchen. As I walked through it, realizing what lay before me, I said out loud, "I hate to push my luck, but I need one more little favor. What I need now is energy". I was far removed from the "energizer bunny" I had been on the trains. My body had been through so much, I knew I would never be as strong, or have the endurance I once had, plus (doggone it) I kept getting older! I felt a bit greedy asking for more after receiving the gift of strength and courage and the miracle of my life, but again there was a "poof" and I felt an instantaneous physical response. Over the next two years, whenever I was at work, I had the energy of a teen-ager. I shouldn't have been able to do what I did after all I had just been through, especially at my age (in 2010 I was sixty-eight).

The cafe space was bright and cheerful with the sun-flower wall-paper and yellow wainscoting. We wanted it to look like a friendly grandmother's kitchen —a place where you would feel welcome and safe.

Besides the vases of silk sunflowers, we had chickens in every form imaginable, and after we opened people kept giving me chickens to add to the collection. I used to give a free box of cookies to any child who could count all of the chickens (there were over fifty). The best chicken was our mascot named Cliff!! He was made of wood and was about a foot high with hinged legs. We moved him all over the place and had a whole wardrobe for him for special occasions. For Halloween we suspended a small broomstick from the ceiling and Cliff rode it with a little black cat behind him. He had outfits for Christmas, New Year's. Valentine's Day, 4th of July, Memorial Day, Labor Day, Veteran's Day, Thanksgiving, and Easter. The most unique costume was for the occasion of the royal wedding when William and Kate got married. We had Cliff the chicken sitting on top of the drink cooler wearing a tiara and a long bridal veil that hung all the way down the side. We even found him a blue ring to wear on the tip of his wing. Our customers used to come in and look for him. When I told my waiter Cliff that I had named the chicken after him, he indignantly said "You didn't!". But after a while, every time I talked with him he would ask what his namesake was wearing and I could hear a little pride in his voice.

Michael waited on the customers, did most of the shopping, and took care of the business end. I was the cook. Our food was old-fashioned American and I prepared a lot of the dishes I'd served on the private rail cars. We also did catering and special occasion dinners.

We had some yellow "Connie's Kitchen" soup and travel mugs made (proudly "made in the USA"). Once someone bought one, they could have a free refill of soup or coffee every day. We had a rack on the wall to hang the soup mugs, with the owners names displayed. We also started a "Casserole Club". After purchasing a Corning Ware casserole from us, they could bring it it and purchase a take-home meal prepared in it. We kept a record, and after so many, they would get a free one.

We didn't serve "health food", but we did serve healthy food. We bought as much organic as we could and served nitrate-free bacon and ham. We even corned our own corned beef so it too could be nitrate free. Only canola and olive oil were used, and we didn't even have a deep fryer. It was also important to me to offer our food at reasonable prices. I personally knew what it was like to exist on a shoestring, and I felt strongly about every-day people, especially families with children, having the opportunity of eating out. One time, a gentleman came in, clearly down on his luck and clearly hungry. I watched as he pulled a few coins from his pocket and counted them, trying to see what he could afford to buy. I told him, as it was the end of the day, I was about to dump the rest of the minestrone soup and offered to give it to him rather than throw it away. (It wasn't really true, but remember, I'm an actress!). He was elated. He then emptied his pockets on the counter and I got the impression this was the sum of his worldly possessions. Among his treasures was a chain bracelet with little colored rocks charms and he gave it to me. I learned a valuable lesson about dignity and cherish that bracelet to this day.

We had a sense of fun in Connie's Kitchen. One time,

Michaels's little daughter, Sierra, was upset when she saw "dev-iled eggs" written on our chalk-board menu on the wall. We changed the name to "angel eggs" and the name caught on. We used to serve eggs Benedict, but our version was called "eggs Bogart". We made the two coddled eggs on top look like eyes with a slice of black olive and parsley for eyelashes. When we would serve the dish, we would say, "Here's looking at you, kid!". Our food was wholesome, delicious, and unique and we had a lot of repeat customers. The building manager, Jimmy, used to come in every morning for his oatmeal. We would cook it with raisins and dried cherries, and serve it with a small pitcher of half and half and ramekins containing fresh strawber-ries and bananas, chopped walnuts, and brown sugar. A lot of people are allergic to nuts, so we kept them separate and op-tional.

My private car standards were ingrained in me and was re-flected in how we ran "Connie's Kitchen.

I got a call from Darrel who was working at Key Holidays. He had a private rail car request for the *Tamalpais*, and wanted Cliff and me to work it. As busy as we were, I missed working with Cliff terribly and with a new business, the inflow of cash would be welcome. It was very tempting and I decided to do it. I figured I would make a whole lot more money from the trip than at Connie's Kitchen, so I cooked a lot of food in advance and left Michael running the restaurant for eight days.

I hadn't worked on a train since before I got sick and didn't know how I was going to do. After being laid up for so long, my back was weakened, so I brought along a heat/massage back rest. But I had no problems. In fact my back felt better than ever. I think the movement of the train as I slept in my bunk at night worked like a constant massage. Cliff set up my backrest in the rear lounge and the guests (all seniors) loved it. They were re-tired railroad presidents, (boy, did they know the railroad!), and we went from Oakland, to LA, to San Antonio, to Chicago, and back to Oakland. The group was pretty specific with their dining requests, evoking their collective memories of train travel, and it was quite a challenge to find pickled watermelon rinds and rhubarb for a freshly baked pie.

It was wonderful being on the *Tamalpais* with Cliff again. I'm so glad I went. I didn't know it at the time, but this was to be not only the last private car trip I would take with Cliff, but also my last private car charter as well and I will be forever grateful for that trip.

When we got back, I had a whole lot of cooking to do to get caught up, but it was worth it. We had a chalkboard back in the kitchen where we wrote down items that needed to be prepared. Michael had taped our entire menu to the board!

Both of us worked hard at our new venture without any salary, but after a year, Michael (who had a wife and two kids) had no choice but to leave and get a paying job. Now, on my own, I was doing everything—the shopping, cooking, cleaning, paying bills, paperwork, and was working seven days a week, leaving before it was light and getting home around 9:00 pm.

What kept me going was the belief that my life had been spared for a purpose. Not only was I providing healthy food but several of my customers either had cancer or had friends and family with cancer and my successful outcome was an inspiration to them. I was even asked to be a speaker at a local Soroptimist Club. I honestly believed I was right where I was supposed to be.

One day, I noticed the last two fingers on my left hand were drooping toward my palm. By the end of the week, they were down completely, and I couldn't raise them. I went to a doctor and was told my wrist bone had developed a bone spur, and it had severed the tendons to my fingers. I considered trying to work with the condition, but was told, if left untreated, the bone spur would similarly affect my middle finger. The solution was surgery, but I would be in a cast for three months. I told the doctor that I had never, in my entire life, ever given anyone the finger, but if I ever got angry enough to do so, I was pretty sure I would want both of my hands functioning, so I opted for the surgery. The problem was, I couldn't afford for the restaurant to be closed for three days, let alone three months.

Connie's Kitchen had a Facebook page with quite a few friends and I posted what was going on and my need for help. I couldn't afford to pay a salary, so I said if anyone wanted to help me, I would teach them how to cook. The first response came even before the surgery. Steph was 26 years old, and we hit it off from the beginning. I only had to show her something once, and she got it. She was easy going and had a great sense of humor. Connie's Kitchen was closed for only two days when I had the surgery. Because of Steph, everything kept running smoothly. Soon, all kinds of people came to help me. One man, Bill, owned his own company and he insisted on washing all of the dishes. He was so generous, even replacing a broken printer for the restaurant office and all four wheels on my van. His wife, Shirley, came and helped me cook as well. There are no words to describe or explain such people, but I am convinced God has a very special place waiting for them in Heaven, where they will feel right at home with all the other angels.

After three months the cast was off, and I was on my own again—well, not completely. Steph kept coming to work part time, and Jade's third daughter, Jessica, helped me during the summer. She was only thirteen, but was already taller than I, and everyone thought she was older. Jessie has the best work ethic I have ever seen. She took all of the orders and payments, kept the front stocked and clean, and baked all of the cookies and breads. I never once had to tell her what to do. She is poised (and pretty) like her Mother, and has a wicked, adult sense of humor. One time, she was spraying a cookie sheet with Pam and said "You can never use too much Pam". "You know, Jessie" I said "When I was a little girl, they didn't have Pam". Without missing a beat, she said "When you were a little girl, Grandma, they did-n't have electricity!" Zinged by my own Granddaughter!

I talked with all of my customers (probably way too much) and my relationship with trains was well-known. One of them brought me a framed poster of the *Lahaina Kaanapali and Pacific Railroad* in Maui, Hawaii, that I put up on the wall. The people of Martinez are so friendly and down to earth, and I was given many more gifts too, while I had Connie's Kitchen.

The town itself is quite historic. Originally an Italian fishing village, it had several third and fourth generation Italian families still living there. Its claim to fame is that it was where Joe DiMag-gio was born, where the martini was invented, and it is the loca-tion of the largest bocce ball tournament in the world. And Martinez, being the county seat, had some classically beautiful public buildings downtown.

Henry and I were looking to downsize from our house in Walnut Creek, and Henry was interested in Sunol. Although it was forty miles from Martinez, I knew it would make him so happy to be close to the NCRy and I resigned myself to the long commute to Martinez. One of my customers was from Sunol and had a rental property that was going to be available. We were contemplating the move, when the deal fell through, so we started to look at Martinez as a possibility.

The customer who had given me the poster came in, and we started talking about trains. I told him I was looking for a place in Martinez where Henry could hear the trains. He said he owned a house, where you not only could hear the trains, but you could see and feel them. His tenant had just moved out and he was looking for new tenants. As soon as we saw the house, we knew it was for us and planned our new move. Michael and Michelle moved into our house in Walnut Creek and became our new tenants.

The house in Martinez was built in 1918, in the craftsman cot-tage style of the day. It is built on a hill, and at the back of the property, there is a road paralleling the main line train tracks. Living there we saw all of the passenger trains and a lot of freight trains passing through Martinez. On the other side of the tracks, are four baseball fields, the marina and the Carquinez Straights, where huge ships ply the waters. There is a large refinery in Martinez, and we could see the dock where the super tankers moored Across the Straits, and huge car carriers offloaded their cargo. The waters there are alive with ships, tugboats, barges, sailboats, and pleasure crafts. The area between our house and the water was extensive and devoid of power lines. This, along with the winds coming through the Carquinez Straights, made it a perfect kite-flying locality and the deck on the back of our house was like a grand box in a theater—affording us unparalleled views and enjoyment—the climax of which was on the Fourth of July where we could see the fireworks from five different locations

At night, as I lay in bed, I listened to the whistle of trains, the cuckoo clock in the kitchen, and, on foggy nights, a fog horn echoing guidance for the ships in the Straits. My mind was propelled backwards through time, and I was a child once more.

One door closes....

I've had such an amazing and fulfilling life. Many people live their entire lives in a self-imposed box, never experiencing so much that life has to offer. I guess they feel it's safer not to venture outside what is familiar. It's not really fair to criticize this, since what might seem boring or limited to one person, is comfortably adequate for someone else. I don't think I've been offered so many more opportunities than anyone else, I've just been open to them. It's said that when one door closes, another door opens. The trick is to walk through that door. If things don't work out, take away from it a lesson learned, and walk through the next door.

When I was thirteen years old, and a freshman in high school, we had to do a report on what we wanted to do in life ("what do you want to be when you grow up, little girl?") We had to interview someone in our chosen profession, and my choice was a newspaper reporter. In all of the jobs I've had during my life, not one of them was working for any publication. Looking back, I think what an absurd and ludicrous question it was for a thirteen-year-old. Perhaps it is this inquiry that put so many people in that self-imposed box.

I had managed to stay in business for a year after Michael left, but it got harder and harder. It is difficult to have a small business in California (especially a restaurant), but with the economy so fragile, for me it became impossible. I had people advising me to raise my prices and buy non-organic, cheaper food. From a business standpoint, this made sense but to me it would have been an obscene assault on my integrity and negated the very purpose of Connie's Kitchen. I finally had no choice but to close up shop.

I succeeded in so many ways to achieve my dream. I never compromised my standards and quality and have absolutely no regrets. I have nothing but fond memories of that endeavor. Life itself is a series of the temporary occupation of places and time and to stay stagnate is to not live to ones fullest capacity.

Just when I thought Henry and I were settled into our final home in Martinez, we heard that a house in Sunol was going to be available to rent. It was located right next to the train tracks and had a wrap-around porch that looked directly across the street to the NCRy depot. Not only was it Henry's dream house, but it was more practical to live there. Now that Connie's Kitchen was closed there was no reason to live in Martinez. We were driving several times a month to the NCRy anyway.

My new adventure included raising chickens! I hadn't planned on keeping chickens, but the former tenants left five hens and they came with the house. They had been very inadequately housed, so, before we moved, my handyman, Jim, and I commuted to Sunol to build a new abode for them and I enjoyed having fresh eggs (organic, of course). Who would have thought my new door would lead into a hen house. You just never knew what life was going to throw at you.

Sunol is a tiny town, consisting of a post office, antique store (since closed), convenience store, cafe, restaurant, events center, and railroad depot. The depot which had once been moved and used as a residence, has been restored by the PLA and is back in almost the original spot it occupied when it was built in 1884. There were only two eating establishments in Sunol—Bosco's (a large restaurant and bar) and The Sunol Railroad Cafe.

Bosco's was named after an international famous dog! Years ago, a couple of men were running for the position of Mayor of Sunol. Apparently, the locals weren't crazy about either one of them and wrote in their chosen candidate—Bosco, a friendly black labrador who was the "town dog". Well, Bosco won and became the official Mayor of Sunol. The story spread and Bosco's fame spread. His only negative review was in a Chinese newspaper which cited his mayoral office as the "proof" that America was a degenerate country where people could elect a dog as a mayor. I think the review was "proof" that the Chinese needed to work on their sense of humor! Today there is a statue of Bosco next to the Post Office, commemorating Sunol's most illustrious citizen.

The Sunol Railroad Cafe was a longtime landmark in Sunol and the locals hung out there to enjoy local camaraderie and delicious food. Yet I noticed it was only open for breakfast and lunch. Even though Connie's Kitchen was closed, I wasn't quite ready to retire, so I came up with a plan. I talked the owner, Jeff, into letting me come in after closing time and open the cafe for dinner on the weekends. I decided to serve one entree each night and would advertise the menu on a board in the cafe and also out front. I was competing with Bosco's Restaurant and knew I had to offer something unique. Every Friday night I served fish and chips, as this had been wildly popular in Martinez. Saturday was "International Night" and changed every week. I have the best borscht recipe and served it with beef stroganoff for my Russian Night, and shepherd's pie and watercress soup for British Night but my most popular menu was my German meal—rouladen, potatoes, carrots and red cabbage with Black Forest cake for dessert, I would finished the week-end with all-American "Sunday Fried Chicken." If you love what you're doing, it's not work at all, and when I cook I am full of energy and I'm happy.

After a year, the novelty of living the country life across from the depot had worn off, and although we enjoyed our time in Sunol, we realized that renting was not for us. Having owned our own home for so long, we missed the freedom to garden and decorate to our own tastes. We had been considering selling our house in Walnut Creek, but decided to move back there. We'd completed a full circle and returned to our home. Our old dog, Lucky, who had made the moves to Martinez and Sunol with us, was especially happy be back home!

Kaleidoscope

When we were children, we were delighted by an old-fashioned toy—a kaleidoscope. Basically, it is a tube that contains mirrors and colored glass. When eyed through a lens in the end and rotated, a myriad of beautiful and fanciful shapes would appear. I believe my life has been a kaleidoscope. With every twist and turn, a new pattern has appeared—new experiences, new places, and new people. Realistically, not everything in life is good and beautiful, but we do have the choice to prioritize our memories, and my memories of the trains in my life (and in my heart) are lovely to dwell on.

Off and Running

When other couples Henry's and my age would be quite content to sit in a rocking chair and stay put, we are contemplating a new dream. We've been scouting out RV shows. We're not interested in anything elaborate (we've seen some that even have a fireplace and marble floors). Our needs are modest, but we would like two beds, a small stove top and refrigerator, and a bathroom with a shower. We found a couple of styles that are the size of a pickup truck and fit our needs. Our aim is to drive around the country, see friends and family, and visit railroad operations and museums. We're not quite ready to embark on our new venture, but just imagining it is giving us pleasure. I have just learned a new saying—KOKO. I believe it originated in England and means: Keep on keeping on—quite a good and appropriate recipe for life.

> My heart is warm with the life that I've led;
> With trains and friends and adventures in it;
> Yet there isn't a life that I'd rather have had;
> Life's short—be happy—have dreams and live it.

Connie Collins Luna (1942 -)

The Cast of Characters

My waiters and the private car owners played such a huge part in my life, I wanted the opportunity to introduce them to you, and asked them to include any stories they might want to share. I have not included waiters who only worked for me on one or two trips, as these were friends or relatives of my regular waiters, and were used only occasionally.

Waiters

Mike Biehn	Morris Lyons	Jim Ramos
Ron Torres	Ollie Beaudry	Michael Luna
Darrel Saunders	Todd Utikal	Richard Evans
Cliff McDaniel	Shawn Saunders	George Heflin
Tom Nelson	Michele Stevens	Greg King
Mike Perry	Grant Stubblefield	

Mechanic
Will Walters

Car Owners	Private Car
DeWitt Chapel	The Chapel Hill
Doug Ebert	The Sierra Hotel
Jon Kirchanski &	
Lou Bradis	The Tamalpais
John Kirkwood	The Yerba Buena
Tom Lantry	Business Car #33 (*formerly*
	The Tamalpais)
Wade Pellitzer	The Virginia City
Dave Rohr	The Native Son (Bella Vista)

Randy Schlotthaur-	The Columbia River
Roy Wullich	The Silver Solarium
Wayne Yetter	Royal Gorge & The Plaza Santa Fe

In Their Own Words

Mike Biehn, the Other Michael

It was a warm spring afternoon. I was driving through Sunol and I saw two men working on a railroad track. I stopped and asked them what they're working on. I thought this track was abandoned rail line. One man (Phil Orth) told me they're building a tourist railroad. I asked if they had any heavy equipment. They said yes, they have one, but we don't know how to work it. I asked what it was and one replied, "We have a backhoe but do not know how to work it". I said that I have many hours working one for my Dad. They then showed me where it was. What you could say is, the rest is history.

From then on, I joined the Pacific Locomotive Association. After some months working, I went on one of the excursions with a group of members. One we went on was a trip to Los Angeles on Amtrak. That was fun. I didn't know how much fun 'til we got all the way back home and I wanted to do more so I talked to the group leader, Henry Luna, about doing more and was introduced to his wife Connie. Connie introduced me to "Private Rail Cars'. For the first trip, I believe I got to work on the *Native Son*, a Dome car. We went to Reno to watch the Reno air races with a group of lawyers. Not ONE bloody tip did I get! That was an experience. Customer/First Class Service was number one? When we got to Reno, feeling like I had walked the whole way, I just collapsed in my room at the hotel. I was so tired I don't even recall dreaming. The next day we went to the air races and I enjoyed the whole day watching the airplanes and that started another part of my life and a whole different story.

I became a 'RailFan'.

Through the years I got to work on several private railcars. The *Royal Gorge, Plaza Santa Fe* and *Native Son*. Each car brought its own challenges to service. One of my favorites was the *Tamalpais*, currently the BC33, a business car. Spending nights on board was another thrill. I wasn't much of a bartender, but I learned quick. Connie was amazing in the galley. She introduced me to her best 'Railroad Recipes' including her famous 'Ramos Fizz', with ice cream no less. Ice cream substituted for the cream, sugar and egg. Super! She knew a lot of short cuts and secrets needed to manage a rail car galley. Everything was great. Leftovers didn't exist, well sort of. They became 'Crew Food'. That is if there were any leftovers. Quite a few charters were repeats and they knew what to expect, nothing but the best. Most times we were fishing for crackers and jam after parking the car in Reno. Connie prepared the biggest part of these recipes with 'Fresh' ingredients. A 'shopping' trip was included with every trip. Restocking the galley, bar and pantry was a must. We hit many stores, both liquor and grocery, to get the best for the customer. Some galleys were very small and the *Tam* was no bigger than a closet. No more than one person could fit in the galley or pantry side. You could do some dishes and glasses while bar tending on the pantry side while the chef was in the galley. The dining table only fit eight persons. Normally 16 were booked. This made for a busy day. First, you would serve refreshments to all after boarding. Later (after playing the chimes), when the meal was served, it was in several courses. I remember the stove burners acting up and sooting up the galley a bit. Didn't affect the food but the whites we wore didn't fare well. Refreshments had to continue to the second seating awaiting their meal while serving the seated guests. Man was that work.

You had to remember that you were riding on the Rails. This was a great moment for any railfan. During the trip, I would make the rounds for refreshment leaving the Rear Observation

Deck for last to steal a moment in the fresh air and enjoy the world going by. It was a very special time on the 'Tam'. There was always a way to find a safe opening on any car to feel the wind on your face and steal that 'Railfan moment'. I wouldn't change or give up a thing. That was fun! Every private car had its good and bad points. On the *Native Son*, currently known as the *Bella Vista*, the galley was huge by comparison (under the dome floor) and working in it wasn't too bad. Going up to the Dome with a full tray was the killer. Balancing a tray of anything on a moving train was a challenge but those stairs were really awkward. The rail got polished every time I went up or down, to keep me upright. The dome was a great place to take in the scenery and the world passing by. But duty calls.

Another great memory that I find myself still doing today is singing "Don't worry, be happy" if someone gives me a tip for anything. When the tips were divided after a successful trip, Connie would put that song on the music system of whichever car we were working. I also remember the good moments after the trip with Connie regaling us with stories of other trips and rail adventures she had traveled and just chatting about life. It was good to relax and decompress from the journey.

In 1991, I started working on the *Reno Fun Train*. After a few years the private cars were attached as they were chartered. I didn't work those too much, mostly as host on board. But it was funny to look into the *Fun Train* and see the other passengers looking down the aisle wondering "what's going on in there"? It was probably the best sales tool for the private cars when Connie would allow a 'tour' of the cars by a select few.

Connie had a son named Michael. He was in high school and then college when I went on those trips. I retired from BART and moved out of state. That made it hard to return for further trips. He started going on the trips and did a fantastic job. That' why I was the 'Other Michael'.

AHHH the *Fun Train*. But that's another story too.

Richard Evans

Life on the Train

When I spoke to Connie back in April about her project, I was exited to hear about her book. Now, here I am, 2 days before she needs my "stories", trying to remember those madcap moments! Let's see... Well, I'm not putting them in any order, so her it goes.

I remember one trip to Reno and we had gone shopping on the Saturday, and were coming back to the Fun rain. I believe there were some cars, trucks blocking the way to the train, so Connie decided (she was driving) to 'go to the side" of the parked vehicles. There was a little embankment, so there we were, probably going a little faster than was needed, and taking the "hill' at speed to get by!! IT was definitely a "Dukes of Hazzard" moment—Loved it! We were all cracking up! We even made it to the train in one piece!

OK, I need to keep this short, as I've been told one page only. Connie said no "turkey sandwich" story, so forget that one. I remember an "overnight" on board the train—Reno bound—and stuck in the Sierras. Locomotives had broken down. So, once we informed all the passengers of the delay, we hastily set-up our passengers in each compartment, and settled in for the long ride ahead. I think we arrived in Reno around 9:00 am, quite bleary-eyed and ready for bed! We got to the hotel around noon!

All right, that wasn't the greatest of stories, but I'm thinking of one last quick one where I accompanied Connie on a "Fam" tour to Monterey and Yosemite. I was quite enjoying the trip, until Connie handed the microphone to me, and wanted me to "lead" the group. Being a little 'Wet behind the ears" at that time, I mumbled and winged my way through it (all 5 minutes of it) if I remember rightly! I promptly handed the microphone back to Connie! I was her "assistant" after that! The group was accommodating though, and thankfully took me under their wing.

I'm starting page two here—naughty, naughty! One last

word: I'd like to say I've been very privileged to have worked with Connie and her amazing group of "guys" over the years. I miss seeing them and the camaraderie we had. They are all funny, hard-working, and caring people. Friends for life...

Good luck with the book Connie! Love, Richard X

George Heflin IV

My first outlet for my interest in trains came when I joined the railroad museum in San Diego at about age thirteen. I worked in the gift shop to start. I helped with track work when they began maintaining a section of old track and building a siding to facilitate a tourist train. When the first passenger train ran, I was too young (fourteen) to be in the operating department. It was suggested that I take care of the cars and provide information to the passengers. Soon, I was operating the concessions, followed by lunches for the crews, and even an occasional Saturday night dinner for them. A couple members of the board were involved with private cars, and I was making my first trips by age sixteen. In six years, I traveled over 250,000 miles and already had my dream career under my belt. I soon realized that there would be no home life in this, so I transitioned to fifteen years in various food service post ions on solid ground. A few trips have fit my schedule since, but I'll always have my memories of my gilded youth.

The story that I do not wish to be remembered for is indeed the one that my old friend Connie Luna has requested. I hope that this will be the final telling, even though I think that she may be hoping that the element of scandal will sell more copies.

I was set to deadhead the *Tamalpais* from New Orleans to Los Angeles. Unbeknownst to me, someone had opened the fresh air intake for the air conditioning. The propane Waukesha Ice Engine was running around the clock and not doing any good against the summer heat. My best friend Jim had been chef as far as Jacksonville and flown home from there. The owners asked if I wanted to have a friend join me as we were allowed two "crew" on deadhead trips. I flew my girlfriend at the time to New Orleans. After I had made all the arrangements, they told me that one of the owners could join me at any point in the trip. When he hadn't shown up by departure in New Orleans, I thought we were in the clear.

I suggested that we stay up late the first night and enjoy the rear platform, as the scenery of west Texas the next day was not as nice. After sleeping-in past Alpine, Texas, I thought I'd sneak to the crew room shower in my underwear. When I passed my girlfriend's room, the door was open and she wasn't there. I then saw that she was on the rear platform with the door propped open. I couldn't stand this with my air conditioning problem, so I released the doorstop and stepped out to say "Good morning". It was when I heard the door click that I realized that the 1920s lock with the push buttons on the side had been set to lock. This was bad. I knew there was a spare key hidden under the rear platform, but I had to wait for the train to stop.

I started to negotiate. My girlfriend was wearing a bathrobe, and only that. I somehow convinced her to let me borrow it to get off the car and get the key. In exchange, I offered her the hand towel that I kept out there to wipe the handrails whenever we stopped at a station. This grimy thing barely covered the essentials. If she stayed seated, no one would ever know she was there because of the solid platform surround. We were now covered in several hours of sweat and road dirt of the summer in West Texas. For once in its life, Amtrak #1 never stopped until we arrived in El Paso station. I hauled myself off the side opposite the station, trying to be discreet, when who appears but the car owner.

I started a new negotiation when he opened with "What on earth is going on?" I was trying to convince him to give me his keys to open the door before he got on the car to give the poor girl a chance to get inside first. When I shut the platform gate behind me, he just pushed it back open, thrust out his hand and introduced himself to the poor child with "Hi! J.B.B.!" She managed to raise one hand in greeting whilst maintaining her coverage. Sally Rand could not have done a better job of backing up down the hall to the shower at breakneck speed to temporarily avoid her new acquaintance and the curious filing back to see who was aboard the private car.

Even though no sin had taken place, I knew from his entertainment from our peril that I had better start telling the true story before his embellished version became established as fact. The story spread along the rails faster than I could imagine. My professional image was now softened with the wry smiles of those wanting to know if something so fantastic could be true. Ah yes, my gilded youth!

Dave Rohr, reminiscing about the *Native Son* and Connie.

I first met Connie over 30 years ago. She used the *Native Son* many times in the 1980s and 1990s with trips on the *Coast Starlight* to and from Los Angeles and on trips to Reno.

I acquired the *Native Son* in 1984 from Anbel Corporation in Brownsville, Texas. They acquired the car from Auto Train who purchased it from the Union Pacific. The car was originally built as a dome lounge observation car for the Union Pacific's City of Portland as their car number 9006. I added seating in the dome, a kitchen under the dome, 4 dining tables and lounge seating in the rear. The car originally had windows in the rear, which were blanked in after only a few years on the Union Pacific. Surprisingly the metal frames were still in when I purchased the car and were put back for rear viewing.

She (Connie) was a great promoter of Key Holiday Tours and the *Fun Train*. Connie approached me about getting a new paint job for the car. She wanted the Casinos to sponsor the private car on the *Fun Train* to Reno and she proposed a new paint job for the car, in return she put decals on the car for publicity for the casinos. I was glad to get a new paint job. The car never looked better.

Connie is a great cook and she has a bubbly personality, so it was a pleasure to travel with her. The kitchen in the *Native Son* was not fancy and I felt it was never completely finished, but Connie's meals out of that kitchen were fabulous. She knew how to use what was available. Kitchens in most private cars are small and to get out meal after meal for 20 or more is quite a feat that Connie did with ease.

I was always surprised at the quantity of food Connie brought onto the car and how much cooking and preparation was done ahead of time. Early on, I went to her house before a trip to help her bring provisions to the car in Oakland and I found Connie still working and organizing all she would bring. It was a lot. No passenger on her trip would ever go hungry.

I remember many times passengers would stick their heads in the kitchen and let her know what a great meal they had. Connie would beam at the complements. And that went for the crew too. We were all well fed and pampered. It was a joy to work with her.

Roy Wullich

Roy J. Wullich is a native of Batavia, NY and is a Certified Public Accountant. A graduate of St. Bonaventure University he is the owner and President of Rail Journeys West Inc.—a luxury private rail travel company that provides various passenger rail management and consulting services. The Company founded in 1998, also owns the former *California Zephyr* dome-observation car *Silver Solarium*. Like many people, Roy's interests with trains began with a Lionel train set around the Christmas tree. A Past President and Board member of the Railroad Passenger Car Alliance since 1988, Mr. Wullich started working with the Western

New York railway Historical Society in Buffalo, NY with railcar preservation and excursion operations in the early 1980s. Roy has continued working with various excursions, charter and special trains; historical preservation projects; as well as various roles in both museum and operations management. He is also a contractor to several Class One Railroads. Roy also has served, and continues to serve, as an Officer of and on the Boards of several non-profit organizations and railroad preservation organizations. Roy has owned over 24 pieces of historic rail equipment throughout his preservation efforts.

The *Silver Solarium* is one of the six originally Budd built dome observation cars built in 1948 for the famed *California Zephyr*. The car is the only one of the six still to be operational and it has been restored to reflect the era in which she was built. The car sleeps nine passengers plus two crew. It has a full bar and a lounge area, as well as a dome area that seats twenty-four.

One of Roy's favorite memories is traveling to Reno aboard one of the *Reno Fun Train*s. Due to storms in the Sierra and various delays it took almost 24 hours to get to Reno. One of the guests on the trip was an NFL player who had to bend over while standing at the bar due to his height. Since the train was late we spent the night on the train. We provided a place for him to lie down and he took up a lot of space. Everyone survived and they were all very understanding, given Mother Nature, etc. Our reward was a beautiful sunrise and lots of fresh powder snow at Donner Lake, which was simply spectacular.

Author's note: Although Roy wrote the above narrative, he wrote it in the third person. Not wanting to use the word "I" is indicative of his unassuming and modest nature. Although he accompanied his car on all of the trips, passengers rarely knew they were traveling with the owner. All of the owners and waiters with whom I worked could all be described by the same word—Gentlemen.

ABOOKS

ALIVE Book Publishing and ALIVE Publishing Group
are imprints of Advanced Publishing LLC,
3200 A Danville Blvd., Suite 204, Alamo, California 94507

Telephone: 925.837.7303 Fax: 925.837.6951
www.alivebookpublishing.com

CPSIA information can be obtained
at www.ICGtesting.com
Printed in the USA
FSHW010212011218
53966FS